The Making of Wordsworth's Poetry, 1785–1798

Paul D. Sheats

The Making of Wordsworth's Poetry, 1785-1798

Harvard University Press   Cambridge, Massachusetts   1973

821.7
Sh 3m
8 9377
July 1974

Publication of this book has been aided by a grant
from the Hyder Edward Rollins Fund

Library of Congress Catalog Card Number 72-90645

SBN 674-54375-0

Printed in the United States of America

For my parents

Contents

	Preface	ix
	Short Forms of Citation	xix
I	Hawkshead: 1785–1787	1
II	Cambridge and France: 1787–1792	43
III	Salisbury Plain and Windy Brow: 1793–1794	75
IV	Racedown: 1795–1796	105
V	Racedown: 1797	136
VI	Alfoxden: 1798	162
VII	Return to the Wye: 1798	205
	Epilogue	246
	Notes	255
	Index	287

Preface

The first recorded inquiry into the making of Wordsworth's poetry arrived at Dove Cottage in the early spring of 1801. Impressed by the "genuine simplicity" of the *Lyrical Ballads* and the originality of the Preface, an admiring and curious Londoner, Anne Taylor, wrote to the poet, asking him to identify the influential events that had shaped his opinions and his style. How, she wondered, had such an art come to be?

Such questions have lost none of their power to fascinate Wordsworth's admirers. They have been asked in every decade of the present century and will be asked again in this book. But it is prudent, before doing so, to consider Wordsworth's reply to Miss Taylor. A year earlier, in the fragment that would become *The Prelude,* he had mocked the presumption of those who reduce the mysterious growth of the human mind to single and extrinsic causes, who "point, as with a wand" and say, "This portion of the river of my mind / Came from yon fountain" (II. 213–215), and now he accedes to Miss Taylor's request for influential events only to refuse it. He politely deprecates such attention to himself—"you do me too much honor"—and then summarizes his life as a series of places, dates, and distances, irreducible facts that blunt the quest for cause or influence. "I was born at Cockermouth, about twenty-five miles from the place where I now dwell. Before I was nine years of age I was sent to the Grammar School of Hawkshead." He mentions Cambridge and his retirement to the Lakes, and then adds an apology: "In what I have said I am afraid there will be little which will throw any light on my writings, or gratify the wish which you entertain . . . but in truth my life has been unusually barren of events, and my opinions have grown slowly and, I may say, insensibly."

The poet thus tactfully rescues his reader from what R. D. Havens has called "that inclination, common to all scholars, for tracing influences and developments," * and in the remainder of his letter redirects her attention to his poems. If Miss Taylor wishes to understand the growth of his mind and art, he suggests, she might turn to two forgotten works of 1793. "They would perhaps interest you, by shewing how very widely different my former opinions must have been from those which I hold at present." With unusual expansiveness, he then proceeds to demonstrate his present "opinions" by revising particular words and phrases in another early work, in the explicit assumption that style, closely examined, is morally, philosophically, and psychologically significant, and that in this case it embodies the operations of a mind that looks steadily at its subject (*EY*, pp. 327–328).

Miss Taylor's response to this lesson in criticism has not survived, but its moral, I would suggest, is clear. This poet would have us read his poems rather than his biography; here and in later years, despite growing fame and repeated accusations of personal egotism, he consistently urged would-be students of his life to look closely at his poems instead. If we insist upon inquiring into his development, an inquiry that might be forgiven by a poet who made it the subject of many of his greatest poems, he would strenuously oppose the quest for single and extrinsic influences, be they psychological, philosophical, or political in nature. Finally, he would resist an approach that withdraws attention from the texts of his poems. Here, he implies, in the words selected and arranged by his mind at a particular time, we will find the most accurate record of his growth.

This book attempts to put these injunctions into practice, and to base a reinterpretation of Wordsworth's poetic development during the early years on a close and sympathetic reading of his

* R. D. Havens, *The Mind of a Poet* (Baltimore: Johns Hopkins Press, 1941), p. 47.

poems. It traces the fruition of a great mind, from a perspective that seeks to emphasize the active as well as the passive elements in that mind, its achievements as well as its debts. And these achievements deserve notice. Wordsworth's apprenticeship spans an epochal transition in Western thought and sensibility, and his early poems record an intellectual odyssey that is not idly compared to those of Darwin or Newton. Between 1792 and 1797 he was forced by his own experience to identify the central moral and philosophical dilemmas bequeathed to the modern poet by the rise of empirical science and rationalism; "sounding on / Through words and things a lone and perilous way," he questioned and rediscovered the sanctions of his art. At the same time, as a practicing poet, he forged a poetic language adequate to this perception, a language that continues to provide the dominant idiom of serious modern poetry. Both prophetic and representative, his career during these years might be described in the words Keats gave to Shakespeare: he led a life of allegory, and his works are the comment on it.

I have also attempted to honor Wordsworth's commitment to his poems, and to suggest the relevance of the early life to the criticism of his mature work. A history of the way he learned to make poems can provide a useful critical perspective on the great decade, and aid in defining the essential characteristics of a genius that was as progressive as the stream to which the poet so often compared it. Although it may be objected that the obvious place to begin such a study is in the "golden prime" that Matthew Arnold so influentially delineated, it is in his masterpieces, above all, that Wordsworth's art poses problems of interpretation that are massive and perhaps intrinsically insoluble. From the beginning, these poems have exhibited a characteristic power to generate precise and lasting critical antinomies and to expose the limitations of the assumptions brought to them by the critic, whether these concern his philosophy or his art. His "paradoxes," as A. C. Bradley wrote nearly seventy years ago, "still remain paradoxes." * Al-

* A. C. Bradley, "Wordsworth," in *Oxford Lectures on Poetry* (London: Macmillan, 1909), p. 101.

though I do not presume in this book to resolve these paradoxes systematically, I do believe that our best hope of comprehending them—of affirming their presence and value without explaining them out of existence—lies in an understanding of their origins, in poems that render them comparatively amenable to discussion.

Such aims have shaped the strategy of this book in several ways. The merit of a close reading obviously depends upon the authenticity of the text; not a few influential assessments of the poet have been based on inaccurate or misdated texts, including some revised when he was in his seventies. Whenever possible, therefore, I have employed Wordsworth's manuscripts to correct and when relevant to supplement the published texts. In dating the poems I have generally relied upon an aid hitherto unavailable, Professor Reed's exhaustive chronology of the early years.

A careful reading of the early poems requires, too, that we suspend the aesthetic condescension typified in the nineteenth century by Arnold and in the twentieth by H. W. Garrod, who regarded them as "endless arid tracts" through which the critic trekked on toward the "oasis" of the great decade.* It may readily be agreed that none of the juvenile works justifies close attention on aesthetic grounds alone; most of them stand Janus-like between the ages of sensibility and romanticism, and the tastes they presume have generally passed into oblivion. But we may usefully remember that the young man who made them considered them poems, not biographical or philosophical documents, and that he by no means regarded them as failures. If we hope to understand his growth, we must reconstruct a point of view that allows us to sympathize with his ends if not his means.

From the beginning, furthermore, he was a self-conscious craftsman whose technique was the product of decision, informed or misinformed. At the age of seventeen, on the occasion of his debut before the reading public, he chose the pseudonym of "Ax-

* H. W. Garrod, *Wordsworth: Lectures and Essays,* 2nd ed. (Oxford: Clarendon Press, 1927), p. 14.

iologus," or "word's worth," and along with the doodles and declensions of a not-too-attentive schoolboy his earliest notebook preserves ambitious and technically adroit imitations of the poets he admired. As his later advice to Miss Taylor suggests, his style provides a continuous and virtually unexplored record of practical decisions that in turn illuminate his changing conception of poetry and its purposes. This is not the place to debate what John Danby has called "the fallacy of the 'fallacy of intention,' " * but it should be noted that Wordsworth's changing purposes are of obvious importance to an understanding of his development and that they may be inferred with some probability from the way he made and then revised his poems, however offensive these poems may have become to tastes of another era.

Partly, one suspects, because they have been judged poetic failures, the early poems have seldom been examined for their own sake, but have been pressed repeatedly into the service of hypotheses that originate elsewhere, in the later poetry or in the controversies of modern scholarship. In interpreting these poems, therefore, I have tried to suspend what Wordsworth called "our pre-established codes of decision," and to retrieve the purposes and feelings of their author. Success in such a venture is neither easy nor verifiable, but it is nevertheless possible to avoid assumptions that involve evident historical anachronisms. Such, for example, are those that derive from Wordsworth's later poetry, and especially *The Prelude*. Although no student of the early work can afford to neglect this great poem, it is not and was not intended as a biographical *vade mecum,* and its emotional and intellectual perspective is its own. Consistently assumed, for example, in the later books of *The Prelude*—those of 1804 and 1805—is a philosophical perspective that contrasts sharply with that of earlier poems. In recalling such episodes as the crossing of the Simplon Pass, Wordsworth employs categories that are idealistic and dualistic. He celebrates an imagination that transforms and exalts the

* John F. Danby, *The Simple Wordsworth* (London: Routledge & Kegan Paul, 1960), p. 15.

visible world, a world he sets in sharp contradistinction to the supernatural. Assumed as critical norm and applied to the early
poems, such a perspective renders the younger, naturalistic
Wordsworth something of a Blake manqué, a poet in whom the
natural man rose up against the spiritual man to the detriment of
the visionary poetry he was capable of writing.* Though provocative, such a view is anachronistic; like *The Prelude,* it interprets
the young poet in the light of premises he articulated only in his
maturity.

Another and more obvious anachronism issues in part from
Wordsworth's success in creating the taste that has judged him:
from the rise of romanticism and from Victorian and modern rein-
terpretations of romanticism. It is often assumed that he was a romantic poet from birth and that his early poems may therefore be
read as if they were naïve effusions of personal feeling. Such an
assumption enabled Herbert Read, for example, to cite the following lines from an early version of *Guilt and Sorrow* as the "key-
note" of his thesis that much of the poet's early work exhibits a
"morbid spirit of guilt and remorse": †

* An influential statement of such a view is Geoffrey H. Hartman's
Wordsworth's Poetry 1787–1814 (New Haven: Yale University Press,
1964). Hartman relies primarily on poetry composed after 1800, and
particularly on the Simplon Pass episode in *The Prelude,* in deriving a
mode of approach to the early poems. He fully develops the corollaries
of the premise: Wordsworth's philosophy of nature becomes the imped-
iment it seemed to Blake, a binding materialism generated by psychic
division, and his development a belated discovery of the true autonomy of the visionary or apocalyptic imagination from nature. A
similar method yields very different conclusions in F. W. Bateson's
Wordsworth: A Re-interpretation (London: Longmans, 1954). Bateson derives a working model of the poet's "two voices" from three
poems of 1798, and then applies that model to the entire development.

† Herbert Read, *Wordsworth,* 2nd ed. (London: Faber and Faber,
1949), p. 10. One may note that Read misquotes this passage, reading
"Flies fast" for Wordsworth's (and Virgil's) "Flies first" in the second
line.

Unhappy Man! thy sole delightful hour
Flies first; it is thy miserable dower
Only to taste of joy that thou mayst pine
A loss, which rolling suns shall ne'er restore.

(*PW* I, 105; MS 1)

One may question Read's identification of "guilt and remorse" in these lines; the speaker, a narrator commenting on the misfortunes of his characters, seems rather to be stating a general condition of human life and directing sympathy toward that condition. More significant, however, is Read's assumption that this emotion, whatever its name, is personal, and that it warrants straightforward psychological diagnosis. Wordsworth no doubt endorsed the sentiments of his narrator, but so did Virgil:

Man's sweet and pleasant time, his morn of life,
Flies first. . . .

(*Georgics,* III, 66–67)

and Catullus:

But we, when once our [   ] light
Is set, must sleep in endless night.

(V. 4–6)

The translations, furthermore, are those of Wordsworth, who imitated these and other *loci classici* as a schoolboy, long before the French Revolution and the event to which Read ascribes the remorse of these lines, his supposed desertion of Annette Vallon.

It would seem, then, that psychological interpretation of the early poems ought to be undertaken with some caution and in the light of Wordsworth's probable understanding of poetic decorum. In this passage he deliberately employs "sentiments" that had been polished and verified by centuries of imitation; he appears in the role of poetic "maker," and the theoretical justification of his poem is not expressionistic but mimetic and pragmatic, to use

those terms in the sense given them by M. H. Abrams.* Given
pragmatic theory, a passage that is pathetic (or terrific) in effect is
not *prima facie* evidence that the poet was troubled or (as has
been suggested) neurotic. In theory, at least, the construction of
such a passage is quite irrelevant to the poet's personal feelings at
the time, being justified by the assumption, common to the poets
the young Wordsworth admired, that to evoke pity is to inculcate
virtue and to give pleasure, or, in the words of Horace and Samuel
Johnson, to instruct by pleasing. In practice, Wordsworth's choice
of genres and effects does have psychological significance. But it is
seldom simple, and at times would seem the reverse of what we
might expect of a naïve expressionism.

Aside from such tactical precautions, the plan of this book is
straightforward. I begin at the beginning, in the schoolroom where
Wordsworth was assigned his first poems, and survey the intellectual and literary culture implied by those poems. Here I introduce
three aspects of his thought that form major and controversial
themes in his mature work: his conception of the mind and its relation to its objects, of the natural universe and its relation to
man, and of the problem of sustaining hope within the natural and
temporal world. Following chapters trace the development of the
poet's thought and technique as he passes through three successive
phases of his career, in each of which an abrupt crisis of disappointment initiates a renewed struggle toward psychological integrity and hope. My last two chapters survey the third of these consummations, the *annus mirabilis* of 1797–98, and conclude by
examining a poem that remains an enduring testament to the
poet's mastery of himself and his art, *Tintern Abbey*.

This book could not have been written without help from several quarters. I am grateful to the Trustees of the Wordsworth Library, and especially to Mrs. Mary Moorman, Professor Basil
Willey, and Mr. Jonathan Wordsworth, for granting me permis-

* M. H. Abrams, *The Mirror and the Lamp: Romantic Theory and
the Critical Tradition* (New York: Oxford University Press, 1953),
pp. 6–26.

sion to consult the poet's manuscripts. The same privilege was extended in the United States by the Cornell University Library. Financial support at various stages was provided by the English Department of Harvard University, the Research Committee of the Academic Senate at UCLA, and the Humanities Institute of the University of California. Timely advice was given by Miss Nesta Clutterbuck, Professor Mark Reed, and the late Professor John Finch. Three of my colleagues took the time to read and comment on the manuscript: Professors Maximillian Novak, Florence Ridley, and Peter L. Thorslev, Jr. Among those who helped prepare the typescript were Patricia Jones Adams, the Reverend Edward A. French, Beatrice Gould, Constance Luke, Steve Sharp, and Jeanette Dearborn. That this typescript became a book is due in large part to the labors of my editor, Miss Kathleen Ahern. My wife, Audrey Hathaway, gave her editorial acumen freely, although circumstances rendered time more than usually precious.

This study is peculiarly indebted to the distinguished body of Wordsworthian scholarship, editorial and critical, that extends from Émile Legouis' *Early Life* to the present day. This obligation is not least where I diverge from the conclusions of my predecessors; Professor Hartman's rather different portrait of Wordsworth has in particular helped focus my thinking. My greatest debt is to Professor David Perkins, who introduced me to the study of the romantic poets ten years ago, and who in the years since has given aid and encouragement with unfailing generosity.

P.D.S.

Santa Monica, California

Short Forms of Citation

BL   *Biographia Literaria*, ed. J. Shawcross, 2 vols. (London: Oxford University Press, 1907).

DCP   Dove Cottage Papers.

DWJ   *Journals of Dorothy Wordsworth*, ed. Ernest de Selincourt, 2 vols. (London: Macmillan, 1941).

EY   *The Letters of William and Dorothy Wordsworth, The Early Years, 1787–1805*, ed. Ernest de Selincourt, 2nd ed., rev. Chester L. Shaver (Oxford: Clarendon Press, 1967).

LY   *The Letters of William and Dorothy Wordsworth, The Later Years*, ed. Ernest de Selincourt, 3 vols. (Oxford: Clarendon Press, 1939).

Moorman   Mary Moorman, *William Wordsworth, A Biography, The Early Years, 1770–1803* (Oxford: Clarendon Press, 1957).

MY   *The Letters of William and Dorothy Wordsworth, The Middle Years*, ed. Ernest de Selincourt, 2nd ed., rev. Mary Moorman and Alan G. Hill (Oxford: Clarendon Press, 1969–70).

Prelude   *The Prelude*, ed. Ernest de Selincourt, 2nd ed., rev. Helen Darbishire (Oxford: Clarendon Press, 1959). Unless otherwise specified, all citations are taken from the text of 1805.

PW   *The Poetical Works of William Wordsworth*, ed. Ernest de Selincourt and Helen Darbishire, 5 vols. (Oxford: Clarendon Press, 1940–49).

Reed   Mark L. Reed, *Wordsworth, The Chronology of the Early Years, 1770–1799* (Cambridge, Mass.: Harvard University Press, 1967).

STCL   *Collected Letters of Samuel Taylor Coleridge*, ed. Earl Leslie Griggs, 6 vols. (Oxford: Clarendon Press, 1956–1971).

The Making of Wordsworth's Poetry, 1785–1798

". . . the discipline
And consummation of the Poet's mind."   *Prelude* XIII. 270–271

I   Hawkshead: 1785-1787

"Song was his favourite and first pursuit."—James Beattie

The history of Wordsworth's poetry begins in the single class-room of the Grammar School at Hawkshead, a small market village in the heart of the Lake District. It was probably in the autumn of 1784—his fifteenth year and his fifth at the school—that he was assigned his first poem, on a topic most of his readers have composed upon, the summer vacation. His talents did not go unrecognized; his headmaster, William Taylor, assigned other poems, and in the following June invited Wordsworth to compose and deliver a formal panegyric on the occasion of the bicentenary of the school's foundation. This "School Exercise" was "much admired," and shortly afterward he began to compose verses as a free agent, "from the impulse" of his "own mind." In his last years he was something of "the poet of the school," a reputation he confirmed by publishing a sonnet in the *European Magazine*.[1]

The "strong indentures" that bound Wordsworth to his muse were thus the product of education: his gifts were educed and molded by an academic community that at once introduced him to the literary and intellectual culture of his age and offered a sympathetic and encouraging audience, a prototype of those smaller enclaves of trust and dedication he would seek and find at Nether Stowey and Grasmere. As a result, the poems and fragments that survive from the Hawkshead years are both active and passive in character. They record the exuberant awakening of genius to the exercise of its own powers and help us to define those powers. But they point as well to the conditions imposed upon that genius by its historical milieu, and to a number of conventional assumptions that Wordsworth shared with his community and his age. Because the few critics who have commented on these poems have done so quite selectively, we may begin with a brief survey of the characteristics of the poetry and then look more closely at the schoolboy's understanding of the three main regions of his mature song: the relation between mind and its objects, the significance of nature, and the course of human life through time.

I

With the exception of the "School Exercise," all of the poems that survive from the Hawkshead years are products of Wordsworth's later, active phase. The "Exercise" alone suffices, however, to suggest the existence of a profound contrast between the two groups of poems, those imposed by Taylor's fiat and those that sprang from the impulse of the young poet's mind. Endorsed by the assembled community, it may be taken as a spirited summary of the school's purposes and values. And it reminds us that the culture Wordsworth inherited from this "ancient and respectable seminary of learning," as his younger brother called it a few years later,[2] comprehended several traditions that we today regard as disparate or even contradictory. An allegorical vision in heroic couplets, the "Exercise" presents a personified "Power of Education," who surveys the history of the school from its foundation under Elizabeth, summarizes its ideals, and delivers a spirited exhortation to "Britain's sons" to pursue virtue, fame, and truth. The conception of human nature implied by this speaker is at times molded by classical humanism. One task of education, for example, is to

guide the fluctuating youth
Firm in the sacred paths of moral truth,

To regulate the mind's disordered frame,
And quench the passions kindling into flame.

(ll. 77–80)

Here Wordsworth affirms the ideal of the rational man as it had descended to him from Plato, Cicero, and Milton; he assumes that the human reason is an intuitive and ethical faculty capable of knowing the good, free from epistemological aberration, and endowed with authority, providential or natural, over the passions. Elsewhere in the poem, however, he celebrates the power of education

To teach, on rapid wings, the curious soul
To roam from heaven to heaven, from pole to pole,
From thence to search the mystic cause of things,
And follow Nature to her secret springs.

(ll. 73–76)

Given their date, these lines imply the authority of the discursive or demonstrative reason, a power that since the earlier seventeenth century had been conceived as analogous to "mathematical demonstration," as Locke had written.[3] Like Coleridge and Kant, Wordsworth would learn to discriminate between these two conceptions of "reason" and would ultimately describe the second as a "false secondary power." Here, however, he assumes their compatibility, as he does that of two other branches of human knowledge, religion and natural science. The theology of the poem is Anglican; Wordsworth extols the progress of "pure Religion" since the Reformation. But equally evident is a consciousness of vigorous participation in the enterprise of enlightenment that derives from the empirical and scientific tradition. The school itself is the house of "Science," of certain and demonstrable knowledge, and the one thinker Wordsworth names in the poem is Francis Bacon.

Behind such confident syncretism lies the Hawkshead curriculum, which mingled the classical studies inherited from the Renaissance grammar school with a rigorous study of mathematics. As B. R. Schneider has pointed out, Hawkshead was an intellectual outpost of the University of Cambridge, which provided its masters and received its scholars, and like Cambridge it was committed to the scientific and empirical tradition exemplified by Bacon, Newton, and Locke. By the time he graduated Wordsworth had mastered five books of Euclid's *Elements* and had proved on his own pulses the ineluctable certainty of the Euclidean *quod erat demonstrandum,* a certainty to which he would turn for reassurance, as a touchstone of sanity, in later years. One would judge from the "Exercise," furthermore, that he now believed, as he would in later years, that the geometrical method "held acquaintance with the stars" (*Prelude* V. 104) and in Bacon's words buckled the mind to "the nature of things." [4] Here, too, he probably learned to assume the applicability of mathematical demonstration to moral questions, and that, in Locke's words, "morality" lies among the "sciences capable of demonstration" (IV, iii, 18), a "truth" he would question and give up "in despair" within ten years.

Wordsworth's acquaintance with the empirical and scientific tradition may, indeed, have been first-hand. Like his brother, he may have been familiar with Locke's *Conduct of the Understanding.* Philosophical and scientific allusions appear occasionally in the poems composed at the time, and autobiographical passages of later years suggest that the schoolboy was familiar with the fundamentals of contemporary geology as well as the "laws of light." [5] Whether or not his interest in such subjects was sufficient to guide his reading, he lived in a community in which it would have been difficult for a curious and speculative boy to have escaped a rudimentary understanding of the fundamental assumptions of empirical psychology and natural science. Equally important, his access to this tradition was direct. He did not encounter Newton, for example, in the popularized versions of the *Principia* that had graced the drawing rooms of mid-century. His Cambridge masters were certainly familiar with both the *Principia* and the *Optics,* as well as the mathematical language which Newton elaborated for the description of natural law. And this consideration grows in significance when we distinguish between the Newton deplored by later advocates of an organic vitalism—the architect of a dead and mechanistic universe, effectively abandoned by its creator—and the author of the *Optics,* whose conception of the universe was consistent both with revelation and Wordsworth's later vision of a nuministic and vital "nature." [6]

The dominant impression given by the "Exercise," then, is harmony. Wordsworth assumes the compatibility of natural science, Protestant faith, and a humanism that owes as much to the classics and the Renaissance as to the Enlightenment. The later and spontaneous poems, however, provide a contrasting view of the intellectual and psychological divisions that cut across the waning decades of the age of reason. Here, working from the "impulse" of his own mind, Wordsworth forcefully rejects the techniques of the "Exercise" and the attitudes associated with them. He abandons the heroic couplet for lyric measures, and displays great fondness for the meter of *L'Allegro* and *Il Penseroso,* the octosyllabic couplet. With two exceptions he chooses genres that are lyrical: the ode, stanzaic and irregular; the sonnet; various kinds of elegy; and the ballad. The exceptions, both narrative, are marked by lyrical feeling: a fragmentary heroic tale in Ossianic prose, and the most considerable of the surviving poems, *The Vale of Esthwaite,* a compromise between topographical and narrative genres that seems intended to exemplify the tastes and activities of a Hawkshead minstrel, that is, an enthusiastic lyric poet. His models, modern and ancient, are all lyric poets: Anacreon and Catullus, the young Milton, Collins, Gray, and a number of Gray's imitators, including James Beattie, Charlotte Smith, and Helen Maria Williams. In all these poems, Wordsworth dedicates himself to ends that are hardly hinted in the "Exercise": to the art of lyric poetry, and to the evocation of powerful and at times violent feeling.

The quality of this feeling is characteristically melancholy. Although the schoolboy attempted on occasion to strike what a contemporary student of the lyric, John Aikin, called "the graver and sublimer strains" appropriate to such genres as the ode, and twice experimented with ingenious amorous compliments, most of the later poems exemplify that taste for the "tender and pathetic" that Wordsworth would acknowledge as his own in the Preface of 1800 (*PW* II, 402). As their collective epigraph we might take Virgil's half-line, which the schoolboy prefixed to his lament for the fall of a starling: "sunt lacrimae rerum." His "Ballad" precisely fulfills Aikin's definition of the "modern pastoral": a "pathetic tale of the peaceful village," it describes the slow decline and death of a maid from unrequited love, and as her dying speech quotes the last words of his headmaster. In the "Dirge" a minstrel mourns the death of a boy in the manner of the "Minstrel's Song" from Chatterton's *Aella*. In one sonnet a husband mourns his wife, and in the pastoral elegy, a "Song" later dignified as a Theocritan "Idyllium," Wordsworth himself mourns the imagined death of the "rough terrier" who so joyously welcomed him back to Ann Tyson's cottage in the summer of 1788. The author of *The Prelude* by no means exaggerated his youthful fealty to the "Lady Sorrow" (VI. 486), and before he was a poet of nature he was emphatically a poet of the human heart. His ear for the "still, sad music of humanity," however sentimentally he transcribed it, was by no means a product of his maturity, as he would claim in *Tintern Abbey*.[7]

Such a poetry clearly lies at some distance from the "paths of fair majestic Truth," as Wordsworth pointed them out in the "School Exercise." There, in effect, he laid claim, for the first time in his career, to what he would call "truth . . . general, and operative" (*PW* II, 394). Here, in his first independent efforts, he implicitly gives up the attempt to "quench" the passions and instead endorses them. In *The Vale of Esthwaite* he goes further, and at times explicitly repudiates the values of the "Exercise." He declares his apostasy from truth and reason, to which he prefers "Fancy" and "Youth" (ll. 296–297). He now cultivates the irrational:

And moody Madness aye was there
With wide-rent robe, and shaggy hair.

(ll. 395–396)

Instead of rejoicing at the banishment of Superstition by an age of light, he seeks "gloomy glades," "brooding Superstition," and her "druid sons" (ll. 25–34). Elsewhere in *The Vale of Esthwaite* the speaker suffers mystic or melancholy visions, approaches a mysterious castle in a storm, explores a dungeon, and descends into the bowels of Helvellyn, where he or his ghostly guide witnesses visions that recapitulate the bloody history of Cumberland.

Abstracted from their age, such effects have encouraged the supposition that Wordsworth was psychologically unbalanced. One modern reader suggests that he suffered from neurotic guilt; another detects a radically disturbed understanding of the physical world. But it is more probable, I believe, that these Gothicisms reflect the response of an integrated sensibility to a divided culture. The schoolboy's appeals to terror and the irrational are organized not by neurosis but by genre; they appear only in *The Vale of Esthwaite,* and contemporary poems obey quite different patterns of decorum. Such effects had been assiduously cultivated, furthermore, by poets and critics of "romantic" sensibility since the beginning of the century. In an essay very probably read by Wordsworth, to cite only one example, John Aikin had explicitly recommended exaggerated appeals to terror: "the more wild, fanciful, and extraordinary are the circumstances of a scene of horror, the more pleasure we receive from it." To a modern reader Wordsworth's menacing Druids may suggest a fear of "apocalyptic wounding":

And lo! her druid sons appear.
Why roll on me your glaring eyes?
Why fix on me for sacrifice?

(*Vale of Esthwaite,* ll. 32–34)

But they would probably have seemed less idiosyncratic to Helen
Maria Williams, or to the many subscribers who enjoyed her "Irregular Fragment, Found in a Dark Passage of the Tower":

> Pale spectres! are ye what ye seem?
>   They glide more near—
>   Their forms unfold!
> Fix'd are their eyes, on me they bend—
>   Their glaring look is cold! [8]

Such parallels, which are extensive, suggest that Wordsworth's
Gothicisms represent an ambitious and enthusiastic response to
the most evocative models of the age,[9] a first instinctive aspiration
toward poetic subjects that are "carried alive into the heart by
passion" (*PW* II, 395). They are quite compatible, in other words,
with the ample evidence that Wordworth's years in this "beloved
Vale" were among the happiest in his life, and with the character
adumbrated by the *Memoirs,* the letters, and the later poems: a
young man violent in his affections, stiff, moody, and proud in response to constraint, and intensely ambitious, but not psychologically unbalanced. This point deserves emphasis, not only because
Wordsworth would look back on this period as one in which he
enjoyed integrity, but because later poems exhibit symptoms of
psychological disintegration that are by no means conventional.

We need not, furthermore, regard Wordsworth's *volte-face* in
the spontaneous poems as evidence of a personal rebellion against
the age of reason. Along with the "baleful influence" of Gothicism, as de Selincourt described it, Wordsworth inherited the assumption that the province of lyric poetry was essentially divorced
from reason and truth, and that the indulgence of the irrational
was therefore essentially poetical. When he claims to prefer
"Fancy" to "Truth" he is speaking as an enthusiastic minstrel, and
stating the conditions of his art. As we shall see, there were other
options open to him, positions that offered a greater measure of
epistemological integrity to the poet; and that he at times embraced this assumption points again to the influence of his commu-

nity. It was Bacon who had definitively formulated the epistemo-logical impotence of an art that submits "the shews of things to the desires of the mind," and the enthusiasm with which Wordsworth cultivates the irrational in poetry is the complement, and not the contradiction, of an unquestioned adherence to the truths he stud-ied in the classroom. We may recall that the headmaster who taught him to honor Bacon also encouraged him to imitate the poet of "moody madness," Thomas Gray.[10]

An overview of the Hawkshead poems thus points to two simul-taneous commitments on the part of the young poet: he upholds an amalgam of moral and scientific truth that derives as much from the Renaissance as from the Enlightenment, and he enthusiasti-cally devotes himself to a late eighteenth-century conception of lyric poetry. A central task in the years to come was the reconcili-ation of these commitments, the forging of an art that honored both "truth" and passion, and reclaimed "the desires of the mind," in Bacon's terms, from the "shews" to the "nature of things." But Wordsworth would also struggle simply to keep faith with the to-tality of what he had been at Hawkshead, and to preserve an in-tegrity that must be inferred from the divided compositions of the time. It is suggestive that the last line of the Immortality Ode al-ludes to the poem he was commanded to imitate on one of his first "school-assignments": Gray's "Ode on the Pleasure arising from Vicissitude." The impulse given by the Hawkshead commu-nity was a lasting one.

II

The subjectivity of Wordsworth's mature poetry has provided matter for critical debate since his own times, a debate that at once raised the related questions of his egotism and his solitude. Because both parties to this debate have with few exceptions pre-sumed the personal significance of the poet's concern with his own mind,[11] however, it is particularly useful to remind ourselves that he inherited a pronounced subjective bias from his age. Like the empirical philosophers who molded their conception of the mind, the poets of sensibility assumed that their proper concern lay with consciousness rather than with the objects of consciousness. For a young and enthusiastic minstrel of the 1780's the true voice of feeling was a profoundly introspective voice, which took for granted the priority of mind over its objects, and employed a language that, as Josephine Miles has shown, permitted description of mind apart from its objects. In all the early poems, to repeat Matthew Prior's comment on Locke, it is the mind that "rules the roast." [12]

The practical effects of such assumptions on the composition of poetry may be illustrated by a number of passages in the early notebooks, passages that record Wordsworth's attempt to describe an emotion he cherished, pity. He may have begun in prose: "There are times when the heart feels itself affected by a kind of twilight sadness, without fixing on any determin'd object" (DCP). His attention is devoted solely to the mind, which he isolates with studied vagueness ("a kind of") from any object whatsoever. The heart "feels itself," and the existence of an object-world is only hinted by an adjective ("twilight") that functions as descriptive analogy. His first metrical version was equally introspective:

> Now too, while o'er the heart we feel
> A tender twilight softly steal,
> Sweet Pity gives her forms array'd
> In tenderer tints and softer shades;
> But soon we mourn the fading view:
> Soon all is fled,—but Pity's dew.
>
> (DCP)

He elaborates the analogy to twilight without positing any relationship, syntactical or epistemological, between the mind and the outer world. A personified "Pity" offers "forms" that are described in a language of painting that probably reflects the influence of Gray, who had painted the "sabler tints of woe" and many

other emotions. The disappearance of these vague "forms" evokes a concrete sign of feeling, a tear, which Wordsworth describes in a periphrasis ("Pity's dew") borrowed from a sentimental ballad by one of his favorite models, John Langhorne.[13]

Later revisions witness a growing proficiency in this highly conventional art of poetic introspection. In one version Wordsworth brightened his palette, opposing the "golden tints of joy" to "sorrow's softly brooding shade" (DCP). In another he borrowed the words of Gray's Bard, who after imploring the phantoms of "Edward's race" to "Stay, oh stay!" had observed that "they melt, they vanish from my eyes" (ll. 101–104):

> Stay, sadly-pleasing visions, stay—
> Ah, no, they melt, they fade away.
>
> (DCP)

An alternative to this couplet derives from a sentimental ballad by Helen Maria Williams, in which impoverished children "weep, unknowing why," at a heroine's benevolence.[14] Wordsworth again transfers the phrase to the mind:

> The heart, when passed the Vision by,
> Dissolves, nor knows for whom nor why.
>
> (DCP)

In still another version he imported a complete landscape into the mind:

> When o'er the mind's naked withered scene
> The gales blow bleak and keen . . .
>
> (DCP)

Such experimentation may seem tedious and hardly justified in modern eyes, which have long since outgrown a "vocabulary of emotion" that in Josephine Miles's words rendered the "active description of the passions . . . new and challenging and absorbing to a poet who desired to contribute delight and moral advantage and contemporary emphasis to literature."[15] But the young

Wordsworth appears to have regarded this passage, and others like it, as something of a challenge, and he was not ashamed of his results: at least five versions survive in early notebooks, and a final version appears six years later in print. The example thus offers us some insight into the direction in which we must alter our presuppositions if we are to understand the subjectivism of Wordsworth's poetry, whether in this early form or the later and more celebrated form of the "egotistical sublime." He takes for granted the extreme subjectivity of lyric poetry and devotes his attention to the technical problem of describing consciousness, a problem he solves by appropriating devices from the poets he admired, and applying them, with deliberate innovation, to his own subjective experience.

The highly figured style of the early poems suggests, furthermore, that Wordsworth shared with his models the nearly ubiquitous belief that poetry was essentially directed to the imagination, that is, that it dealt in "lively" and "vivid" images rather than abstractions and that the activity of the poet's imagination was in some sense creative.[16] A precise definition of what Wordsworth meant by the imagination, or the "fancy," as he consistently calls it in the early poems, is as difficult to come by here as it is in later poems, but it is possible to draw several useful parallels between his work and the prevailing assumptions of his time. In *The Vale of Esthwaite,* for example, "Fancy" mediates both vision and madness, roles exemplified in Beattie's *Minstrel* (1770–1774), a compendium of moral and aesthetic commonplaces that Wordsworth loved. When he asserts, in another context, that "fancy's rays the hills adorn" (l. 177), he calls, in imitation of Beattie's salute to "sweet Fancy's ray" (*Minstrel,* II. 39), upon the widespread view that the imagination mediates intuitive response, emotional, aesthetic, and moral, to objects of immediate sense perception—a view that would become a central tenet of Wordsworth's creed.[17] Several passages suggest, too, that he was familiar with the associational power of the fancy. As he pictures his return as an old man to the Vale of Esthwaite,

for example, he implies the association of feelings and memories with natural objects: "from every rock would hang a tale" (l. 495). In "Beauty and Moonlight: An Ode" he portrays a lover who is unable to resist the associational power of an amorous fancy, which transforms natural landscapes into the features of his beloved. This first of Wordsworth's attempts to describe the association of ideas in a state of excitement assumes what the associational critics called the principle of resemblance, and illustrates the truth that "wherever the fancy supposes [such resemblance], it readily, and with a kind of eagerness, passes from one idea to its associates." [18]

There is evidence, finally, that Wordsworth attributed a more radically creative power to the poetic imagination, and that he conceived of it as essentially autonomous from nature. His clearest description of the image-making power comes in a passage at the close of the "Idyllium," which he began in the language of Locke:

> If, while I gaz'd to Nature blind
> On the calm Ocean of my mind
> Some new Idea rose . . .

(DCP)

At first sight a "new Idea" would seem to suggest an ideal form assembled, according to orthodox neoclassic theory, by the rearrangement of remembered images. Its "novelty," in Johnson's words, could issue from "varied combinations," or from what Reynolds called the "close comparison" and "reiterated Experience" of sense-impressions. Wordsworth's revisions of the passage, however, suggest that this is not what he meant. He altered "new Idea" first to "naked image," emphasizing its concrete integrity, and finally to a "new-created image," which "rose"

> In full-grown beauty at its birth
> Lovely as Venus from the sea . . .

This final version, which he would virtually repeat in *The Prelude* (IV. 104–105), may reflect the more extreme idealism of Collins, who in the *Ode on the Poetical Character* had regarded Fancy and Heaven as "kindred Pow'rs" (l. 74), or of Akenside, who had personified the "living image" of beauty as "Venus, when she stood / Effulgent on the pearly car, and smil'd, / Fresh from the deep." In short, Wordsworth would probably have agreed with John Aikin that there is in the mind "an internal eye constantly stretching its view beyond the bounds of natural vision, and something new, something greater, more beautiful, more excellent, is required to gratify its noble longing. This eye of the mind is imagination—it peoples the world with new beings, it embodies abstract ideas, it suggests unexpected resemblances, it creates first, and then presides over its creation with absolute sway." [19]

That the schoolboy sought to exercise a power that "bodies forth / The shape of things unknown" is evident from his style, which consistently employs images to represent what is literally invisible. As we have seen, he shifts images from the external world to the mind, as analogies or metaphors that in the words of the popular critic Hugh Blair (1783) render "intellectual ideas . . . visible to the eye, by giving them color and substance and sensible qualities." He delighted in the figure Lord Kames (1762) distinguished as "descriptive personification," which corporealizes the invisible or animates the inanimate without implying conviction on the part of the speaker, and he employed it not for an orthodox neoclassic purpose, to render abstract truths available to the senses and emotions, as in Johnson's poems, but to fabricate quasi-allegorical pictorial tableaux in the manner of *L'Allegro* and the odes of Gray, Collins, Beattie, and others. His "School Exercise" offers an example:

> Now flush'd as Hebe, Emulation rose;
> Shame follow'd after with reverted eye,
> And hue far deeper than the Tyrian dye.
>
> (ll. 20–22)

Most of these personifications, as we would expect, refer to emotions: Pity, Fear, Melancholy, Hope, and others. All are derivative. In judging the young poet's predilection for such personifications, we should remember that, like the figure of Venus rising from the sea, they were sanctioned by their very independence of sense-perception, and that they attested to the radical creativity of the imagination. We should remember, as well, that their existence was entirely subjective; they reflect what Lord Kames called the imagination's "singular power of fabricating images without any foundation in reality." [20]

A similar justification may be invoked on behalf of the figure that is perhaps Wordsworth's favorite, analogy. As we shall see, he employs several conventional varieties of analogy. Here it is sufficient to note that he employs the figure for a primarily descriptive and "imaginative" purpose, to embody the invisible, and that he betrays virtually no sense of its ontological significance, whether it links mind and its objects or other levels of being. He exemplifies with some force what Earl Wasserman has described as the decadence of the "analogical myth" the eighteenth-century poets inherited from pre-Enlightenment culture, and repeatedly displays the self-consciousness of poets who, in Wasserman's words, are "thinking about thinking analogically." [21] The figure is indeed the principal locus of his most ambitious attempts to surpass his models. In composing a passage in *The Vale of Esthwaite,* for example, he began by describing Pity as the "autumn of the heart," and in succeeding revisions added a "laughing" summer of "Mirth" and a "long winter of the poor" that is warmed by Charity. Elsewhere in the poem he compared his sentimental response to a "tender tale" to the gathering of flowers:

> Pluck the wild flowers and fondly place
> The treasure in the bosom's vase.

One wishes he had stopped here, but he elaborates the conceit:

> Yet, ah! full oft the enchanting while
> We croud the heart with pile on pile
> [And grief's waters] rising high
> Well from the heart, they droop, and all is dry.
>
> (*Vale of Esthwaite,* ll. 180–185; DCP)

Wordsworth here describes the "spontaneous overflow of powerful feelings," an expressionistic conception of emotion and art that he by no means discovered but inherited, and the poetic effects of which, as this passage suggests, he was to discipline. The mode of his description, however, is analogical; he sets up a continuous and complex relation between subjective reality and a group of images that render that reality visible to the "eye of the mind," imagination.

In these analogies we sense the pride and ambition that would inspire the reported prediction that at Cambridge he would be a "senior Wrangler or nothing" (Reed, p. 75 n12). Like Keats, who in his early works broke the couplet more vigorously than his models, the young Wordsworth begins by taking for granted the value of the literary modes available to him, and displays his ability by pressing them to new extremes of intricacy, hyperbole, and intensity. We must assume that these extremes were deliberate; the young man who on his first appearance in print transliterated his name into the Greek must have been aware of what a recent critic has called the "divine joke" of his name.[22] And the focal point of this ambition lies in his conception of the imagination, a power that creates and manipulates imagery, and in so doing testifies to the hegemony of the mind over the sense and the sensible world.

If Wordsworth inherited a view of poetry that in practice and theory encouraged a profound subjectivism, we have complementary evidence that his own deepest instincts tended in the opposite direction, toward a realism that looked for moral and psychological support to the object world beyond the mind. In his well-known gloss on the Immortality Ode he recalled that he was "often unable to think of external things as having external existence."

I communed with all that I saw as something not apart from, but inherent in, my own immaterial nature. Many times while going to school have I grasped at a wall or tree to recall myself from this abyss of idealism to the reality. At that time I was afraid of such processes. In later periods of life I have deplored, as we have all reason to do, a subjugation of an opposite character, and have rejoiced over the remembrances (*PW* IV, 463).

Other accounts survive, including the poet's words to Bonamy Price, as he pushed against the top bar of a gate: "There was a time in my life when I had to push against something that resisted, to be sure that there was anything outside me. I was sure of my own mind; everything else fell away, and vanished into thought" (*PW* IV, 467). All accounts focus on the ninth stanza of the Ode, and the remembered "fallings from us, vanishings" that offer the aging poet hope. Modern readers have regarded this experience as evidence of extreme subjectivism, or a first version of a "visionary" experience, and it is worth reconstructing in some detail.[23] It is clearly not the kind of "vision" that terrified the young Blake, who saw the head of God peering through his bedroom window; Wordsworth continued to see exactly what he saw every day on his walk from Colthouse to the village school, a "beauteous scene of hills and water." But he saw it in the temporary and frightening conviction that it was "in" his own mind. The agency of vision ceased, in other words, to convey the "outness" of its objects, and visible images paradoxically blinded the mind to whatever lies beyond the self. Judging from the metaphors of "falling" and "vanishing," which suggest both vertigo and sensory deprivation, what lay beyond these subjective images would seem to be a void, an "abyss." Wordsworth's response, to grasp at a tree, is at once the response of someone about to fall and someone who cannot see, and it succeeds, by touching something, in re-establishing the "outness" of the visible world.

This experience was pre-literary; it did not find its way, in any obvious sense, into the poetry Wordsworth was writing at the time. But it clearly bears on the subjectivism implied by that poetry, and on several central assumptions of the empirical philosophy itself. What "vanished and fell away into thought" is what tended to vanish in the Lockean system: the "substance," knowable only in part, that underlies and accounts for the ideas of sense that present themselves to consciousness. The experience furthermore reflects the instability of Cartesian dualism, which during its uneasy history had repeatedly collapsed into a monism that was either materialistic or idealistic. It is quite accurately described, in fact, as a Berkeleian "subjective idealism," in which, to quote Coleridge, "not only the mind's self-consciousness, but all the other things perceived by it, are regarded as modifications of itself, as disguised but actual modes of self-perception." [24] That the dissolution of the material world should take place within the modality of vision and be reconstituted within that of touch is equally consistent with the premises of the empirical philosophy. The ambiguous status of "fancy" throughout the century issued in large part from the assumption that vision most vividly demonstrated the mind's power to create "secondary" qualities, such as color, in contrast to those "primary" qualities which Locke, following Galileo, Boyle, and others, had assumed to be real and measurable properties of external substance. It was to the sense of sight, for example, that Berkeley appealed in arguing that there are no primary qualities at all. Among the materialistic and dualistic followers of Locke, on the other hand, the modality of touch was consistently assigned the epistemological authority that common sense demands. Locke regarded "solidity"—which he defined as a power resisting penetration—not only as a "primary" quality, but as one of the few "original ideas" from which "all the rest are derived" (II, xxi, 75), and refuted Berkeley in advance by requesting an idealistic reader who doubts the reality of a fire to *"feel* it too; and be convinced, by putting his hand in it" (IV, xi, 7). Samuel Johnson accomplished the same end by "striking his foot with mighty force against a large stone, till he rebounded from it"—by "pushing," in Wordsworth's terms, "against something that resisted." [25]

Such parallels are of course only suggestive. At most, like the late nineteenth-century dreams studied by Freud, they exemplify the truth that the form of a psychic experience is to some extent shaped by its historical milieu. It is significant, however, that powerful feelings were focused on categories we can call epistemological, categories that would become one of the poet's grand themes. Unlike Locke or Johnson, Wordsworth was afraid, and he reached out toward the substantial object-world not to demonstrate a point of argument but to rescue himself from a fearful solitude. And we are further justified in describing the instincts revealed here as realistic, and in observing that the idealism presumed by the poetry he was imitating at the time would in future years prove less than congenial to him. The experience of the "abyss of idealism" indeed prefigures one dimension of Wordsworth's accomplishment in the coming decade, which was to reorganize the purposes of his art around an insight into the ethical and psychological significance of the epistemological object and to develop a poetic language that could convey this insight truthfully, a language that was epistemologically critical. If the Hawkshead schoolboy responded to an isolating subjectivism by touching a tree, the poet of 1798 would confront his readers with "substantial things," or exhort them, more simply, to "touch gently."

It is, however, an oversimplification to describe the significance of this experience, and of the development to come, as a straightforward reaction against the subjectivism of the later eighteenth century. The schoolboy's goal, in reaching out toward the object, was less to assert the exclusive value of the object than to compensate for an alarming disequilibrium of relationship between mind and object. He sought, that is, to recover a relationship in which both poles, inner and outer, guarantee and support each other. If his instinctive response to an idealistic monism is to reassert the existence of the external world, he is no less insistent in later years on upholding the existence and the power of the mind against an object-world that threatens to overwhelm it. His career, then, may be regarded as a continuing attempt to perpetuate this balance, in circumstances that are consistently relevant to the intellectual history of his times and ours. What abides throughout the career is the inherited frame of reference within which these changing hopes take poetic form, the relation between mind and object.

III

For a number of reasons, including Wordsworth's fear of an extreme subjectivism, we might expect the Hawkshead poems to celebrate the psychological and epistemological authority of the external world, or—in one of the word's many senses—of "nature." In the second book of *The Prelude,* in particular, the poet presents his later "school-time" as a period during which his relationship to nature, hitherto "intervenient" and "secondary," became a direct and conscious love (II. 206–207). The "common range of visible things" grew dear to him (II. 182–183), and his observation of those things and their "minuter properties," their "differences" and "affinities," became attentive and exact (II. 301–320). It was in his seventeenth year—the year during which many of the Hawkshead poems were composed—that this "religious love" perceived universal Being wherever it looked: "I saw one life, and felt that it was joy" (II. 376, 405–430).

Although most students of Wordsworth's development have accepted this account, the evidence of the early poems requires that we qualify it in several significant ways. We are not, perhaps, entitled to dispute the poet's own memory of a "religious love" for nature. Nor do the poems written at the time fail to record occasional "Sentiments of Affection for inanimate Nature," as he entitled one of the selections he took to Cambridge (*PW* I, 369). In an unpublished passage of Ossianic prose he bids farewell to the "spirit of these mountains," and acknowledges that it had instructed him in the "love of nature" (DCP). At the close of *The Vale of Esthwaite* he imagines a future return to the scenes of his youth and binds up his "local attachment" to the place with his affection for his sister and his closest friend, in a movement that prefigures the close of *Tintern Abbey*. But aside from these few explicit and not unconventional sentiments, all of which appear to have been written during his last months at Hawkshead, when departure was imminent, there is little evidence of a primary and conscious recognition of nature's value. The poetry suggests rather that, in his role as an enthusiastic lyric poet, he regarded the natural objects of his affection with some condescension and that he consistently understood nature in terms of a decorum that was literary. Nature enters his poems only when the conditions set by those poems permit it.

Among the surviving work, for example, we find none of the genres we might expect from a "religious love" for nature. *The Vale of Esthwaite,* which is his only attempt at the most obvious vehicle for a reverent naturalism, the topographical poem, is less concerned with landscape than with the mind of the poet; like *L'Allegro* and *Il Penseroso,* it seeks to characterize a particular sensibility, that of the Hawkshead "Minstrel," and in only about an eighth of the surviving text does the poet have his eye on the natural object in any serious sense. The poem displays far less attention to landscape, in fact, than the more correct (and prosaic) topographical poem planned a few years later by his brother Christopher, whose poetic itinerary through "the glory of rugged Westmorland" can be mapped.[26] Nor is there any evidence that Wordsworth was moved to imitate the descriptive blank verse of James Thomson, the foremost exemplar of a sustained attention to concrete nature that was justified by religious enthusiasm. He used the seasonal motif only twice, and in both cases transmogrified it in the direction of the poetry of subjective feeling: his fragmentary and unpublished *Ode to Winter* imitates Collins and perhaps Cumberland, but not Thomson; and the elaborate seasonal analogy, described above, is dedicated to the description of mind, not landscape.

Nor does the style of these poems suggest a loving apprenticeship to nature; in most of them, natural imagery plays a role that is quite precisely "intervenient" and "secondary." As we have seen, such images frequently provide the subordinate term in illustrative and ornamental analogies, within generic contexts, such as elegy, complaint, or amorous compliment, that have nothing to do with landscape. And it is in such subordinate roles, paradoxically, that the loving attention to the "minuter properties" of natural objects claimed by *The Prelude* seems to have had its principal effect on Wordsworth's style. When humanistic and literary ends justify attention to landscape, Wordsworth looks at it closely; when, on the other hand, he undertakes to describe natural landscapes for their own sake, his style characteristically moves toward the highly figured and virtually opaque language of excited and creative imagination. In neither case does style reflect a belief that the external object is in itself a locus of value.

Although the weight of critical opinion and poetic practice throughout the eighteenth century emphasized the free manipulation of images by the mind, there was by the 1780's a substantial and growing body of opinion that stressed the poetic value of accurate and detailed representation of natural images. In 1756 Joseph Warton had praised James Thomson for having "enriched poetry with a variety of new and original images, which he painted from nature itself, and from his own actual observations," and a few years later John Aikin pointed to "the boundless variety of genuine beauties, applicable to every purpose of ornament, which nature liberally scatters around us." Hugh Blair (1763) found the descriptive imagery of Ossian "very correct," and "without exception copied from that face of nature which he saw before his eyes." [27]

It is not surprising that Wordsworth should have been sympathetic with this viewpoint. An accident of birth had placed him in a region that had been described in verse and prose for several decades, and that offered daily instruction on the relationship between word and thing. From what he saw with his own eyes, as he recalled in 1815, he recognized that Blair was wrong, and that the imagery of Ossian was "spurious" (*PW* II, 423). In a well-known note to *An Evening Walk* he recalled an evening during his schooltime when he noticed the dark silhouette of an oak against the bright western sky. The image, once revised, is preserved in *The Vale of Esthwaite:*

> The oak its boughs and foliage twines
> Mark'd to the view in stronger lines,
> Appears with foliage marked to view
> In lines of stronger browner hue,
> While, every darkening leaf between,
> The sky distinct and clear is seen.

(ll. 97–102)

"The moment," he wrote, "was important in my poetical history; for I date from it my consciousness of the infinite variety of natural appearances which had been unnoticed by the poets of any age or country . . . and I made a resolution to supply, in some degree, the deficiency" (*PW* I, 319). His language recalls Warton and especially Aikin, who had exemplified the "superior accuracy" with which the Roman poets had described trees, including the oak, in the *Gentleman's Magazine* of 1786 and 1787. If we look more closely at the circumstances under which Wordsworth described this image, however, it becomes apparent that his appeal from literary convention to nature was a very limited one. As de Selincourt points out (*PW* I, 368), Gray had described the "broader, browner shade" of the oak in his *Ode on the Spring.* Wordsworth looks more closely than Gray at the "minuter properties" of the scene; he sees the sky between "every darkening leaf," and notices the gradual intensification of contrast as the western sky brightens. But his attention is guided to this object by the authority of literary precedent, an authority he does not question. The young poet is "out for images," and he displays no sense that the value of this image resides in its empirical relationship to a "mighty sum of things" that has a decorum of its own. Here and elsewhere, he appears to have regarded the visible world as a source of discrete images that he imports under given conditions

into art. He would seem to have shared William Gilpin's condescension toward the external world itself:

> He who works from Imagination . . . culls from Nature the
> most beautiful parts of her productions—a *distance* here; and
> there a *foreground*—combines them artificially; and remov-
> ing everything offensive, admits only such parts, as are con-
> gruous AND beautiful.[28]

A similar spirit is suggested by Wordsworth's use of these "new
and original images" as subordinate terms in analogies. We have
already noticed one function of such analogies—to render subjective feeling apparent to the senses. In the heroic fragments and in
three of the lyrics we find a second type, which draws purely visual comparisons between a landscape and the human figure. As
conventional as other types, such analogies were regarded as characteristic of a primitive and natural style, and were exemplified
for Wordsworth by such poets as Chatterton and Macpherson:

> White her rode as the summer snow
>
> (*Minstrel's Song*)

> Thou art snow on the heath; thy hair is the mist
> of Cromla; when it curls on the hill, when it
> shines to the beam of the west! Thy breasts are
> two smooth rocks seen from Branno of streams.
>
> (*Fingal*)

Wordsworth characteristically elaborates such comparisons into
analogies that, like geometrical proportions, involve several terms
on each side. In his imitation of Anacreon's Ode XXVIII, for example, he surpassed earlier translators such as Cowley and Addison by inserting a series of miniature landscapes as guides to the
"Rhodesian painter" (Wordsworth's "Reynolds") who is painting
his beloved. Where Addison had translated, quite literally,

> Beneath the Shade of flowing Jet
> The Iv'ry Forehead smoothly set,[29]

Wordsworth amplifies:

> Let her forehead smooth and clear
> Through her shading locks appear,
> As at eve the shepherd sees
> The silver crescent through the trees.

(ll. 13–16)

The Prelude does not hint that the "affinities / In objects where no brotherhood exists / To common minds" (II. 403–405) were on occasion so frivolous, and it comes as something of a surprise to realize that the schoolboy's occupation on his rural excursions was to search out equivalents of the man in the moon, to see a row of teeth in a line of breaking waves or a flock of sheep, an eyebrow in an ivied bridge, or a woman's breasts in two swans—quite literally humanizing the "face of nature."

When Wordsworth describes natural landscape directly, in *The Vale of Esthwaite* and the pastoral *Idyllium*, his style remains sensitive to generic decorum, and generally seeks to justify itself by visibly adorning the landscape, or by employing the figured language of intense subjective response. Here, of course, he stands with the majority of poets and critics in his age. In neoclassical theory the argument from the uniformity of nature encouraged what Johnson called the "embellishment" of descriptive scenes, and for the poets of sensibility such scenes invited the exercise of the fabricative imagination. Collins' *Ode to Evening* could be praised by John Langhorne as an "introduction of fictitious life" into a "scenery" of "material objects" that would otherwise be "dull." Hugh Blair regarded the "figured style" as an expression of man's social instincts; "it introduces us into society with all nature." [30]

It ought not to surprise us, then, that few of Wordsworth's direct descriptions of landscape display the attention to visible reality that we find in his analogical landscapes. On several occasions he renders pastoral and domestic landscapes in a style that is deliberately plain, but far more often he resorts to a highly figured style that eloquently embodies the "wish for something loftier, more adorn'd, / Than is the common aspect, daily garb / Of human life" that he recalled, in partial contradiction of Books I and II, in the later *Prelude* (V. 599–601). Both of his explicit tributes to nature, for example, employ personification; the farewell to Helvellyn presents the mountain as a spirit able to remove clouds from its forehead, and his "sentiments of Affection" for inanimate objects are exemplified by the personification of a wreath of woodsmoke rising from a charcoal-hurdle, which, like the departing spirits of Gray's *Elegy,* lingers with "fond delay" at the "dear Spot" it had loved (*Vale of Esthwaite,* ll. 186–193).

When Wordsworth's attention moves from the pastoral to the sublime, from the "pleasures of a softer kind" exemplified even for the schoolboy by "Grasmere's heavenly vale" (*Vale of Esthwaite,* ll. 288–291), to the "mingling storms, roaring torrents, swelling oceans, lightning and thunder" that composed the landscape of *Ossian,* it brings with it a highly figured style that mingles and confuses subject and object, natural and supernatural, animate and inanimate. Here Wordsworth employs the "nobler" form of personification that Lord Kames termed "passionate," and that Ruskin would call the "pathetic fallacy": personification of natural objects with belief.[31] To the poet's "fear-struck mind," an aisle of sable firs seems "gigantic Moors in battle joined" (*Vale of Esthwaite,* ll. 211–219). In a significant admission that the "common range of visible things" is inadequate to his purposes, he elevates response to a waterfall, seen by night, by comparing it to a scene from Gothic romance:

> So oft in castle moated round
> In black damp dungeon underground
> Strange forms are seen that, white and tall,
> Stand straight against the coal-black wall.
>
> (*Vale of Esthwaite,* ll. 39–42)

Like the poets he imitated, he peoples his landscapes with ghosts, demons, spirits, and spectres. In the murmurs of an impending storm Charlotte Smith had heard the "Spirits of the Tempest"; in a "dying storm" Wordsworth hears the "Spirit of the surge" singing the "tempest's dirge" (*Vale of Esthwaite,* ll. 230–231). Through the "breaches" of a tempest in *Fingal* "look forth the dim faces of ghosts"; in *The Vale of Esthwaite* "the Demons of the storm in crowds / Glar'd through the partings of the clouds" (ll. 319–320). In another storm "scene" (ll. 274–283) the poet's excited imagination generates ultimate personifications: the God of the whirlwind, the Nature that is His instrument, and, in the background, Hell and Death.[32] These personifications may represent the "spirits" and "powers" Wordsworth would recall with gratitude in 1798. At times in the early notebooks we come across figures that remind us of Blake's early prophecies: "and I saw a mighty Spectre standing by the edge of a black cloud" (DCP). But in 1787 their origin is clearly literary, and their function ornamental or expressive. "The Yew-tree," Wordsworth recalled, "had its Ghost . . . for ornament" (*Prelude* VIII. 528–529).

An entirely different descriptive decorum governs the only pastoral elegy that survives from the Hawkshead years, the *Idyllium*. In this poem Wordsworth experiments with another literary mode he would soon abandon, that of classical mythology. Its two epigraphs quote Catullus on Lesbia's sparrow and Horace's pledge to immortalize the Bandusian Spring, and suggest Wordsworth's sense that the classical landscape was the site of both beauty and credulous animism.[33] He begins with a close imitation of the address to the nymphs in *Lycidas,* a passage Warton had praised at the expense of Pope's version of the same original, the first idyll of Theocritus:

> Where were ye, nymphs, when the remorseless deep
> Clos'd o'er your little favourite's hapless head?
>
> (ll. 1–2)

Milton's reference to the "famous Druids" in the next line evoked a miniature landscape:

> nor did ye mark the white moon beam
> Pace like a Druid through the shaggy wood
> Of Derwent.

In subsequent revisions Wordsworth suggested the credulity of the perceiving consciousness, as was appropriate to the pastoral elegy:

> For neither did ye mark with solemn *dread* . . .

Then, probably moved by memories of Milton's *Nativity Ode,* in which a landscape of "haunted spring and dale"—the landscape of Horace's Ode—is abandoned by the "parting Genius" of pagan superstition, he replaced the conventional epithet for a romantic wood, "shaggy," with the euphonious and suggestive "haunted steep":

> For neither did ye mark with solemn dread
> In Derwent's rocky woods the white moonbeam
> Pace like a Druid o'er the haunted steep;
> Nor in Winander's stream.

(ll. 3–6; DCP)

The effect, as John Jones has noted in his fine appreciation of this passage,[34] briefly looks forward to the style of Wordsworth's maturity. In the attempt to conform to the decorum of classical pastoral, he abandons the standards of "truth" that had shaped the intricate and ambitious analogies and personifications of his Gothic and Christian poems. His style becomes comparatively clear because the mode of perception being imitated—a pagan credulity and an imagination that is "lord/Of observations natural," as he would describe the ancient mind in *The Excursion* (IV. 707–708)—is false. Toward the end of the poem, as he hurls Horatian imprecations at the perfidious waters, his tone verges on the playful: "And may the dog star with his tonge of fire lap [?thy] waves; May no virgin lave/Her white limbs in thy cursed waves" (DCP).

The *Idyllium* therefore constitutes a partial exception to the descriptive style most characteristic of the Hawkshead poems, which freely, often violently, and quite seriously subordinates natural to human and supernatural form, and suggests on Wordsworth's part virtually no conscious recognition that external nature is a locus of independent and primary value. Whether he is describing the external world or the mind, he pays little attention to the relation between subject and object, and continues to embody the priority of subjective response over external form. The relationship between mind and nature is thus characteristically confused in these early poems, which fully justify Earl Wasserman's statement that descriptive poetry in Wordsworth's age either "evaded or left uneasily indecisive" the problem of "the transaction between the perceiving mind and the perceived world." [35]

Of particular interest, therefore, are those few passages in the Hawkshead poems that, seemingly without conscious intention, succeed in conveying the sense of nature's abiding presence, beyond the mind and its humanizing powers, that we associate with Wordsworth's mature work. Several passages display a marked sensitivity to the loss of visible imagery, and to the kind of sensuous deprivation that took an extreme form in the schoolboy's experience of the "abyss of idealism." He sees not the "dirt" in Mammon's mine, as Beattie had (*Minstrel,* I. 56), but its "dreary gloom" (*Vale of Esthwaite,* l. 562), and avails himself of several conventional gloomy Gothic enclosures. In imitation of Virgil and Thomson,[36] an evening landscape in *The Vale of Esthwaite* emphasizes the loss of visible forms, which

> From the blunt baffled Vision pass
> And melt into one gloomy mass.
> (*Vale of Esthwaite,* ll. 115–116; DCP)

Other passages in this poem celebrate the continuity of the line of sight between eye and object, as in an extended analogy between the rising moon and Hope (ll. 165–170), or between the longing retrospection of age and the beams of the setting sun:

My soul shall cast the wistful view
The longing look alone on you.
As Phoebus, when he sinks to rest
Far on the mountains in the west,
While all the vale is dark between
Ungilded by his golden sheen,
A lingering lustre fondly throws
On the dear hills where first he rose.

(*Vale of Esthwaite,* ll. 506–513)

Wordsworth memorialized the circumstances that inspired this image in *The Prelude,* where he finally and reluctantly attributed it to the inferior power that he had by then come to call the "fancy" (*Prelude* VIII. 454 [1850]), and he placed a polished version at the head of his collected poems, where it looks across the work of a lifetime to that other, more famous sunset that takes its coloring from an eye "that hath kept watch o'er man's mortality."

Such sensitivity to the availability of visual objects recalls the instinctive fear of solipsism displayed by Wordsworth's response to the "abyss of idealism." A few passages repeat the circumstances of that experience more exactly. Throughout the reverie that produced the "new-created image" of the *Idyllium,* as Wordsworth stood "blind" to nature, his dog stood guard at his side. Return from the trance issues in a spontaneous reaching-out of the hand, and a submerged appeal to the sense of touch:

Then, while my glad hand sprung to thee,
We were the happiest pair on earth.

(ll. 23–24)

In *The Vale of Esthwaite* a sound intrudes upon the "wondrous dream" of a minstrel:

Then fancy, like the lightning gleam,
Shot from wondrous dream to dream

> Till roused; perhaps the flickering dove
> Broke from the rustling boughs above.[37]

Although these images derive from Beattie's "Retirement," where the "scar'd owl on pinions gray / Breaks from the rustling boughs" (st. 7), this involuntary disruption of a subjective trance clearly endows the "common range of visible things" with heightened significance.

In another passage Wordsworth chides a noisy river for intruding upon his melancholy reverie, the "dirge within" (l. 399), and then attempts unsuccessfully to transform it into an appropriate analogy:

> Cease, cease, or rouse that sullen roar
> As, when a wintry storm is o'er,
> Thy rock-fraught heavy heaving flood
> Sounds dee [p], and creeps along the freezing blood.
>
> (ll. 404–407; DCP)

Ultimately, however, he gives up the attempt to impose literary conventions upon the river and acknowledges its autonomous happiness in rhythms borrowed from Gray's *Progress of Poesy* (ll. 31–34):

> Upon thy bosom pleasure dancing,
> Still retreating or advancing,
> Still art thou dear, fond prattler, run,
> And glitter in to-morrow's sun.
>
> (ll. 412–415; DCP)

A natural object actively resists the conventional forms the poet seeks to impose upon it, and reminds us that beyond the internally consistent and largely subjective decorum of these early poems there was indeed what Wordsworth would call a "real solid world / Of images" (*Prelude* VIII. 604–605)—a world in which image was based in solid substance, and could intrude upon and disrupt the dreams of a subjective and solipsistic "Fancy."

With the advantage of hindsight, we can recognize in such passages a dim prophecy of the naturalistic "creed" of 1798. In 1787,
however, such significance was clearly excluded by Wordsworth's
conception of his art. Each of the passages above concerns an object that fails to meet the standards of decorum set by the majority
of Wordsworth's poems. They are common, domestic, and familiar: a pet, a river addressed as if it were a pet, and a dove in a
tree. They thus offer a brief glimpse of the quotidian reality of the
schoolboy's relationship with nature: an affection for things he
takes very nearly for granted, and considers largely irrelevant to
the task of making poems. It is therefore a mistake, I believe, to
regard the early poems as evidence that the young Wordsworth
was psychologically incapable of seeing nature straight, as a recent
critic has suggested.[38] As he tells us in *The Prelude,* he imitated
books "knowingly" (VIII. 518). Like a medieval illuminator who
embroiders his margins with precisely detailed sketches from life,
and yet does not begin to question the propriety of conventional
stylization in the text, he saw nature quite clearly, but he did not
yet see the point of describing "the common range of visible
things" for its own sake. He knew perfectly well that the imagery of *Ossian* was spurious, and he imitated it all the more enthusiastically because it was poetic. A dedicated lyric poet, he was
drawn to none of the modes of literary realism that had been elaborated during the century, modes suggested by the names of
Thomson, Burns, Cowper, and Crabbe, and he could not yet begin
to perceive the sublime significance that the next ten years would
lend to the landscape about him.

IV

As inheritors of a romantic individualism that elevates the
unique above the typical, we are apt to forget that the categories
within which Wordsworth understood his own life, in prospect and
in retrospect, were bequeathed to him by his age, and that his

greatest poems confront moral and psychological problems that he regarded as representative. In the Hawkshead poems we find the assumptions about the growth of the individual mind that dominate his career: that the normal course of human life involves a crisis of transition from naturalism to an orthodox dualism; that this crisis threatens spiritual and psychological decay; and that the task of man and poet is to survive it, to relinquish youthful vision without loss of hope.

Virtually all the poets the young Wordsworth imitated make such assumptions, and they do so in a particular form: the belief that the power of "fancy" is dominant in youth, and that maturation involves a transition to a mature reason and the truths it reveals.[39] A detailed survey of their views lies beyond the scope of this book, but it is useful, before looking at Wordsworth's poems, to point out that conventional attitudes toward this transition varied widely and significantly. What may be called an orthodox and optimistic humanism was exemplified throughout the century by Alexander Pope, who in several celebrated distichs had affirmed his own passage from "Fancy's maze" to "Truth," and assimilated it to the Virgilian passage from pastoral to didactic genres, from "description" to "sense." Among later poets, however, and particularly the poets of sensibility, such optimism is rare; entrance into rational maturity becomes an occasion for passionate complaint. As the young Minstrel gaily pursues the rainbow, emblem of delusive hope, the adult narrator is touched by pity and envy:

> Perish the lore that deadens young desire!
> Pursue, poor imp, th' imaginary charm,
> Indulge gay hope, and fancy's pleasing fire:
> Fancy and hope too soon shall of themselves expire.

(I. 31)

Both situation and feeling could be duplicated in the work of John Langhorne, Helen Maria Williams, Charlotte Smith, or Thomas Gray, whom Beattie here imitates. All share his assumption that youth is blessed with hope, a hope mediated by the fancy and therefore solipsistic and delusive. For all, maturation brings a crisis that is epistemological and moral, a painful exposure of these illusions by reason and truth. Gray's figure for this crisis is particularly vivid: like the sacrificial lamb of the *Essay on Man,* the boys of his Eton College ode are "little victims" who await an "ambush" set by truth.

The loss of innocence and youth is a perennial subject for human complaint, but such complaints were clearly intensified by the philosophical and psychological doubts of the later Enlightenment, and in particular the crisis of confidence in reason and natural law. To grow up in Locke's world, as we have seen, was to accept the authority of a demonstrative reason that generated universal but nominal abstractions, or what Locke called "creatures of the understanding" (III, iii, 11), and to relinquish a "truth" that inhered in sensible images, a truth available to intuition as well as reflection. And to grow up was to confront the problem of reconciling evil with the inexorable processes of natural law, a law no longer generally apprehended within the context of revelation. Maturation therefore forces the surrender of a naïve and enthusiastic naturalism, and a recourse to other and more problematic grounds of hope: inference or faith. In the absence of revelation, Locke's system allowed the pure in heart to see God only by means of the divine analogy, which may have offered what Edward Young called "man's surest guide below" (*Night Thoughts* VI. 734), but which nevertheless remained a process of heuristic inference from visible to invisible, natural to supernatural. When the advent of autumn suggests to the Minstrel that all joy is mortal, his "simple Sire" responds with analogy:

> Heaven's immortal Spring shall yet arrive,
> And Man's majestic beauty bloom again.

(I. 27)

This heavenly "spring," though concrete, is factitious; it results from the transposition of natural images to invisible hopes. A franker and equally orthodox response to the ambush of youthful fancy was a blind fideism, which openly acknowledged man's blindness to ultimate objects of hope. When the Minstrel's complacency is shaken by a reading of "The Children in the Wood," a ballad that vividly unveils the gulf between natural law and human hope, Beattie himself intervenes with consolations drawn from the *Essay on Man:*

> Dark even at noontide is our mortal sphere;
> But let us hope; to doubt is to rebel.

(I.   47)

Neither of these orthodox consolations offers a psychological or poetic recompense for the loss of revelation. In each case rational maturity is effectively blind. Milton's Adam, it may be recalled, had feared a material world that blinded him to God:

> In yonder nether world where shall I seek
> His bright appearances, or footstep trace?
> (*Paradise Lost* XI. 328–329)

But Michael had reassured him, offering a hope that ministered to the senses as well as the reason:

> Adam, thou know'st heav'n his, and all the earth.
> Not this rock only; his omnipresence fills
> Land, sea, and air, and every kind that lives,
> Fomented by his virtual power and warmed.
> All th' earth he gave thee to possess and rule.
> (*Paradise Lost* XI. 335–339)

For many of the poets admired by Wordsworth, departure from what Gray had called the "paradise" of youth required the surrender of this numinous world. It is the youthful and delusive fancy that paradoxically offers man his only concrete experience of a "nature" that is in some sense adequate to the desires of his spirit.

The poets of sensibility are therefore characteristically divided in their allegiance; they uphold the truths of Newton and Locke only to deplore them, and their indulgence of youthful fancy becomes a self-conscious truancy. This dilemma could be resolved, of course, as Berkeley had resolved it, on idealistic grounds. By declaring that "Vision or Imagination is a Representation of what Eternally Exists [,] Really & Unchangeably," [40] Blake rendered the ambush of hope a sham, a solipsistic illusion generated by a fallen reason, and effectively reclaimed for poetry the spiritually significant object-world of pre-Enlightenment culture. The question that remained, however, was whether such epistemological and psychological integrity could be reclaimed on realistic grounds as well, without surrendering the traditional claim of Western humanism to the dignity of the reason. That this required great courage is suggested by Samuel Johnson's *Vanity of Human Wishes,* a poem that systematically exposes the temporal hopes of men, and then asks the logical but painful question:

> Where then shall Hope and Fear their objects find?
> Must dull Suspence corrupt the stagnant mind?
> Must helpless man, in ignorance sedate,
> Roll darkling down the torrent of his fate?
>
> (ll. 343–346)

Where, in the sensible world, is the mind to look for images of hope, concrete "objects" of sense and feeling that can be approved by the enlightened reason? Johnson rejects the orthodox consolations—the "objects" of hope manufactured by the divine analogy, the easy and yet ultimately hopeless comfort of nostalgia for a lost fancy, or a retreat into what seemed to him a protective subjectivism. Like Juvenal before him, he turns to the one empirical object that continues to offer hope, the "healthful mind" itself, and, as a Christian, celebrates its power to speak to God if not to see Him. He insists that hope, if it be won at all, be founded on the common "sense" of men.

The price of such integrity is fortitude, a fortitude that was rarely mustered by the poets of sensibility. As befit the champion of truth against the skepticism of David Hume, Beattie dedicated the second part of *The Minstrel* (1774) to an energetic defense of rational hope. The naïve and enthusiastic hero of the first part is here "humanized" by a philosophic sage, who directs him to Science, Art, and History, and exhorts discipline of the imagination and the passions—a course of studies that recalls the Hawkshead curriculum, as Wordsworth realized at the time.[41] Beattie seeks to demonstrate, in short, that a rational hope can survive the ambush of youthful fancy. At the height of his argument, however, the poet himself is ambushed by a menacing truth—the death of a close friend. And although his poem had exhorted a stoic fortitude that braves the "deadliest blow" of Fortune (II. 12), Beattie responds like the man of feeling he is, convulsively. The light of reason flickers and dims to a "funereal gleam" of mourning, as he melodramatically bids adieu to a poem that he now includes among the "lays that Fancy's flowers adorn, / The soft amusement of the vacant mind" (II. 62), and collapses into a grief-stricken silence. Reminded of Parson Adams or the stoic philosopher in *Rasselas,* the reader is left with the impression that, in his role as poet, neither Beattie's aesthetics nor his ethics can withstand the approach of truth. If Johnson had argued of *Lycidas* that authentic grief forbids pastoral artifice, for Beattie it would seem to forbid art itself. Given his assumption that poetry is dedicated to the "amusement" of the mind, or in Bacon's words, to the "desires of the mind," his most eloquent rhetorical response to pain is to lay down his pen. Changing conceptions of nature, reason, and art here act jointly to force the realistic poet into silence, a silence that raises the further question of whether there remained a place for a poetry that was at once, in Milton's words, "simple, sensuous, and passionate," and at the same time faithful to reason and truth.

Wordsworth inherited these questions and the dilemmas they imply, and the loss of youthful fancy is a major theme in *The Vale of Esthwaite.* As we might expect, the seventeen-year-old who seemed to his sister to resemble Beattie's Edwin assumed that the exercise of fancy was characteristic of youth as well as of lyric poetry, and he openly indulged it.[42] Fancy charms "life's tear-glister-ing morn" (l. 176), and throws a "rainbow on the cloud of grief" (DCP). But he was equally faithful to the epistemological assumptions taught him in the classroom, and although he attributes the power of creation to the fancy, he never follows Collins and Blake into an assertion of its veracity. He is, on the contrary, continuously conscious of its vulnerability to the truth, and, even as he celebrates the fancy, acknowledges its power to deceive:

> Through what sweet scenes did fancy rove
> While thus her fairy dreams she wove.
> Compared with fancy what is truth?
> And Reason, what art thou to Youth?
>
> (ll. 294–297)

Succeeding lines intimate the ambush that awaits such "dreams":

> Soft sleeps the breeze upon the deep
> Sweet flowers, while all in peace you sleep
> Dream of the tempest, which may blow
> Tomorrow, and may lay you low.
>
> (ll. 298–301; DCP)

On the inside front cover of the notebook he took with him to Cambridge he copied Beattie's lines:

> Indulge gay hope, and fancy's pleasing fire:
> Fancy and hope too soon shall of themselves expire
>
> (DCP)

and at the close of *The Vale of Esthwaite* he acknowledged that time would force him to "resign" even the "one timorous winking ray" with which Fancy might cheer his toil in "Mammon's joyless mine" (ll. 556–559; DCP), that is, a law office.

In other passages, however, he adopts a more prophetic stance: that of the realist who has survived the ambush of hope, and who openly repudiates the fancy. He acknowledges, for example, that a Gothic adventure, a descent into a dungeon, is one of the "idle toys" of a "sickly Fancy" (l. 269), an epithet that would remain accurate when he reviewed this period from the perspective of 1804 (*Prelude* VIII. 609). He repeatedly employs the divine analogy, transferring hope from natural to supernatural objects in the mode required by the dissolution of youthful fancy. He was particularly fond of the Catullan analogy between night and death, which he supplemented by postulating, as had Beattie in his "Ode to Hope," an eternal morn to come, or a moonlight of religious hope. In a passage he excerpted from *The Vale of Esthwaite,* he professes his willingness to share human pain (ll. 536–541). His more general indulgence of pathetic subjects may reflect an implicit assertion of maturity, a passage beyond the carefree paradise of a youthful fancy that like the Mirth of *L'Allegro* is "blind" to "Melancholy" (l. 550).

Wordsworth's most notable attempt at a humanistic seriousness, however, is personal: near the close of *The Vale of Esthwaite* he reconsiders his own response to his father's death, three years earlier. From *The Prelude* we know that at the time he had regarded this sudden reversal of his desires as an ambush, a divine "chastisement" of excessive hope (XI. 370). In 1787 he briefly recalls his wait for the horses, and the enigmatic landscape that portended and yet veiled the future, and then protests his present grief:

> Flow on, in vain thou hast not flowed,
> But eased me of a heavy load;
> For much it gives my heart relief
> To pay the mighty debt of grief.
>
> (ll. 428–431)

He here echoes the last line of *The Minstrel,* where Beattie had urged his tears to "flow forth afresh" (II. 63), and associates himself with a deliberate relinquishment of the "lays that fancy's flowers adorn"—a line he quoted at the head of the selections from *The Vale of Esthwaite* he took to Cambridge. On the eve of his departure for the university, he thus presents himself as a man who has already survived the ambush of hope, and dedicates himself, by implication, to a poetry of reason and truth.

Like his response to the "abyss of idealism," Wordsworth's rejection of the delusive fancy is prophetic. Although his language and his sentiments are colored by the poetry of sensibility, he instinctively detaches himself from the idealism that would feed the poetic theory of the romantic age to come, and associates himself with a chastened realism that has more in common with Johnson than either Gray or Blake, and that would become a characteristic posture of his genius. He would interpret the great psychological and moral crises of his career as "ambushes" of hope, and on each occasion would struggle not only to confront but to affirm what he regarded as the objective truth. Such sentiments end his affectionate farewell to Esthwaite in 1787, and they end his elegy for his brother John in 1806, where he again acknowledges the loss of the "Poet's dream" and claims that a "deep distress" has "humanized" his soul.[43] Although he has repeatedly been viewed as a naïve optimist, he was thus at the outset of his career deeply suspicious of an optimism that was potentially solipsistic and treacherous, and in later years he interpreted the course of human life as a process of relinquishment, in which the task of both man and poet is to look boldly on painful things, without surrendering the power and the dignity of speech.

It would appear, furthermore, that Wordsworth assumed from the beginning that a naturalism mediated by the fancy was unstable and temporary, and that in the normal course of human life the "ambush" of truth forced the transfer of hope from the natural to the supernatural world. At the close of *The Vale of Esthwaite* he adopts the stance of a man who has already passed beyond the delights of a childish naturalism and who rests his hopes on supernatural objects that are rendered visible by the conventional language of analogy; he was, in short, a "transcendentalist" at the age of seventeen. If, as readers have pointed out since his own time, the history of his work after 1800 reveals a gradual transition from a reverent naturalism to an orthodox dualism, this transition is not the end-point of a linear development, but a repetition of the crisis Wordsworth had already survived in 1787. He did not, that is, gradually discover that nature leads beyond nature, as is frequently assumed; he began with this conventional assumption, and in the years after 1800 returned to it.

From this perspective the crucial fact in his career becomes the interruption of this representative odyssey of hope by a vision that transformed the natural universe into a literal incarnation of divine power and love, and rendered an orthodox dualism supremely unnecessary. For six years Wordsworth would be granted an intermittent revelation of the "bright appearances" of God, under circumstances that permitted him to regard it not as a projection of youthful fancy but as self-evident fact. The central drama of his career lies in his struggle to perpetuate this revelation, and, as time gradually revealed that it, too, was a subjective illusion, to survive its loss.

V

I have discussed these "toilsome songs" in some detail because, when seen in their own terms and those of their age, they establish the significance of the changes to come. An equally important lesson to be learned from them, however, is that these changes, immense and influential as they were, very seldom involved a repudiation of the ideas and assumptions Wordsworth took for granted as a schoolboy. The well-known stances of his later years— naturalism, transcendentalism, Christian stoicism, and a forceful affirmation of the imagination's autonomy from nature— all develop conventional assumptions he had articulated at Hawkshead. Nor did his poetic character undergo fundamental change; he remained a poet of the human heart and a man of "lively sensibility" (*PW* II, 393), who almost necessarily took as his major task the return of poetry to the "paths of fair majestic Truth."

In each case what the schoolboy lacks is not the ideas of the mature man, but a sense of the significance of those ideas. The immense changes that would take place in his art and 'philosophy' during the next thirteen years do not, therefore, generally record the impact of new "doctrines" upon his mind, but his deepening understanding of old ones, and his increasingly radical application of such understanding to the purpose and technique of his art. This is not to discount the powerful extrinsic influences on his development, but to point out that they were seldom purely intellectual, that they quickly ceased to be purely literary, and that they subserved the larger end of enabling him to reconstruct the beliefs and hopes of the past. Under the pressures of his times, of personal crisis, and ultimately of the "necessity of growing old," he reinterpreted and reaffirmed one and then another of the conventional positions he had gathered together in his first poems, much as he returned, in outward life, to the landscapes that perpetuated the past and reconciled it to the present.

II   Cambridge and France: 1787-1792

"Enough: for now into a populous Plain
We must descend."

—The Prelude

The first of Wordsworth's many wanderings began in the fall of 1787 when he boarded the coach that would take him from Hawkshead to Cambridge. The prospect of this departure had already begun to endear his "native regions," as is evident from the several poetic farewells of 1787; but he could not have predicted the significance it would take on in retrospect. It was at this point that *The Prelude* virtually halted for four years, from 1800 to 1804, when Wordsworth finally described the departure from Hawkshead as a descent from an eminence into a "populous Plain" (III. 169–195). Books III and IV eloquently communicate the loss he suffered at Cambridge: the absence of outward objects of respect and veneration, his sense of the superficiality and the laxness of his joys and pastimes, and of a buried life that slept, untouched by "the surfaces of artificial life / And manners finely spun" (III. 590–591). The institution itself he compared to a theatrical performance, a "theatre / For Wake or Fair" (III. 607–608), or a "wide Museum" where variety and pleasure are casual and transient (III. 653). Virtues he had praised in his "School Exercise"—"generous Emulation," "Industry," and "Ambition" —all turned inward during these years, away from the public goals offered by the academic community and prized by his own

relatives. He failed to read for honors, surrendered his chances for a fellowship, and, perhaps in proud loyalty to the memory of William Taylor, refused to distinguish himself in the spring of his first year by eulogizing a master he neither knew nor honored. It was at Cambridge that Wordsworth first became what he would later call a "Borderer of his age" (*PW* V, 6, ll. 98 / 99 *app. crit.*).

I

The poetry Wordsworth wrote during the Cambridge years, from 1787 to 1791, suggests that he indeed attempted to put the "flowery lays" of a childish fancy behind him. Although his work remains derivative, his models change. Instead of the octosyllabic couplet, for example, he now experiments with the weightier and more stately pentameter line, in both blank verse and heroic couplets. Despite a continuing interest in the lyric of sensibility, and particularly the elegy, he now employs descriptive and narrative genres that reflect the influence of Virgil, Thomson, and the elder Milton, and prophesy his virtual abandonment in the next few years of lyric modes.

Along with Beattie's farewell to a flowery fancy, in the notebook he took with him to Cambridge, Wordsworth quoted the closing lines of Virgil's *Eclogues,*[1] and it is not surprising that one of his principal models during these years was the more mature, realistic, and responsible poet of the *Georgics*. Virgil had his eye on the object, as Wordsworth would acknowledge (*EY,* p. 641), and in each of his several translations of the *Georgics* Wordsworth disciplines the subjectivism of the poetry of sensibility. In his translation of Orpheus, for example, he goes out of his way to emphasize descriptive imagery and dramatic dialogue, devices that invest pathos in the object.[2] His own narratives are equally objective; in a group of fragments that apparently derive from a single story, a mother suffers from cold in a moonlit forest:

Regardless of her woes another babe
Sat by and smiled delighted [,] for he beheld
A glowworm in his little gleaming hand.
He touch'd it with his finger—while his face
Was bright with laughter, wildly did he talk
With the pale fire; and toss'd it to and fro
Then gaz'd the stars that on the brow of night
Dim twinkled.

(DCP)

This scene clearly attempts to evoke pathos; "I could a tale re-late," Wordsworth added to one fragment, "Of that unhappy fam-ily, more sad / More piteous in its circumstance . . . [*cetera de-sunt*]" (DCP). But it follows Virgil in doing so by means of objective "circumstance." [3] Elsewhere, Wordsworth adds a con-crete and literal dimension to the allegorical tableaux he had de-lighted in at Hawkshead. He recasts a portrait of "moody Mad-ness" in a slow-moving blank verse, for example, and inserts a simile that reflects the influence not of Gray but of Virgil and the elder Milton:

And madness barking on his hands and feet
While foam'd his mouth; and through his shaggy hair
His green swoln eyes glar'd dismal; as at night
The stranger wildering o [']er the dreary moors
Starts at two lights expiring on the ground
As moves the rustling wind the long dank grass.

(DCP)

Elsewhere he draws on a literal description in Erasmus Darwin's *Botanic Garden* to elaborate a single metaphor of *The Vale of Esthwaite* ("the shipwreck of the thought," l. 547) into an allegory for madness: a parent "Reason" becomes the victim of shipwreck, and is helpless to "relieve the pain" of the other powers of the mind: "Fear, Religion, Charity and Love, / Pity and Hope." [4]

Both allegories reflect a new reluctance to indulge the irrational, as does the original version of the "Remembrance of Collins," a sonnet that Wordsworth composed during a "solitary walk" along the banks of the Cam (*PW* I, 324). Here he puts his favorite source of analogical imagery, the sunset, to a new use, and compares the coloring of the evening sky to the "fairy views" that "smile before/The poet [heedless] of the following shades" (DCP). At the poem's close he locates the scene on the Thames, and alludes to Collins' "Ode on the Death of Mr. Thomson":

> Witness that son of grief who in these glades
> Mourned his dead friend: suspend the dashing oar.

He thus converts a landscape emblematic of the inevitable and treacherous decay of poetic fancy into a comment on the madness and early death of the visionary poet he had imitated so enthusiastically at Hawkshead. Like his other work at the time, the poem reflects the disillusioned realism of a young man whose hopes had "melted fast away" at Cambridge (*Prelude* III. 437). Unlike the poets of sensibility, however, Wordsworth refuses to convert this recognition into a self-indulgent lament for a lost paradise of delusive fancy. He tends rather toward an ironic and implicitly bitter juxtaposition of hope and reality, which avoids the utterance of personal emotion altogether.

The positive energies of the Cambridge poems, on the other hand, are directed toward natural landscape, and by implication the "native regions" Wordsworth had put behind him. And here, too, he was guided by the *Georgics,* from which he translated several passages that reveal marked changes in his attitude toward landscape. In one he bids shepherds to be kind to their flocks, in a style that seeks to recreate the sensuous reality of an absent landscape: "Give them to taste the cooling rural vale/While yet the star of Morning glimmers pale" (DCP; *Georgics* III. 324). In another he freely expands Virgil's celebrated encomium of rural virtue:

> To them the acts of falsehood are unknown
> And nature's various wealth is all their own.
> And living lakes and caves of coolness . . .
> All nature smiles.
>
> (DCP; *Georgics* II. 467–469)

Passing over a line that described his situation at Cambridge with some precision, in which Virgil protests his "love for the waters and the woods" though "fame be lost" (*Georgics* II. 486), Wordsworth continues: "Let me lie /Far in some vale, on Haemus cool and high . . ." (DCP; *Georgics* II. 488–489).

That Wordsworth should choose these passages suggests the influence of the inevitable comparisons between Cambridge and Hawkshead, between the "grave Elders" of the university and the "Shepherd Swains" of Westmorland (*Prelude* III. 574–580), as well as his memories of the natural beauties of the north, which, a classmate would recall, he praised "with a warmth indeed which, at that time, appeared to me hardly short of enthusiasm." [5] Clearly, he now values a "common range of visible things" that he took for granted in 1787. From the standpoint of Cambridge, furthermore, his moral perspective merges with that of Virgil, with whom he rejects the idle pleasures of a Theocritan Arcadia and instead celebrates the virtuous industry of the Roman or Westmorland farmer. Here, for the first time, he moralizes and objectifies the conventional nostalgia of "local attachment" that had characterized his farewells to Hawkshead a year earlier, and appears to have proved upon his pulses the beliefs that would encourage him to greet the French Revolution as a "work of nature," and in later years justify the subjects and the diction of the *Lyrical Ballads*.

A similar appreciation for concrete nature appears in the original compositions of the time, many of which adhere to the decorum of the loco-descriptive poem and adopt a style far more literal and detailed than that of the Hawkshead poems. In several of these, furthermore, Wordsworth draws for the first time upon the conventional theme of natural sympathy. A popular motif in descriptive poetry throughout the eighteenth century, the predication of some form of emotional relationship to an objective landscape obviously requires a poetic style that can distinguish subject from subject, a condition seldom attained by the Hawkshead poems:

> Now o'er the saddened heart we feel
> A tender twilight slowly steal.
>
> (DCP)

This "twilight" is analogical; it exists purely in the mind. When Wordsworth alters "saddened" to "accordant," however, and qualifies this twilight as "sympathetic," as he did at Cambridge,[6] he is clearly insisting upon the simultaneous existence of an external and objective world, and focusing attention upon the mind's empirical relationship to that world.

Like their probable models, the sonnets of William Bowles, Wordsworth's Cambridge sonnets progress from a literal description of a particular landscape to some assertion of sympathy for that landscape, and to what the young Coleridge admiringly called "a sweet and indissoluble union between the intellectual and the empirical world." [7] The three quatrains of the unpublished "When slow from pensive twilight's latest gleams," for example, enumerate details in an evening landscape. The couplet echoes the speaker of Bowles's first sonnet (who had been "sooth'd by the scene") and a *je ne sais quoi* motif recalled from Hawkshead:

> Soothed by the [?stilly] scene, with many a sigh
> Heaves the full heart, nor knows for whom nor why.
>
> (DCP)

A pastoral scene exerts a similar power in "Sweet was the walk along the narrow lane", as it "agrees" with the poet's "Soul" (*EY*, p. 74); and, in "Written in Very Early Youth," evening inspires a "strange harmony" between mind and nature. In each sonnet Wordsworth devotes closer attention than Bowles to the landscape and less to subjective response. All suggest that the relationship of speaker to landscape is not simply analogical but empirical.

II

Although, according to *The Prelude,* Wordsworth returned to the Lakes with unfeigned joy, this "auspicious . . . outset" was soon belied by a recognition of change and loss, not only in the landscape but within himself. Though not unrelieved by "moments of conformity" to what he had been, there seemed to be a "falling-off" and "inner weakness" (IV. 270 [W]). He gave himself up to what seemed in retrospect a "vague heartless chace/Of trivial pleasures" (IV. 304–305), and was afflicted by a "swarm/Of heady thoughts" (IV. 272–273). He could not forget himself:

> The very garments that I wore appear'd
> To prey upon my strength, and stopp'd the course
> And quiet stream of self-forgetfulness.
>
> (IV. 292–294)

The Prelude does not specify the deeper causes for this distress. We may remember, however, that Wordsworth was returning from a disappointing year at Cambridge to scenes that had very likely become a source of hope and expectation in themselves, a return which may have thrown the extent of his disappointment into painful relief. Whatever its causes, this equivocal and unsettled state of mind was apparently that in which he turned again to the poem he had written to celebrate his departure a year earlier, *The Vale of Esthwaite,* and began to transform it into the topographical poem that he would publish in 1793 as *An Evening Walk.*[8]

Wordsworth and most of his critics would regard this poem as an egregious capitulation to conventional stylistic vices, and take it as a striking contrast to the work of 1798 and after. But when we compare *An Evening Walk* to the Hawkshead poems it takes on a broader and more positive significance as a vivid and, at times, extreme example of the kinds of discipline suggested by the minor poems and fragments of the Cambridge years. It is, in the first place, a correct and polished topographical poem, which testifies to the unabated ambitions of its author. It accepts and exploits the conventions common to the genre during the century, and employs the closed heroic couplet, the most obvious vehicle for a demonstration of poetic skill, as well as for the moralization of the octosyllabics of a year before.[9]

As virtually all its readers have noted, the most striking aspect of the poem is its imagery, and more broadly its devotion to the description of landscape.[10] Except for an introduction that casts the poem as an epistle to a dear friend, it consists entirely of descriptive scenes, ordered, like those of *The Vale of Esthwaite,* in a temporal sequence from noon, through sunset, to the concluding appearance of the moon. Some scenes are picturesque compositions: a "cascade scene," "sunset," or, as an example of local superstition, the appearance at sunset of phantom horsemen on the slopes of the hills. Others exemplify the mode Wordsworth would call "bricklaying," or the "formal accumulation" of particular images as members of a class (*LY,* p. 307): "twilight sounds," or various objects touched by the light of the sinking sun. In all, Wordsworth seeks effects that in the words of a contemporary guidebook "please the eye by richness of tints or variety of shades."[11] To a circumstantial account of the "visionary horsemen," for example, he added light, shade, and color:

> Anon, in order mounts a gorgeous show
> Of horsemen shadows winding to and fro;
> And now the van is gilt with evening's beam
> The rear thro' iron brown betrays a sullen gleam.[12]
>
> (ll. 183–186)

This is indeed the most colorful of any of Wordsworth's poems; there are more "blue," "red," and "purple" things in its 446 lines than in the whole of the final version of *The Prelude.*[13]

Comparison between work of 1788 and that of 1787 suggests,

furthermore, that Wordsworth deliberately corrected his earlier imagery, presumably by looking more closely at the landscape about him. In 1787, for example, he had entered into affectionate dialogue with, but did not describe, a "dear brook"; now he describes a "dear rill," which he identifies in a note as the lower fall at Rydal, in minute detail:

> To where, while thick above the branches close,
> In dark-brown bason its wild waves repose,
> Inverted shrubs, and moss of darkest green,
> Cling from the rocks, with pale wood-weeds between;
> Save that, atop, the subtle sunbeams shine,
> On wither'd briars that o'er the craggs recline;
> Sole light admitted here, a small cascade,
> Illumes with sparkling foam the twilight shade.
>
> (ll. 73–80)

As de Selincourt points out, this "visto" recalls Thomson's description in *Spring:*

> With woods o'erhung, and shagged with mossy rocks
> Whence on each hand the gushing waters play,
> And down the rough cascade white-dashing fall
> Or gleam in lengthened vista through the trees.
>
> (ll. 910–913)

But it is far closer to the portrait drawn by Mason of the actual scene, as quoted in West's *Guide to the Lakes:*

> Not a little fragment of a rock thrown into the bason, not a single stem of brush-wood that starts from its craggy sides, but has a picturesque meaning; and the little central current dashing down a cleft of the darkest coloured stone, produces an effect of light and shadow beautiful beyond description.[14]

Wordsworth's eye is more attentive to the object than Mason's; by enumerating visual details, he seeks to describe what is "beyond description." [15]

Such preoccupation with imagery has an obvious effect on other dimensions of Wordsworth's style: it intensifies the bravura with which he manipulates diction and syntax. Instead of bodying forth the shape of things unknown, he demonstrates his skill by choosing the unusual epithet or periphrasis, or, more frequently, by rearranging the order of the English sentence. Such vices were summarized in detail by Legouis,[16] and need not be catalogued here, but we may note that they follow in part from Wordsworth's commitment to the natural image. In his attempt to pack concrete details into the couplet, he placed inordinate emphasis on adjectives and substantives, and seriously weakened the power of his verbs.[17] Other vices, however, were clearly sought for their own sake. In the *Idyllium* Wordsworth had described the islands of Winander,

> Which hear her far-off ditty sweet,
> Yet feel not ev'n the milkmaid's feet.

(ll. 9–10)

In 1788 he dignifies this image simply by distorting syntax:

> Where, tho' her far-off twilight ditty steal,
> They not the trip of harmless milkmaid feel.

(ll. 225–226)

In *The Vale of Esthwaite* an owl had greeted the rising moon:

> The moaning owl shall soon
> Sob long and tremulous to the moon.

(ll. 200–201)

A year later Wordsworth deliberately renders his language "knotty and contorted," in Coleridge's phrase (*BL* I, 56):

> The bird, with fading light who ceas'd to thread
> Silent the hedge or steaming rivulet's bed,
> From his grey re-appearing tower shall soon
> Salute with boding note the rising moon.

(ll. 389–392)

One senses that Wordsworth looks with some contempt upon the style of the Hawkshead poems, a style that by comparison seems the real language of men, and that his alterations bespeak the pride that in 1800 he would criticize all the more harshly because it had been his own.

Wordsworth's tolerance of obscurity does not carry over into his poetic epistemology. In *An Evening Walk,* as in the minor poetry of the Cambridge years, he insists upon clarifying the distinction between subject and object. Landscape no longer serves largely as an analogy for mind; instead, and in striking contrast to his practice a year earlier, he imposes a rigorous discipline on all figures that distort or obscure the relation between mind and landscape: analogy, personification, and metaphor. Virgil offered a practical model for such discipline, but theoretical guidance appears to have come from a modern critic, John Scott of Amwell. In a note subjoined to his sunset scene, Wordsworth refers the reader to Scott's *Critical Essays* (1785),[18] and in particular to Scott's commentary on a sunset in Thomson's *Summer:*

> Low *walks* the sun, and broadens by degrees,
> *Just o'er the verge of day.* The shifting clouds
> *Assembled gay,* a richly-gorgeous train,
> In all their pomp attend his setting throne.
> Air, earth, and ocean, *smile immense.* And now
> As if his weary chariot sought the bowers
> Of Amphitrite, and her tending nymphs,
> (So Grecian fable sung) he dips his orb;
> Now half-immers'd; and, now a golden curve,
> Gives one bright glance, then total disappears.
> (*Summer,* ll. 1620–29)

The italics are Scott's, who commented that the passage "is truly poetical but very incorrect," and the imagery "beautiful" but "inconsistent." "The sun's walking," he continued, "is an act that can relate only to the real visible globe of fire: the mention of the 'setting throne' again indicates a prosopopoeia, and the 'dipping' of 'the orb' again implies a reference to the natural object" (p. 347).

Scott does not object to figures per se, but to a style that mingles them without regard to the literal truth, imposing decorative personification (the 'throne') in one line and withdrawing it in the next. Moved by a Quaker's suspicion of ornamental falsehood, he censures the "poetical" confusion of subject with object, of what he elsewhere called "the product of the Poet's imagination" with "circumstances . . . actually existent in nature" (p. 299). He would therefore correct Thomson by segregating the literal from the figurative:

> This would have been a most masterly piece of composition . . . if the gradual descent and enlargement of the sun, its immersion within the horizon . . . (all fine natural and picturesque circumstances) had been regularly connected, and the romantick idea of "Phoebus's" chariot [had] . . . been kept entirely distinct, and introduced last as an illustrative allusion (pp. 347–348).

As an example of what Thomson might have done, he then quotes a sunset scene by Moses Browne.

Such principles, which rigorously discipline the use of figures, are characteristic of Scott,[19] and they are respected throughout Wordsworth's poem. In his own sunset scene (ll. 151–174), for example, Wordsworth follows Scott almost to the word. His sun does not "walk" but "sinks," and rests not on a metaphorical "verge of day" but on a "steep," an image Scott had praised in Browne's sunset. Wordsworth even quotes Browne (l. 158), and deletes the decorative personifications of the throne and the chariot. A similar discipline is evident throughout the poem. Although it contains as many personified abstractions as *The Vale of Esthwaite,* they are clustered within a few passages that describe subjective phenomena: the author's introductory "regret of his Youth" (ll. 17–52), and the fear and suffering of a female beggar (ll. 242–300). Here his style is fully as figurative as in the Hawkshead poems. Elaborating an image in Gray's ode on vicissitude (ll. 29–36), for example, he finds an analogy to the life of man in a sundial:

With Hope Reflexion blends her social rays
To gild the total tablet of his days;
Yet still, the sport of some malignant Pow'r,
He knows but from its shade the present hour.

(ll. 39–42) [20]

In the descriptive passages of the poem, however, he consistently avoids the personification of abstract ideas. He also disentangles natural objects from the passionate personifications he had fabricated a year earlier. He had seen, for example, a wreath of wood smoke as a spirit reluctant to leave its home; now it curls "from the trees" in an afternoon landscape (l. 108). When he does animate natural objects he emphasizes natural function; to the speaker's eyes the cliffs "aspire" (l. 157), and to the terrified imagination of the vagrant the lightning seems to hold a torch (l. 298). Although such discipline relaxes somewhat after sunset, when the absence of visible objects encourages surmise, Wordsworth never imposes new visible forms upon nature: murmuring streams, for example, become "far-off minstrels of the haunted hill," but they remain sounds (l. 326); streaks of moonlight on a lake imply "fair Spirits" (l. 347), who themselves remain invisible. The only extended analogy in the poem survives from *The Vale of Esthwaite:* a comparison between the rising moon and hope. The Gothic motifs of the earlier poem disappear, and the only reference to "fancy," which implies its delusiveness, was deleted before publication (l. 255 *app. crit.*).

Neither of the stylistic changes we have noticed—an intensified devotion to the natural image and a rigorous discipline of the subject-object relationship—is surprising at this time. Like *Tintern Abbey* and *Home At Grasmere, An Evening Walk* celebrates reunion of the eye with a beloved landscape, a landscape endowed with new significance by separation. In contrast to the Hawkshead poems, it assumes the intrinsic value of "the common range of visible things," and its emphasis on imagery may be viewed as a poetic response, framed within the available conventions, to Wordsworth's homecoming. That he should call his reader's attention to his correction of Thomson, who in Warton's words had "painted from nature herself," points not only to the survival of his literary ambitions, and the loss of "dread awe / Of mighty names" (*Prelude* VI. 72–73), but to a new conception of himself as a serious nature poet. The mode of this correction, moreover, no longer assumes that "accuracy" is simply a matter of fidelity to visual appearance; description now requires the clear segregation of mind from nature, as would have seemed appropriate to a young man who sensed that "objects hitherto the gladsome air / Of my own private being" were subject to independent destinies (*Prelude* IV. 226–227), and who now refused to humanize a nature he valued for itself.

Such interpretations seem insufficient, however, in the light of other aspects of Wordsworth's style in this poem. These suggest that this centrifugal movement toward nature was intensified, consciously or unconsciously, by the unsettled state of his feelings at the time. At the poem's outset, for example, the speaker's language is rich in references to his own consciousness. Looking back on his youth, he professes a nostalgic melancholy, and promises to review these scenes with Memory at his side (l. 43). The descriptive parts of the poem, however, are virtually devoid of subjective reference. Style now exerts a rigorous discipline over the statement or dramatization of consciousness; as Wordsworth wrote when reintroducing it in 1815, it lacks "thought, sentiment, and almost . . . action" (*PW* II, 434 *app. crit.*). The speaker exhibits no melancholy; he never reflects, never recollects. He does not mention the moral virtues of rural life, nor does he state his own affection for "inanimate Nature," as he had done at Hawkshead. Except for a few professions of delight in observation ("I love to mark," l. 141), he once describes his heart as "accordant" (l. 381) and follows Bowles in attributing to evening sounds the power to compose the breast (l. 309). Only one emphatic personal feeling is voiced in the poem: his hope that he and his "dearest friend" may find a home in a distant cottage revealed by the moon (ll. 413–422).

Nor does this style succeed in implying feeling, by means of repetition, for example, or through significant shifts of attention. As it traces the contrasts and lines of composition prescribed by the canons of picturesque beauty, his eye shifts with clock-like regularity in time to the couplet, marking what Samuel Johnson called the "intersection" of rhyme.[21] And the landscape itself is largely devoid of subjective references. The only human being in the foreground of the poem, a female vagrant, suffers and dies. Described in violently figurative language, her turbulent consciousness contrasts abruptly with the tranquillity of the natural order. Her death is followed by the most violent transition in the poem, as the eye moves from her infants,

> Thy breast their death-bed, coffin'd in thine arms
>
> (l. 300)

to a series of "evening sounds":

> Sweet are the sounds that mingle from afar,
> Heard by calm lakes, as peeps the folding star.
>
> (ll. 301–302)

Other human figures are distant, like those that work or muse in the landscapes of Claude. These seem to have little or no subjective existence:

> Their pannier'd train a groupe of potters goad,
> Winding from side to side up the steep road;
> The peasant from yon cliff of fearful edge
> Shot, down the headlong pathway darts his sledge.
>
> (ll. 109–112)

In each respect this poem effectively reverses the dominant affiliations of the Hawkshead poems to sensibility and the subject. In them, Wordsworth had presented the heart itself without reference to "any determin'd object." Now he presents the object without reference to the heart.

Of the two virtually symmetrical forms of epistemological imbalance, the passionate objectivity of *An Evening Walk* would seem the more compulsive, a product of the fear of self-consciousness recalled in *The Prelude*. What pure sensation, and its rhetorical equivalent, imagery, offers in this poem is not only relationship to nature but forgetfulness of self. The objectivity of the poem is therefore unstable; it enacts that form of psychological division and degradation in which, as Wordsworth would write, the eye is "master of the heart," and the will rejoices to "lay the inner faculties asleep" (*Prelude* XI. 172, 195). For all their subjectivism and terror, the Hawkshead poems seem by comparison to be the products of integrity. They spring from a mind that takes its own activity for granted, and exults in the articulation of feeling and sentiment. In them we sense a self; in much of *An Evening Walk* we sense only a silently moving eye.[22]

This poem, then, presents something of a paradox. In its devotion to the sensible world, and to the resolution of epistemological confusion, it clearly points toward the future. To give only one example: Wordsworth's clearest definition of the function of the imagination in 1798 or shortly thereafter is quoted from Scott. And yet such prophetic changes are in part the product of psychological distress, and they effectively suppress the most enthusiastic commitment of the Hawkshead poems, to sensibility. The psychological dilemma implied by *An Evening Walk,* therefore, is that a compulsive naturalism deprives the mind of freedom, dignity, and identity. Its technical corollary is that a language of empirical transcription—a picturesque Dutch realism—is entirely inadequate to the description of relationship between mind and nature, and of the excursive activity that embodies the dignity and identity of the mind. The most obvious symptom of maturity and psychological integrity in Wordsworth's later verse, and the goal toward which his development after 1788 tends (in a progress by no means linear), is a capacity to affirm both the freedom and power of the mind and its dependence upon an order external to it. And it is in this direction that he most obviously moves, within a genre and a language still predominantly conventional, in his next poem, the *Descriptive Sketches.*

III

Although the second of the two poems that Wordsworth "huddled up" and "sent into the world" in January 1793 shares the contorted syntax of its predecessor, and has been repeatedly grouped with it as evidence of his early stylistic vices, the differences between *An Evening Walk* and *Descriptive Sketches* are manifold and profound. The latter poem proceeds not from immediate observation but from the memory of a landscape—the scenes Wordsworth and his friend Jones viewed on their Alpine walking tour of 1790. Although (with one exception) these scenes are presented in the order in which they were viewed, and may be said to recall the aesthetic impact of the Alps on the mind of the picturesque traveler of 1790, they are consistently reinterpreted in the light of Wordsworth's ideological commitment to the French Revolution during the summer and fall of 1792, when the poem was composed.

As an example of the impact of the Revolution on Wordsworth's descriptive style, one may take a passage that seemed to Coleridge "an emblem of the poem itself, and of the author's genius as it was then displayed" (*BL,* I, 57), a sunset scene:

> 'Tis storm; and hid in mist from hour to hour
> All day the floods a deeper murmur pour,
> And mournful sounds, as of a Spirit lost,
> Pipe wild along the hollow-blustering coast,
> 'Till the Sun walking on his western field
> Shakes from behind the clouds his flashing shield.
> Triumphant on the bosom of the storm,
> Glances the fire-clad eagle's wheeling form;

Eastward, in long perspective glittering, shine
The wood-crown'd cliffs that o'er the lake recline;
Wide o'er the Alps a hundred streams unfold,
At once to pillars turn'd that flame with gold;
Behind his sail the peasant strives to shun
The west that burns like one dilated sun,
Where in a mighty crucible expire
The mountains, glowing hot, like coals of fire.[23]

(ll. 332–347)

Although several details from the sunset of *An Evening Walk* persist, such as the dilated sun, this passage embodies a selective yet forceful rejection of the epistemological discipline preached by Scott. Wordsworth once again mingles "the productions of . . . imagination" with "circumstances actually existing in nature." He humanizes the visible world, interpreting the sound of the storm as the cry of a spirit, as he had at Hawkshead, personifying the sun with the very verb ("walks") he had self-consciously deleted from Thomson's sunset in 1788, and adding a decorative appurtenance, the "flashing shield."

In structure and movement, furthermore, the passage clearly transcends the balanced antitheses of light and shade praised by the proponents of the picturesque. The "new images" presented in the sunset of 1788 had emphasized such contrasts: the "long blue bar" that divided the orb of the setting sun, and the "steep" whose "edge" flamed with gold. Now, however, Wordsworth avoids painting shades altogether, and proceeds in a mode that is incremental, not antithetical. The movement from darkness ("mist") to light is not a balance of opposites, but a dynamic progression, hinted by sound that is building to intensity ("deeper murmur"), and embodied by images of light that mount steadily to a climax. The eye moves from west to east and back again—from a personified sun to light that "glances" from the eagle overhead (a verb that implies but does not name a contrasting shade), to the light reflected from the eastern waterfalls, where it is intensified further by numerical and visual hyperbole. Attention then returns to the west, is intensified further en route by the efforts of the peasant to seek a shade, again unnamed, and finally beholds a sun stripped of personification and enlarged to a preternatural size. The last couplet carries Moses Browne's hyperbolic "prospect all on fire," quoted in *An Evening Walk,* to an extreme that precludes all contrast whatsoever.

If the variegated landscapes of the earlier poem recall those of Claude, this points with some force to the impressionism of Turner—a comparison that recalls the significance, to the age of Locke and Pope as well as Claude, of the assumption violated here: that order, natural and political as well as aesthetic, resides in a *discordia concors* that encloses and balances antithetical extremes. This is, in short, a revolutionary style, which suggests that Wordsworth's vision of landscape was profoundly changed by the events of 1791 and 1792. He defended such extremity in a formal note to this passage, which may be taken as a considered reply to the English critics who had influenced his earlier descriptions, Aikin, Warton, and especially Scott. Appealing to a mode of visible reality that transcends theirs, he argues that the "sublime features" of the Alps are "insulted" by the term "Picturesque" (*PW* I, 62n), and takes his stand with Ramond de Carbonnières, who in his commentary on William Coxe's *Travels in Switzerland* had emphasized the futility of a pictorial rendering: "Whatever could represent these mountains lacks grandeur, and grandeur is what characterizes them" ("Tout ce qui pourroit représenter ces monts, manque de grandeur, & la grandeur est ce qui les caractérise").[24] In particular reply to Scott's insistence on a clear separation of subject from object, Wordsworth argues that the Alps can be adequately rendered only by a style that embodies subjective response: "Whoever . . . should confine himself to the cold rules of painting would give his reader a very imperfect idea of those emotions which [the Alps] have the irresistible power of communicating to the most impassive imaginations." He therefore consulted two authorities—"nature" and his own "feelings"—and sought to portray the "unity of the impression" he had experienced. He does not, it should be noted, surrender the claim to truth, as he had in indulging a delusive fancy five years before. Here and elsewhere in the poem,[25] he returns to a figured style in order to render a phenomenon that is quite objective: the "controuling influence" over the mind that "distinguishes the Alps from all other scenery," and the power he now calls "nature."

He had, of course, encountered an enthusiasm for "nature" that was essentially philosophical in the poetry of Thomson and other celebrants of the Newtonian universe, but had largely ignored it. The term itself appears only sporadically in the Hawkshead poems and not at all in *An Evening Walk*. Now, however, he enthusiastically reverses himself and repeatedly looks beyond the visible particulars of the Alpine landscapes to the power that comprehends them, which he presents as active, normative, and far more sublime than visible appearances alone. "Nature" is morally pure, a "vestal" who guards man (l. 528), a "secret Power" that is profaned by man (l. 424), or a "savage" who humbly joins the ritual of prayer to man's God (l. 554). According to the Swiss mountaineer, "angry Nature" is the instrument of a Divine vengeance provoked by human sin (ll. 486–487). Natural law is "ever just" (l. 490), and offers the beauty and sublimity of its appearances, and "no vulgar joy" (l. 512), to the human heart. A "doubly pitying Nature" offers it "charities" to the pedestrian traveler, who finds a friend in "every babbling brook" (ll. 13–28).

Such sudden exaltation of "nature" not only points to the influence of the French Revolution; it raises, for the first time, the central paradox of Wordsworth's much-debated "philosophy," that it was built out of philosophical commonplaces, transformed by passion and personal experience into ultimately great poetry. What J. W. Beach has shown of Wordsworth's later conception of "nature" is equally true in 1792;[26] it is syncretic, but by no means esoteric or arcane. In the charitable nature that comforts the traveler is the psychological power celebrated by Thomson, Gray, Beattie, and Bowles. A suddenly elevated sense of the justice, power, and benevolence of natural law reflects ideas common to Rousseau, d'Holbach, and other pre-revolutionary political theorists, ideas that were "on every tongue" in the France of 1792 (*Prelude* IX. 202) and which Wordsworth almost certainly discussed with Michael Beaupuy during their walks along the Loire. His explicit appeals to religious feeling and belief remind us, furthermore, that he by no means shared the skepticism of the *philosophes,* and that, like Bacon, Milton, and Newton, he conceived of nature as the creation of God and an instrument of God's will.

Wordsworth's application of such ideas to the Alpine landscape was guided, furthermore, by the commentaries of Ramond, whose precise and detailed descriptions constantly imply a lofty and philosophical conception of nature.[27] His discussion of the various kinds of avalanches, for example, leads to a consideration of the place of evil in nature's "plan," and to an eloquent statement of nature's active presence beyond the multiplicity of visible forms: "So in her large purposes nature disregards particular evils. She spares no cost in the prosecution of her primitive plan, and while she busies herself to hide her immutability behind an inexhaustible variety of forms, what matters it to her if her step displaces, obliterates, one of these beings which she so profusely scatters over the world?" * To Ramond, moreover, the ultimate ends of this plan are benign. Out of death and destruction a fecund nature brings forth life: the "pleasant vegetation" on a desolate slope, or the life-giving waters that flow down from the glaciers, where "like an anxious monarch . . . the mother of the world prepares . . . the flowers she will scatter over our plains." *

* "C'est ainsi que dans ses grandes vues la nature dédaigne les maux particuliers. Rien ne lui coûte quand il s'agit de maintenir son plan primitif, & tandis qu'elle s'occupe à cacher son immutabilité sous une inépuisable variété de formes, que lui importe qu'un de ses pas déplace, anéantisse un de ces êtres qu'elle jette avec tant de profusion sur la face des mondes?" (II, 133).
* "une riante végétation couvre ses tristes débris . . . . ; semblable au Monarque soucieux . . . la mere du monde prépare . . . les fleurs dont ella semera nos plaines" (ll. 43–44, 128).

Throughout his commentary, furthermore, Ramond looks at the Alpine landscape through eyes informed by contemporary geology. Like such geologists as de Saussure, for example, he assumes that the Alps consist of a central core of "primary" and aboriginal mountains, surrounded by a zone of "secondary" sedimentary and fossiliferous mountains that were laid down during the course of a deluge that inundated all but the highest peaks (II, 96ff).[28] He reminds the reader that as he climbs toward the summits he passes through a belt of rocks shattered by the inconceivable fury of the retreating deluge, and, as he looks at the primary peaks, points out that he looks into time, at what Wordsworth would call the "types and symbols of eternity": "The soul, taking the flight that renders her contemporary with all centuries and coexistent with all beings, glides over the abyss of time. . . . The imagination . . . seems to glimpse an image of eternity, which it receives with religious terror." * A follower of Rousseau, Ramond assumes that to look backward in time is to look toward a primitive human innocence, an innocence that survives in the modern Swiss. Although he regards the mountaineer's version of the golden age with some condescension (I, 255), he presents Swiss virtue and liberty as a kind of cultural fossil, preserved from the advances of a corrupting civilization by nature: "There it is that our primitive virtues have taken refuge, virtues that have fled before our enlightenment and that will soon desert this last asylum . . . If you wish, therefore, to recapture the image, not of the *golden age* or *ideal nature* (*belle nature*), but of *simple nature* and the probity of our ancestors, hurry—seek out these privileged valleys." †

---

* "L'ame, prenant cet essor qui la rend contemporaine de tous les siecles, & co-existante avec tous les êtres, plane sur l'abyme du tems . . . [L'imagination] croit entrevoir une image de l'éternité qu'elle accueille avec une terreur religieuse" (II, 138).

† "C'est-là que se sont réfugiées ces vertus primitives, qui ont fui devant nos lumieres, & qui bientôt abandonneront ce dernier asyle . . . Si vous voulez donc vous retracer l'image, non de *l'âge d'or* & de la *belle nature*, mais de la *simple nature* & de la probité de nos ancêtres, hâtez-vous, cherchez ces vallées privilegiées" (II, 62–63).

Such assumptions were not entirely new to Wordsworth. As a schoolboy he had read Milton's description of the flood's furious retreat, and had probably assumed, with English scientists such as Ray and Woodward, that it was verified by geological evidence. On the "bleak and visionary sides" of rocks he may have seen records of

> the day of vengeance, when the sea
> Rose like a giant from his sleep, and smote
> The hills, and when the firmament of heaven
> Rained darkness which the race of men beheld
> Yea all the men that lived and had no hope.
>
> (*PW* V, 384 *app. crit.*)

Nor did he require guidance to see, in 1790, the "terrible majesty" of God in such awesome relics of the downrushing waters as the defile of Gondo (*EY*, p. 34). What Ramond offered the militant republican of 1792 was a way of reconciling this traditional scriptural interpretation of the Alps with a lofty and philosophical conception of "nature," and with the humanitarian ends of the French Revolution.

In *Descriptive Sketches* such assumptions combine to produce a vision of nature that has lasting importance in the history of Wordsworth's poetry. Invested with a power that is at once natural and numinous, the Alpine landscape is framed within a panorama of Christian eschatology that emphasizes three events: the creation, the deluge, and, by implication, the millennium that was being realized before Wordsworth's eyes. As his eye ascends from a pastoral valley to the heights above, he sees a world where "creation seems to end" (l. 289)—a phrase we should take quite literally. As the eye moves upward, it leaves behind the later products of creation—vegetation, animal life, and man—and looks upon a landscape that is stripped to its primitive components, a place where nature's two voices, the mountains and the sea, met in titanic conflict. To a mind steeped in Miltonic imagery and informed by Ramond, the highest summits were quite literally those

that had upheaved their "bare backs" from the primeval sea on
the third day of creation (*Paradise Lost* VII. 285–287). Unaltered
by the flood, they perpetuated the "first world," and suspended the
act of creation that had been begun six thousand years before.
When Wordsworth attributes a "secret Power" to these regions,
and calls them "sacred" and "holy," he responds to a visible sign
of an immanent divine presence.

Similar beliefs contribute to the solemnity and awe with which
he portrays a picturesque scene that had been familiar to him
since childhood, a mist-filled valley:

> A solemn sea! whose vales and mountains round
> Stand motionless, to awful silence bound.
> A gulf of gloomy blue, that opens wide
> And bottomless, divides the midway tide.
> Like leaning masts of stranded ships appear
> The pines that near the coast their summits rear [;]
> Of cabins, woods and lawns a pleasant shore
> Bounds calm and clear the chaos still and hoar.
>
> (ll. 496–503)

Echoing a similar description in Beattie's *Minstrel,* and very probably drawing on his own memory of the ascent of Snowdon a year
earlier, he presents this landscape as a visible reenactment of the
rising deluge, which intimates the destructive power of its terrible
archetype, and yet proclaims itself innocuous and benign.[29] The
scene thus becomes a sign or revelation that testifies to the immanence of the divine power that created the Alps, and confirms the
covenant that ended the deluge, "never to destroy / The earth
again by flood, nor let the sea / Surpass his bounds" (*Paradise Lost*
XI. 892–894).

In succeeding lines Wordsworth traces a similar redemption of
the human past. He describes primeval man in terms that mingle
the naturalistic primitivism of Rousseau:

> Once Man entirely free, alone and wild,
> Was bless'd as free—for he was Nature's child.
>
> (ll. 520–521)

with a Protestant's vision of the moral grandeur of unfallen man:

> As Man in his primaeval dower array'd
> The image of his glorious sire display'd
>
> (ll. 526–527)

He here echoes Milton's description of Adam,

> for in their looks divine
> The image of their glorious Maker shone,
> Truth, wisdom, sanctitude severe and pure
>
> (*Paradise Lost* IV. 291–293)

and displays a "primitivism" that is closer in spirit to that which shaped the English Commonwealth. He then affirms the survival of this divine image in the modern Swiss:

> Ev'n so, by vestal Nature guarded, here
> The traces of primaeval Man appear.
>
> (ll. 528–529)

Original power and glory survive in both "natures," external and human. Like the landscape, man continues to reflect the image of his "glorious sire."

In the concluding Alpine scene of the poem, Wordsworth again fuses geological fact, philosophic naturalism, and scriptural history into a single vision. He stands in the darkened valley of Chamonix, gazing up at the summit of Mont Blanc, which still glows in the light of the setting sun:

> Glad Day-light laughs upon his top of snow,
> Glitter the stars above, and all is black below.
>
> (ll. 700–701)

The scene reproduces a favorite Hawkshead analogy: the last fare-well of a setting sun to the region it loves. But its moral signifi-cance is drastically altered. In looking upward toward the summit of Mont Blanc Wordsworth is again gazing into what Ramond called the "abyss of time," toward a relic of the antediluvian world and a place of original promise and innocence. As his eye moves downward into the darkened valley, to the starving peasants of Savoy,

> . . . poor babes that, hurrying from the door,
> With pale-blue hands, and eyes that fix'd implore,
>
> (ll. 709–710)

it moves not only from natural tranquillity to human suffering—the transition that had violently intruded upon the landscapes of *An Evening Walk*—but from the biblical covenant to man's pre-sent degradation by tyranny. As Wordsworth contrasts the slavery of Savoy to that of Italy,

> That thou, the slave of slaves, art doom'd to pine
> While no Italian arts their charms combine
> To teach the skirt of thy dark cloud to shine
>
> (ll. 706–708)

he recalls the rainbow of the covenant, which Adam had seen as a

> flow'ry verge to bind
> The fluid skirts of that same wat'ry cloud,
> Lest it again dissolve and show'r the earth.
>
> (*Paradise Lost* XI. 881–883)

Such shift of attention implies the question Wordsworth would put to his own origins in 1798: "Was it for this?" (*Prelude* I. 271) Is the covenant to go unfulfilled?

In *Descriptive Sketches,* as in later poems, Wordsworth's an-swer is unambiguous: original power survives, and hope is justi-fied. As the poem concludes, the biblical covenant is fulfilled and extended by a modern deluge of Freedom, the Revolution:

Oh give, great God, to Freedom's waves to ride
Sublime o'er Conquest, Avarice, and Pride,
. . . .
And grant that every sceptred child of clay,
Who cries, presumptuous, "here their tides shall stay,"
Swept in their anger from th'affrighted shore,
With all his creatures sink—to rise no more.

(ll. 792–809)

Like its biblical and geological prototype, the Revolution will sweep down from the high valleys of the Alps, purging the flatlands of corruption with a power that is at once divine, natural, and human. All things move toward the end that Beaupuy indicated to Wordsworth when he pointed to a "hunger-bitten Girl" and said, " 'Tis against *that* / Which we are fighting" (*Prelude* IX. 511–519). To the author of *Descriptive Sketches,* Beaupuy's pronoun, "we," joined man, nature, and God in a single militant and irresistible cause, a "creed / Of zeal by an authority divine / Sanction'd of danger, difficulty or death" (*Prelude* IX. 411–413).

Such a sublime view of nature has several immediate effects. It renders an aesthetic based upon picturesque beauty or purely subjective sympathy pallid and epicurean, and helps us understand why the poet of 1792 makes no mention of the disappointments he suffered when touring the Alps in 1790. His review of this tour in *The Prelude,* twelve years later, is a chronicle of such disappointment, which moves from a first anticlimactic sight of Mont Blanc (VI. 453), to the deeper depression suffered on the summit of the Simplon Pass (VI. 549), and to the final bewildering night on the shores of Como (VI. 629–657). But although *Descriptive Sketches* has been interpreted in the light of these experiences,[30] the poem either ignores or reinterprets them. Wordsworth omits the incident on the Simplon, although he obviously draws upon the religious significance of the descent. He regards Mont Blanc as a superlative example of the sublime, transferring it from its place at the start of his Alpine itinerary to a climactic conclusion. Although he reproduces the night on Como in some detail, he presents it not as an occasion of personal disappointment but as an example of the unnatural solitude suffered by a "Grison gypsey," who is denied the "hope, strength, and courage" that "social suffering brings" (l. 197). While there is no doubt that the disappointments recalled in *The Prelude* were genuine, they were very probably rendered irrelevant by Wordsworth's far more exalted conception of nature in 1792.[31]

In the presence of this conception, furthermore, the orthodox aesthetic and stylistic categories to which he had remained obedient in such poems as *The Vale of Esthwaite* and *An Evening Walk* lose their significance. Opposing modes—the pastoral and the heroic, the beautiful and the sublime—now become varied manifestations of a single power. After the final Alpine scene in the poem, Wordsworth turns from the conventional sublimity of mountain scenery and the virtue and heroism of the Swiss, to the effects of freedom on the humblest French cottager (ll. 724–739) and the pastoral landscape of the Loire:

> A more majestic tide the water roll'd
> And glowed the sun-gilt groves in richer gold.
>
> (ll. 772–773)

All is changed; the most lowly object partakes of sublimity. As in the sublime sunset over the Lake of Uri, incremental diction emphasizes a single power that "rolls through all things."

It is fair to say, then, that the Revolution literally transfigured the way Wordsworth saw the "common range of visible things," as well as his understanding of "nature," and it is not surprising that the only figure he does not resurrect from the Hawkshead poems is the divine analogy. He draws several analogies from natural objects to moral truths; an aged peasant expatiates at length, for example, on the "Alp of life" (l. 593). But Wordsworth does not argue from natural to supernatural objects of hope. The focus of his attention, and the realm of hope, has become

> the very world which is the world
> Of all of us, the place in which, in the end,
> We find our happiness, or not at all.
>
> (*Prelude* X. 726–728)

Nor is this realism in any sense materialistic. *Descriptive Sketches* ends with a prayer to God, and the enthusiasm of Wordsworth's celebration of nature issues from the belief that the physical universe has become the theater of divine power and action, and that it visibly confirms the written promise of Scripture. His transpositions of Miltonic imagery to the Alps are more than literary allusions; as M. H. Abrams has pointed out, like other radical English Protestants, including William Blake, he interpreted the Revolution as a millennium, or, as the Solitary of *The Excursion* recalled,

> a progeny of golden years
> Permitted to descend, and bless mankind.
> With promises the Hebrew Scriptures teem:
> I felt their invitation. . . .
>
> (*The Excursion* III. 757–760)

Although Wordsworth has been opposed to both Blake and Milton as a poet whose naturalism deprived him of a mythological subject matter, it would appear that the Revolution offered him a supremely adequate surrogate for myth, the visible world.[32] In the Alps he found what may be regarded as the empirical obverse of the vision presented in the Praeludium to Blake's *America* (1793), where a deaf, dumb, and blind nature awakens to a vision of revolutionary man:

> Soon as she saw the terrible boy, then burst the virgin cry:
> "I know thee, I have found thee, & I will not let thee go.
>
> (ll. 26–27)

In *Descriptive Sketches* it is man who awakens to a vision of nature that is at once empirical and apocalyptic, a "confusion infinite of heaven and earth," as the Solitary would recall it (*The Excursion* III. 721), and a revelation that in effect restored the "bright appearances" of God to the human senses and recreated the universe described by Michael: "Adam, thou knowest heav'n his, and all the earth" (*Paradise Lost* XI. 335).

Although several critics have regarded *Descriptive Sketches* as the product of acute melancholia,[33] its style bespeaks the psychological integrity that was absent from *An Evening Walk*. Once again enthusiastically articulate, Wordsworth displays the powers of "thought" and "sentiment" in abundance. He again cultivates pathos, for example, but now the pathos of the pain necessarily attendant on Revolution, such as the desecration of the Grande Chartreuse (ll. 53–79). His earlier indulgence of delusive fancy now becomes a humanitarian sympathy for the superstitious hope that brings Catholic pilgrims to the Abbey of Einseidlen:

> If the sad grave of human ignorance bear
> One flower of hope—Oh pass and leave it there.
>
> (ll. 660–661)

The two trances that appear in the poem are not flights of a Gothic or visionary fancy, but the passionate response of a patriot to the heroic deeds of the past. At Cambridge Wordsworth had suspended an oar in memory of Collins, who was betrayed by delusive fancy; now a boatman suspends his oar before the shrine of William Tell (ll. 348–365). Inspired by the "sainted Rocks" of Naeffles, where a small band of Swiss had repelled a host of Austrian invaders, the human spirit towers "beyond the senses and their little reign" (ll. 536–549). Wordsworth by no means ascribes such ecstasies to subjective causes. He takes them as authentic epiphanies, and in the couplet following the Naeffles vision transforms the vague subjectivism of a Hawkshead line:

> The heart, when pass'd the Vision by,
> Dissolves, nor knows for whom nor why
>
> (*Vale of Esthwaite*, ll. 129–130)

to a mode of religious communion:

> And oft, when pass'd that solemn vision by,
> He holds with God himself communion high.
>
> (ll. 550–551)

Such recognition of the mind's hegemony over the physical senses may have been encouraged by Ramond, who had indulged the "seductions of the imagination" far more seriously than most of the poets Wordsworth had imitated at Hawkshead, but its primary inspiration came from the glorious transformation of the human spirit taking place before Wordsworth's eyes.

There is thus considerable evidence that Wordsworth's allegiance to the Revolution was indeed, as he claimed in later years, a natural extension of what he had been and loved:

> a child of nature, as at first,
> Diffusing only those affections wider
> That from the cradle had grown up with me.
>
> (*Prelude* X. 753–755)

Not only the rhetoric but the spirit of the Hawkshead poems reappears: an instinctive proclivity to sensibility and the sublime. The Virgilian naturalism that at Cambridge expressed a growing appreciation for the moral significance of country life now merges with biblical prophecy and the philosophic naturalism of revolutionary ideology, throws off its pastoral guise, and assumes a heroic and triumphant militancy. The Virgil echoed at the poem's conclusion is the prophet of the fourth *Eclogue: Iam redit et Virgo, redeunt Saturnia regna* (Now the Virgin returns, the reign of Saturn returns):

> Lo! from th'innocuous flames, a lovely birth!
> With it's own Virtues springs another earth:
> Nature, as in her prime, her virgin reign
> Begins, and Love and Truth compose her train.
>
> (ll. 782–785)

This triumvirate of values—Nature, Love, and Truth—exemplifies the way in which the Revolution integrated and reconciled the divided claims of feeling and truth, mind and nature, and, like the art Wordsworth and Coleridge would seek to create, brought the whole soul of man into passionate activity. The young poet who had been a "borderer of his age" was now at its center, committed to a "creed of zeal" that was indubitable.

Like the traveler of 1790 who crossed the Alps without knowing it, Wordsworth did not recognize this moment for what it was: a unique consummation in his own life and the life of his age. He took the Revolution as "nothing out of nature's certain course" (*Prelude* IX. 252), and it was not until events suddenly conspired against it that he was forced into the struggle that would dominate his history for the next five years, to perpetuate the integrity, vision, and hope exemplified by the still-conventional couplets of *Descriptive Sketches*.

III   Salisbury Plain and Windy Brow: 1793-1794

> I, who with the breeze
> Had play'd, a green leaf on the blessed tree
> Of my beloved country, . . .
>
>   . . . .
>
> Now from my pleasant station was cut off,
> And toss'd about in whirlwinds.
>
> *The Prelude*

The ambush of Wordsworth's hopes came suddenly, and on a scale commensurate with those hopes. Little more than a month after he returned to it, his native land declared war on France. The profound psychological effects of this event are recalled in *The Prelude,* where it becomes the most dramatic reversal in Wordsworth's life. It administered a violent "shock" to his "moral nature" (X. 234–235), compelled an inner "revolution" (X. 238), corrupted his feelings and imagination, and rendered him vulnerable to the degrading effects of a barren rationalism, and ultimately to despair.

The intensity of this response, which is evident as well in the work of the time, becomes less remarkable when we recall the depth of Wordsworth's commitment to the Revolution and his love for a particular Frenchwoman, Annette Vallon. Although Annette's role is clouded by lack of evidence, it seems probable that her influence in 1792 and 1793 was intimately incorporated with that of the Revolution itself and that each liaison amplified and reinforced the other. Looking back on 1792 in the tale that constitutes his most transparent allusion to Annette, an allusion he perhaps planned at the time (Reed, p. 138), Wordsworth portrayed the love of Vaudracour for Julia in terms virtually identical with those he used to describe his own commitment to the Revolution. Both causes invited an impassioned investment of trust and hope, and offered a reality that surpassed fiction. For Wordsworth, political science became a land of Romance, and Reason an "Enchanter" (*Prelude* X. 695–700); Vaudracour's world surpassed "Arabian Fiction" (IX. 583). Both romance and politics worked alchemy, transforming dross to gold (IX. 587; X. 542, cf. X. 664). Both opened "paradise" (IX. 590; X. 705), discredited "law and custom," and turned to nature for a "happy end of all" (IX. 602–603; X. 610–611).

The after effect of both relationships, moreover, was to place Wordsworth in ardent opposition to "law" and "custom" on behalf of the values to which he had appealed at the close of *Descriptive Sketches*. Given the spirit of that poem, it is probable that he committed his love for Annette to the keeping of the mighty powers that guided the Revolution—nature, love, and truth—and that he parted from her, in October 1792, in hope and trust that they soon would be reunited as man and wife.[1] Their separation may well have seemed a sacrifice imposed by the Revolution, like those he witnessed among the "passing spectacles of Revolutionary life":

> Domestic severings, female fortitude
> At dearest separation, patriot love
> And self-devotion, and terrestrial hope
> Encourag'd with a martyr's confidence.
>
> (*Prelude* IX. 276–279)

But it soon became clear, on Wordsworth's return to England, that his uncles opposed his match with Annette, perhaps seeing in it the proud and rebellious character that had refused to distinguish itself at Cambridge. With the English declaration of war, his opposition to "law" and "custom" became political as well as domestic; he was at once estranged not only from his guardians but from his country. One of the few memories that survives from 1793 attests to the traumatic effect of such estrangement: it was in the fall that he sat in an English or Welsh church and "exulted" over the French victory at Hondeschoote. But such joy was not pure:

> It was a grief,
> Grief call it not, 'twas anything but that,
> A conflict of sensations without name,
> Of which he only who may love the sight
> Of a Village Steeple as I do can judge
> When in the Congregation, bending all
> To their great Father, prayers were offer'd up,
> Or praises for our Country's Victories,
> And 'mid the simple worshippers, perchance,
> I only, like an uninvited Guest
> Whom no one own'd sate silent, shall I add,
> Fed on the day of vengeance yet to come?
>
> (X. 264–275)

Like the "just man" of Blake's *Marriage of Heaven and Hell,* Wordsworth has been forced into spiritual exile. An unknown "Guest" who seeks the destruction of those whose hospitality he enjoys, he refuses to pray to their God and rejoices as their sons are slain. His deepest hopes fix on the future, on a violent reversal and renewal that will vindicate him; but in the meantime he must wait, masking his true feelings and his true identity in silence. The ironic price of loyalty to nature, love, and truth is loss of candor and integrity.

It is probable, furthermore, that as early as 1793 the declaration of war compelled Wordsworth to question the moral authority of "natural" feeling, and to appeal instead to an analytic and judicial reason. In the patriotism, the courage, and the piety of the English, the spirit he had approved in France was marshaled against virtue and the "certain course of nature." His response in the *Letter* to the Bishop of Llandaff, composed in the spring or summer of 1793, is to dismiss English patriotism, in Rousseau's words, as ideological slavery: "tout homme né dans l'esclavage naît pour l'esclavage" (Any man born in slavery is born for slavery).[2] Unthinking and instinctive pity, the virtue of which he had taken for granted throughout his life, now becomes, when directed toward the fallen Louis XVI, "irrational and weak" (p. 83). In 1790 Burke had lamented the fall of French chivalry, "which ennobled whatever it touched, and under which vice itself lost half its evil, by losing all its grossness."[3] Confronted by the desecration of feudal monuments, the republican of 1792 had indulged at least a guarded sympathy for such sentiments, but he now dismisses them as the prattling of an "infatuated moralist" (p. 85). Then he had celebrated communion with the heroes of the past; now he regards Burke's appeal to the historical continuity of the English Constitution as an attempt to "cherish a corse at the bosom when reason might call aloud that it should be entombed" (p. 98). In each case Wordsworth violently repudiates feelings he had cherished in earlier years, in the "School Exercise," for example, and turns instead to the tenets of his revolutionary "creed."

He very probably repressed sentiment on other grounds as well. How could he respond to letters like the following, which Annette sent in March 1793?

> Come, my love, my husband, and receive the tender embraces of your wife, your daughter. . . . Her little heart often beats against my own; I seem to feel her father's; but why, Caroline, are you so insensible? Why does not your heart stir when your mother's is beating so? O my beloved, soon it will be stirred when I shall say to her: "Caroline, in a month, in a fortnight, in a week, you are going to see the most beloved of men, the most tender of men.*

* "Vien, mon ami, mon mari, recevoir les embrassmens tendre de ta femme, de ta fille. . . . Son petit coeur bat souvent contre le mien; je croit sentire celui de son père; mais pourquoi, Caroline, est-tu insensible? pourquoi ton coeur ne s'agitte-t-il pas quand celui de ta mère bat tems? O mon ami, bientôt il le sera agité quand je lui direz: 'Caroline, dans un mois, dans quinze, dans huit jour, tu vas voir le plus chérit des hommes, le plus tendre des hommes.' "[4]

On one occasion such an appeal may have elicited action: a flying visit to France in October of 1792 (Reed, p. 147). But for the most part he could only wait and hope, joining Dorothy, perhaps, in painting to himself a cottage "retreat" where he, his wife, and his sister might enjoy a "Happiness arising from the exercise of the social Affections in Retirement and rural Quiet" (*EY*, p. 93). As months and years passed, however, the very image of a hopelessly patient Annette may have become painful and ultimately unendurable.

It is probable, then, that several influences combined in 1793 to press Wordsworth toward a "Philosophy" that promised to "abstract the hopes of man / Out of his feelings" (*Prelude* X. 807–809). Whatever the formal identity of this philosophy, it was clearly not a cause of Wordsworth's crisis but one of its effects; the sovereign intellect offered what pure sensation had offered in 1788, an alternative to feelings that could no longer be trusted or understood.

I

If Wordsworth composed any poetry during the spring of 1793, as he drifted, waited, and looked for some means of support in London, it has not survived. His first composition after England's declaration of war dates from July, when he spent a month on the Isle of Wight with a Cambridge classmate and patron, William Calvert. In a fragment written at the time, or shortly thereafter, he described the landscape that he recalled in all of his subsequent references to this stay: the view from the north shore of the island across the Solent to where the British fleet was anchored, awaiting orders to sail against France. The sight filled him, he recalled in 1842, with "melancholy forebodings" of war (*PW* I, 94). *The Prelude* is more specific: it was the "sunset Canon" fired each evening from those "gallant Creatures" that seemed an omen of "woes to come" (X. 291–307). Despite lacunae, the fragment of 1793 is more specific still:

How sweet to walk along the woody steep
When all the summer seas are charmed to sleep;
While on the distant sands the tide retires
Its last faint murmur on the ear expires;
The setting sun [   ] his growing round
On the low promontory's purple bound
For many a league a line of gold extends,
Now lessened half his glancing disc de [?scends]
The watry sands athwart the [?forest   ]
Flash [   ] sudden radiance not [   ]
While anchored vessels scattered far [   ]
Darken with shadowy hulks [   ]
O'er earth o'er air and ocean [   ]
Tranquillity extends her [   ]
But hark from yon proud fleet in peal profound
Thunders the sunset cannon; at the sound
The star of life appears to set in blood,
And ocean shudders in offended mood,
Deepening with moral gloom his angry flood.

(PW I, 307–308; DCP)

It is evident that the events of 1793 have had a substantial effect on Wordsworth's style and that these recapitulate those of his earlier crisis of hope, in 1788. He is once again a passive observer; all attention falls on the object. And this object, a landscape, dramatizes a moral breach between nature and man. The possibility of cosmic harmony is implied by several motifs of years past: the first line echoes that of a sonnet of 1789 or 1791, "Sweet was the walk along the narrow lane"; the tranquil sunset recalls Bowles's first sonnet; and the "faint murmur" of the tide might be one of the "evening sounds" that offered a grateful alternative to human suffering in *An Evening Walk*. But such harmony is abruptly shattered, and the premises of Wordsworth's earlier poetry repudiated, by the sunset cannon—a sound that embodies both English violence toward France and human violence toward nature. In the concluding lines, to quote the Swiss mountaineer of *Descriptive Sketches,* an "angry Nature" threatens to "avenge her God" (ll. 486–487). Less than a year earlier, in *Descriptive Sketches,* Wordsworth had invoked a metaphorical deluge of freedom, which would renew the covenant that ended the Biblical deluge. Now, in implicit alliance with both nature and God, he looks to the real sea to perform the same task.

Judging from *The Prelude,* this expectation was disappointed. The elements remained unnaturally tranquil, and for "a whole month of calm and glassy days" the fleet lay vulnerable but unharmed on the surface of the sea (X. 297). We can only guess at Wordsworth's response to this passivity—or indifference—on the part of the power to which he had entrusted his hopes and his destiny. Although by the time of *The Prelude* the political and emotional significance of the scene had changed profoundly (the "shadowy hulks" of 1793 become "gallant Creatures"), something of the young republican's vexation survives in his rhythm: "for a *whole* month" (my italics). Perhaps, like Keats's Hyperion or Meredith's Lucifer, he was forced to measure the gulf that divides human will from natural law, and he may have questioned both will and law. Certainly this, like other landscapes he viewed that summer, left a lasting impression; characteristics of the scene reappear in other landscapes during the next several years, and without exception they witness the disappointment of human expectation by natural law. In this fragment, however, all disappointment has vanished. Nature threatens the act of vengeance Wordsworth so ardently desired.

Such intensified appreciation of the moral power of a literal landscape has immediate and decisive effects on Wordsworth's descriptive style. His organization of space and imagery, in particular, now takes on clearly moral and incipiently symbolic significance. Two sorts of landscape appear in the fragment. The first, as we have seen, recalls those of the Cambridge sonnets and *An Evening Walk.* In color, intensity, shape, and setting it is richly diversified; a broad variety of particulars is comprehended within an overarching harmony and tranquillity. In the seascape that follows, however, Wordsworth's intense and divided feelings focus on a constellation of images that reappear in the poetry of later years. Isolated on a vast, level, and uniform surface, exposed to sun, sky, and sea, the English "hulks" lie at the focus of a landscape that, like the higher Alps, is stripped of variety and gradation. A suggestion of the confrontation of elements perhaps reflects a sense of the imminent return of chaos to a created world that was divided by "partition firm and sure . . . lest fierce extremes/Contiguous might distemper the whole frame" (*Paradise Lost* VII. 267–273). Wordsworth's later epithet for this sea, "glassy," may derive from Milton's description of the deluge at its height, and the tiny ark, "hull down on the flood," while the "clear sun on his wide wat'ry glass/Gazed hot" (*Paradise Lost* XI. 839–845). If made at the time, the comparison would be intensely ironic; unlike the ark, these ships carried a freight of evil and perversity that contrasts not only visually but morally with the tranquillity of the sea, and renders that tranquillity at once enigmatic and portentous.

Language, too, has altered. The first fourteen lines are rigorously literal. Personification of natural objects has disappeared; the "one bright glance" given by Thomson's sun, for example, survives only as a descriptive adjective: "glancing." The response of sun and sea to human vice in the last four lines is modeled on the response of nature to the fall in *Paradise Lost,* but it remains faithful to the visual appearance of landscape as well. Periphrasis becomes thematically functional. The "day-star" of 1788 is now a "star of life," a power that presides over the birth of a new order, and is wounded by human violence ("sets in blood"). The uneasy "shudder" of the "offended" sea suggests an organism that has been awakened to the presence of an alien being within it, which it will purge: "if thine eye offend thee, pluck it out."

Throughout these concluding lines, finally, we sense an attempt to discipline syntactical complexity, which never obscures meaning, and to communicate feeling implicitly, through effects of sound and rhythm. In open defiance of convention, Wordsworth now breaks the couplet, and allows his concluding cadence to overflow into a triplet. The crucial transitional lines,

> But hark from yon proud fleet in peal profound
> Thunders the sunset cannon

employ metrical inversion, assonance and alliteration with some sophistication, and succeed, if briefly, in attaining a Miltonic orotundity. All of these stylistic changes point toward the future rather than the past, and all appear to reflect the passionate intensity with which Wordsworth now observed the "common range of visible things," as an embattled order to which he had entrusted his hopes and his destiny.

II

Wordsworth and Calvert left the Isle of Wight in August, bound for the west of England. An accident to their carriage abruptly ended the trip;. Calvert rode off on the only horse, and Wordsworth was left alone in the midst of Salisbury Plain. For the next three weeks he was once again a pedestrian traveler, as he made his way northward toward Wales along the valley of the Wye, where he viewed Tintern Abbey, met the little girl of *We Are Seven,* and walked for several days with the wild rover who became Peter Bell. By late August he was in the Vale of Clwyd, at the home of the friend who had accompanied him through the Alps, David Jones.

The heightened receptivity of Wordsworth's imagination during this walk is evidenced not only by the three poems of 1798, but by those composed at the time, which witness a sudden influx of new images into a poetry that had been dominated for six years by the scenes of his "native regions." Twice he was moved to composition by the feudal castles that line the Wye, which may have reminded him of their counterparts along the Loire (Reed, p. 146, n

12). Enough survives of both poems, a sonnet and a lyric in elegiac quatrains, to show that Wordsworth no longer sees such
monuments as relics of an old and romantic order. The castle of
the sonnet maintains an active and successful opposition to nature:

> In vain did Time and Nature toil to throw
> Wild weeds and earth upon these crumbled towers
> Again they rear the feudal head that lowers
> Stern on the wretched huts that crouch below.
>
> (DCP)

Attention continues to focus intently on the visible world, and
Wordsworth continues to purge his style of language prescribed by
convention. In his first version it was the "ivy mantle" of Gray's
Elegy that embodied nature's power. But he crossed out this
decorative personification and substituted "wild weeds and earth"
—nouns sanctioned not by convention but by the objects they
name, common things that manifest a sublime moral power.

In the second fragment a "traveller" views a castle by the light
of a gloomy sunset. Its "chasmy walls and broken ridge" recall the
"captive anguish" of past time. But they are tranquillized by time
and nature; the years breathe a "softening gloom," and the "accordant voice" of the Wye touches the ruin with a "tender sadness"
(DCP). Both fragments commemorate the survival of evil and its
continuing opposition to "the certain course of nature."

Another historical vision informs the major product of this
"lonesome journey" (*Prelude* XII. 359): a Spenserian narrative
entitled *Salisbury Plain*.[5] In his preface to the final version of
1842, Wordsworth recalled that the poem was inspired by the
sight of the prehistoric monuments scattered across the Plain,
monuments which led him to compare past and present societies
with respect to happiness (*PW* I, 94–95). Such a purpose molds
the poem's structure: a narrative framed by hortatory addresses to
the reader. After comparing the "unhouzed" savage of antiquity to
modern man, the narrator points out that civilization has brought
two sorts of misery: the envy that attends on class distinction, and

the pain of refined sensibilities (*PW* I, 334–335). To illustrate this decline from primitive origins he then presents his tale: benighted on Salisbury Plain, a traveler seeks shelter from a storm. Warned away from Stonehenge by a mysterious voice, he finds shelter in an abandoned house of refuge, where he meets a vagrant woman. She tells him of the "wonders" of the region, among which are complementary visions of Druidic barbarity and enlightenment that embody the violence and the hope of the French Revolution (which Wordsworth would identify in the *Prelude* as reveries he had experienced on the plain [XII. 320]). The vagrant then relates the story of her life: how her father was dispossessed by an avaricious nobleman; how she lost her husband and children in the American war, and became a hopeless and homeless vagrant. Morning breaks, cheering both characters, who proceed toward a nearby cottage where they will find comfort and nourishment. After bidding them farewell, the narrator delivers a closing address on behalf of reason, truth, and social reform. His final words exhort the "heroes of truth" to complete their work of destroying superstition, injustice, and misery (*PW* I, 340–341).

The explicit mode of the poem may be described as an indignant realism. Wordsworth compares the primitive past to the present, points to the traveler and vagrant as pathetic examples of the extremity of modern suffering, and concludes, as he had in *Descriptive Sketches,* by urging reform. His spirit is Beaupuy's: "it is against *that* / Which we are fighting." But the poem implies a far broader and more complex range of attitudes than this; here, and in the major poems of the next four years, narrative form provides a means of suppressing subjectivity and of dramatizing and objectifying feelings that are implicitly contradictory and probably in large part unconscious. Each of the three characters in the poem —the narrator, the vagrant, and the traveler—exemplifies a different aspect of Wordsworth's recent experience and a different response to it. Each, moreover, employs a rhetoric that is peculiar to its point of view.

The most self-assertive voice in the poem, and the articulate public identity that sponsors it, is that of the narrator. His ideas repeat those of Wordsworth's *Letter* to the Bishop of Llandaff; he responds to the declaration of war and to human suffering by urging reform. In a language that is dense with personified abstractions and analogies, he places his trust in the advancing wave of Freedom and by implication condones its violence. Evil, he assumes, is eradicable. Although he delivers introductory and concluding discourses, during the narrative he becomes a virtually silent reporter who intervenes only to offer moral *sententia* at climactic moments. His benevolent farewell to the two characters —"Adieu, ye friendless, hope-forsaken pair" (*PW* I, 338)— measures his psychological distance from them. He is a poised and controlled spectator; they are his *exemplum*.

Although the vagrant is an invented character whose story Wordsworth may have heard several years before,[6] her response to the war and to separation from her husband clearly draws upon Wordsworth's own experience, and presents it from a point of view more immediate, and in a language more concrete, than the narrator's. The biographical parallels are numerous. Like the republican who refused to pray for an English victory, she was prevented, by grief or indignation, from joining her pious but disappointed father in prayer. She too senses the inhuman tranquillity of the sea: "The very ocean hath its hour of rest / That comes not to the human mourner's breast" (ll. 337–338 *app. crit.*). Like the grief-crazed woman Wordsworth had described in a "Tale" at Cambridge, she is "robbed of her perfect mind," and is the only character to suffer a trance: a "dream" that she had found a "resting-place" (ll. 361–362 *app. crit.*) on board the ship that carried her back to a homeland where like an unknown guest she stands "homeless near a thousand homes" (l. 368). Like the boys of Gray's Eton College ode, she crosses a "mighty gulf of separation" from what she was (l. 352), and protests against the laws that prescribe such loss with fierce intensity: "Oh! dreadful price of being to resign / All that is dear *in* being" (ll. 297 / 8 *app. crit.;* Wordsworth's italics). Although she attacks both war and economic exploitation of the poor, her story pays less attention to the social causes of suffering than to its psychological effects. It is in fact Wordsworth's first attempt to place the trauma of separation and loss in a chronological perspective, his first history of an individual mind.

The vagrant's language reflects her inability to find hope in ideology; largely stripped of analogy and decorative personification, it relies on imagery and metaphor. As she describes her childhood, for example, she simply lists images, much as Wordsworth had listed "evening sounds" in 1787 or 1788:

> Can I forget my seat beneath the thorn,
> My garden stored with peas and mint and thyme,
> And rose and lilly for the sabbath morn,
> The church-inviting bells' delightful chime.
>
> (*PW* I, 106 *app. crit.*)

Unlike the "formal particulars" of earlier descriptions, however, these images are accumulated not as species within a larger genus, but simply because they are loved, a motive that would impel the great "pictures" of the first book of *The Prelude* in 1798, and shape the theory of the "spots of time" two years later.

In the final line above, furthermore, we see an occasion on which Wordsworth deliberately and prophetically altered an example of what he would come to call "poetic diction." In Cowper's "Verses Supposed to be Written by Alexander Selkirk" he had read of the "church-going bell" (l. 29), an epithet he would censure in 1802 as "an instance of the strange abuses which Poets have introduced into their language" (*PW* II, 408). The literal incongruity of Cowper's term, we may note, is the price he pays for ellipsis, the compression of cause (the bell) and effect (going to church) into two words. Wordsworth's alteration to "church-inviting" at once restores the integrity of the literal thing, and shifts attention from a logically self-sufficient conception of cause and effect (and the poet's skill in expressing it) to the power of the concrete thing to cause subjective effects, which it leaves to the reader's imagination. We may call this treatment of imagery *pre-sentational,* because it seeks to reproduce the presentation of phenomena to the mind in experience. The success of such a mode depends not upon the fabrication of imagery or on the manipulation of semantic relationships, but upon the selection of significant literal images and their arrangement in a context that makes this significance clear. It tends, in other words, to render stylistic artifice invisible and to invest concrete images with that power we call symbolic.

The third voice in the poem, that of the traveler, is more enigmatic. He in no way exemplifies the ideological themes of the poem; his suffering is not the effect of war or class, but of the natural environment. His sole identity is that of "traveler," and his sole purpose is to find his way. Except that he too has known "sorrow's deadly blight" (l. 459 *app. crit.*), he has no past and no future. Unlike his companion, he is virtually inarticulate; his only reported words are those which call the vagrant to the window to "view" the cheering sunrise (l. 317 *app. crit.*). Throughout the poem his eye is fixed on the landscape with great intensity and, in the early part of the poem, with great fear.

Confrontation between the traveler's mind and the landscape is violent and elemental. Isolated on a vast, bare, monotonous surface, he searches compulsively for objects that offer the hope of rest, shelter, and human companionship: a meadow, a cottage, a wisp of curling smoke, a light, or simply a "trace of man" (l. 25). His physical appetites inform the intensity of his vision: "By thirst and hunger pressed he gazed around" (l. 24 *app. crit.*). As night falls and the storm rises, his eye is deprived of objects altogether, and his exposure, as the only upright object on a level surface, becomes extreme. Stripped of mediating and protective agencies, the landscape itself belies the hope of shelter. A guide-post (l. 134), his bed (l. 123 *app. crit.*), the walls of Stonehenge (l. 115) and a steep (l. 192 *app. crit.*) are as "naked" as the savage whose sufferings he reenacts (*PW* I, 334).

We cannot doubt, I think, that this character reflects Wordsworth's personal experience. As point of view moves closer to this experience, moreover, consciousness is stripped far more drastically of thought, sentiment, and action than in *An Evening Walk*. Wordsworth compares the plain to an "ocean" (l. 139 *app. crit.*), and in form it closely resembles the exposed seascape he had viewed from the Isle of Wight, with the one ironic difference that the fury he had then vainly invoked now descends upon the character who most obviously represents him, and who is at the focal point of this symbolically significant surface. Any implication that the traveler, or Wordsworth, is in some sense culpable is precluded by his anonymity, and this stormy landscape may have seemed a sudden and terrifying realization of the "whirlwind" of passion he would reduce to a metaphor in *The Prelude* (X. 259), or of the moral and social isolation forced on him by his commitment to France. What is clear, however, is that the effect of natural violence on the traveler is indeed moral: he is driven with irresistible and "unwilled" force toward man (l. 146 *app. crit.*). If the traveler's confrontation with the elements is naked and fearful, it is also indubitably authentic, and it compels a quest for human fellowship that is stripped by extremity of all dissimulation and pride. Put into the context of Wordsworth's memories of this period, natural power humbles the proud isolation that was forced on him by his allegiance to the Revolution, and restores the possibility of a social communion as authentic as the meeting between the traveler's senses and the natural world. Nature forces a compulsive flight from isolation, exposure, and violence toward man, and toward a pastoral landscape that embodies the possibility of harmony with nature.

It was with such an experience fresh in his memory, perhaps, that Wordsworth came to the Wye, a river that "travels through a woody country, now varied with cottages and green meadows, and now with huge and fantastic rocks," as he or Dorothy would describe it five years later.[7] And it was the passionate reunion of his eye with this landscape, which was varied, pastoral, and reminiscent of his "native regions," that he recalled in *Tintern Abbey:*

> I cannot paint
> What then I was. The sounding cataract
> Haunted me like a passion: the tall rock,
> The mountain, and the deep and gloomy wood,
> Their colours and their forms, were then to me
> An appetite; a feeling and a love,
> That had no need of a remoter charm,
> By thought supplied, nor any interest
> Unborrowed from the eye.
>
> (ll. 75–83)

Judging from *Salisbury Plain,* the state of mind recalled here was not the product of an escape from man to nature, as has been repeatedly conjectured. Wordsworth was flying from a landscape that embodied alienation from both man and nature to another that offered the hope of reconciliation with both, and the restoration of the cosmic and psychic integrity that had been destroyed by the "sunset cannon" of war.

And it is such a landscape that greets the traveler's eye in the poem of 1793. The sun rises, "all unconcerned with their unrest" (l. 310 *app. crit.*), rendering human distress subjective and opening the mind to the benevolent discipline of an objective world:

> So forth she came, and eastward looked; the sight
> O'er her moist eyes like dawn of gladness threw.
>
> (ll. 318–319 *app. crit.*)

Familiar sights and sounds, which recall *An Evening Walk, L'Allegro,* and the unfallen nature of *Paradise Lost,* witness the resumption of human activity and its compatibility with the natural order. A wain passes by, its driver whistling "with chearful note"; the rain-swept downs glister in the sun; a cock crows. We last see the two companions as they walk into a landscape that is the antithesis of the vast and vacant plain:

> But now from a hill summit down they look
> Where through a narrow valley's pleasant scene

> A wreath of vapour tracked a winding brook
> That babbled on through groves and meads of green.
> A smoking cottage peeped the trees between. . . .
> <div align="right">(ll. 460–464 <i>app. crit.</i>)</div>

At road's end lies the image that had summarized hope in nearly every poem Wordsworth had written, the cottage.

The traveler's history thus enacts a passionate and successful quest for visible objects of hope, and it is in describing his vision of the plain that Wordsworth advances most dramatically toward his mature style. Here language is stripped of devices that mediate between the external thing and the mind of the reader—passionate or decorative personification, analogy, or periphrasis. Instead, he arranges literal images in a form that endows them with intense but implied significance, and tends to reproduce the appearance of the landscape to the passionately implicated mind of the traveler. In an early stanza, Wordsworth enacts a desperate quest for images by employing a device that reappears in his greatest poems, negation:

> No shade was there, no meads of pleasant green,
> No brook to wet his lip or soothe his ear,
> Vast piles of corn-stacks here and there were seen,
> But thence no smoke upwreathed his sight to chear
> And see the homeward peasant dim appear
> Far off he sends a feeble shout—in vain
> No sound replies but winds that whistling near
> Sweep the thin grass and passing, wildly plain,
> Or desert lark that pours on high a wasted strain.
> <div align="right">(ll. 28–36 <i>app. crit.</i>)</div>

Each negative statement names an image that the traveler seeks, but denies its objective existence. Imagery imitates desire, and syntax the force with which the object-world denies that desire. In the first two lines, furthermore, the visible landscape itself is described entirely by implication. Those of its features that are then named derive an unusual weight of significance from the mere fact of their existence, and, as violent contrasts to what is sought, enact the shock of disappointment. "Vast piles of cornfields" suddenly materialize in abnormally large perspective, but their bulk is ironically qualified by the following line, in which the traveler's quest for hope focuses on a wisp of "smoke upwreathed" that he cannot see. His single action, a "feeble shout," brings an equally ironic reply from the grass and the lark, the inhumanity of which is stressed by a suddenly minute and lingering attention to visual and aural detail.

In the following stanza Wordsworth renders the traveler's interpretation of the image explicit:

> Long had each slope he mounted seemed to hide
> Some cottage whither his tired feet might turn.
> But now all hope resigned in tears he eyed
> The crows in blackening eddies homeward borne.
>
> (ll. 37–40 *app. crit.*)

After naming subjective feeling obliquely ("all hope resigned"), he names its concrete object, the crows. The significance they hold for him is suggested, in turn, by the single adjective "homeward," which informs other details with implied meaning. Earthbound, weary, and lost, he notices and fixes upon the quality of the birds' motion. They seem passive, "borne" to their homes without will or effort by a stream that luxuriates in arabesques of free and unconstrained motion, "eddies" that ironically duplicate and effortlessly resolve his own hopeless wanderings.

In such passages as these Wordsworth solves the technical problem of reconciling object and subject, fact and feeling, in a single rhetorical perspective. He communicates feeling without employing trope; for a humanized "Desolation" to stalk through these landscapes, as in *Descriptive Sketches,* would obscure the autonomy of their existence, and their terrible inhumanity. He accomplishes this as he had in the Hawkshead "Idyllium," by placing a passionately responsive consciousness within the landscape, which he presents as it is perceived by that consciousness. The language of the poet himself is lucidly empirical; whether he is describing the landscape or the traveler, it is never deformed by personal subjective response. The opposite was true in *An Evening Walk,* where another wretched traveler envied a natural creature:

> Fair Swan! by all a mother's joys caress'd,
> Haply some wretch has ey'd, and call'd thee bless'd.
>
> (ll. 241–242)

Point of view is the poet's, an external observer whose language evaluates significance and guides feeling. In *Salisbury Plain* point of view shifts to the character. With great insight, Wordsworth's style imitates the action of a mind compelled by desperation, a desperation we must assume had been his own.

These changes are critical. It was perhaps in the passages quoted above, which remained essentially unchanged in the version he first read, that Coleridge found evidence of the imagination's power, and of the "fine balance of truth in observing, with the imaginative faculty in modifying, the objects observed" that he came to regard as a supreme achievement of Wordsworth's genius (*BL* I, 59). His comment points not only to the contribution of this style to Wordsworth's greatest poems, but to its importance as a technical solution to the epistemological and psychological dilemmas of the age. Wordsworth now possessed a language that, in Bacon's terms, buckles the mind to empirical fact and yet simultaneously acknowledges the power and the authority of the "desires of the mind." Wordsworth himself recalled that about this time he had sight of a "new world . . . fit / To be transmitted and made visible / To other eyes" (*Prelude* XII. 371–373). What he did not volunteer in 1805, however, was that this vision was not the product of a gratuitous revelation or a program of literary reform, but of what would appear to be intense psychological distress. These technical advances cluster about the only character in the poem who lacks an identity; they objectify and discipline feelings that Wordsworth would or could not recognize as his own.

To consider this first version of *Salisbury Plain* in the light of its three characters does some violence to its structure, but it suggests the degree to which events of 1793 resulted in the fragmentation of both technique and identity. In the narrator's voice we hear the language of the demonstrative reason, a language that locates significance and truth in abstractions, which it bodies forth in analogies and personifications. In the descriptions of the traveler, however, we see a language that focuses the quest for hope with great intensity upon objects of immediate intuition, and seeks psychic integrity in the relationship of mind to nature. The first voice comes from the past, and ultimately from Locke; extended and purified, the second voice would become that of Wordsworth's mature poetry and would eventually find philosophic justification in Coleridge's version of transcendental idealism.

In the divergent impulses defined by these characters, furthermore, we find a measure of Wordsworth's growing ambivalence toward the Revolution. The narrator commits himself to his cause with militant fervor; he exhorts the "heroes of truth" to complete their work of purgation and he embraces the moral and social isolation that English apostasy from this cause imposed on Wordsworth. In the words of *The Prelude,* he does not care

> if the wind did now and then
> Blow keen upon an eminence that gave
> Prospect so large into futurity.
>
> (X. 750–752)

But the deepest emotions in the poem, those of the vagrant and the traveler, are less heroic. They point in quite another direction —away from exposure, violence, and division, and toward the cottage and all it implies: the reconciliation of man and nature, man and man, and of man and his own "uneasy heart." If these unheroic feelings are dramatized by the poem, however, they are also disciplined and indeed purged, on behalf of the narrator's unflagging commitment to the cause of France, a commitment that is strained because it no longer offers integrity.

III

In the early months of 1794 Wordsworth's travels came to a temporary end. He returned to the Lakes and for six weeks was reunited with his sister at Windy Brow, a borrowed cottage overlooking the town of Keswick and its celebrated lake, Derwentwater. Here he took up the poem he had begun as a farewell to this landscape and had corrected on his first return to it, *An Evening Walk*. He now revised and enlarged it for a second time, leaving a number of passages that record a distinct, prophetic, and largely unrecognized phase of his poetic apprenticeship.[8]

The prevailing spirit of these additions is a joyful fortitude, a consciousness of present happiness heightened by a sense of trials survived. Wordsworth now opens the descriptive part of the poem not by dismissing the "idle pain" of personal melancholy, as he had in 1788, but by acknowledging the magnitude and dignity of "those passions . . . that rise in mortal minds from mortal change" (A ll. 49–50 *app. crit.*).[9] Among "Grasmere's happy youth," he goes on, there are those

> to whom the buoyant heart proclaims
> That death hath no power o [']er their particular frames [;]
> As the light spirit [,] the perpetual glee [,]
> The spring of body [,] once proclaimed to me.
> <div align="right">(A. l. 49–52 <i>app. crit.; </i>DCP)</div>

In 1804 he would adduce related memories as intimations of immortality, but here, as in the youthful paradise of Gray's Eton College boys, they measure his own survival of the ambush of hope, and his own maturity. Later in the poem his emblem for a virtuous human life becomes the glowworm, a creature that is "sufficed and bless'd" by its "own proper light" (A l. 398/9 *app. crit.*). It recalls the elder Milton:

> In dangerous night so Milton worked alone
> Cheared by a secret lustre all his own
>
> > (A l. 398 / 9 *app. crit.*)

and embodies the isolation of virtue in a world fallen on evil days:

> So Virtue, fallen on times to gloom consigned,
> Makes round her path the light she cannot find.
>
> > (A l. 398 / 9 *app. crit.*)

Although we might at first sight ascribe this spirit of fortified individualism to the influence of William Godwin, whose *Political Justice* Wordsworth openly affirms for the only time in his life this spring, he himself alludes to the stoicism of an older and more august Christian humanism: the elder Milton and Samuel Johnson, whose conclusion to *The Vanity of Human Wishes* he echoes.

The most remarkable feature of these additions, however, is their ardent naturalism. There is no reason to suppose that Wordsworth had lost religious faith, or to doubt that he and Dorothy spontaneously rendered thanks to God for this "good hour," as he recalled in later years.[10] But his attention and his expectations remain where they were in 1792: in the empirical world, where the covenant of God, man, and nature, is revealed. Instead of affirming the purgative violence of political revolution, however, he now looks to the power of an active and progressive nature that itself tends toward the ends of the revolution. He affirms nature not because he is indifferent toward man, as he would imply in *Tintern Abbey* and after, but because nature upholds the covenant of human hope.

Such hopes appear both in the landscapes of 1794 and in Wordsworth's several discursive celebrations of natural influence. The visible world of these additions testifies to the moral harmony of a benign nature and a virtuous man. To the sunset scene of 1788, for example, Wordsworth now added several objects that memorialize the purifying power of time and nature:

> Crested with trees behold yon fortress raise
> His battlements to meet the parting blaze,

Refulgent on the mountain top appear
The naked druid stones, and curling near
From piles of burning fern still smoke aspires,
Where once the savage viewed mysterious fires [;]
The lowly abbey in the purple cove
Hardly betrays his forehead through the grove
Far to the west.

(B ll. 186–191 *app. crit.*)

This fortress is crested not with armed men but trees. Pure light transfigures a Druid monument that distantly recalls the terrifying and "naked" walls of Stonehenge. The barbaric rites of primitive man have become a wreath of smoke, and the abbey, monument of a tyrannic superstition, is humbled and partly concealed by its natural recess. In each case the landscape itself exhibits an active tendency to restore order, tranquillity, and moral harmony to the violently dislocated landscapes of 1793. Elsewhere in the poem, war, pain and violent confrontation of any kind are consigned to the past or the earth, or are shielded or reduced by mediating agencies. A "mountain shepherd" shelters from the noontime sun behind a "mossy mound" in which slayer and slain, the relics of the border wars, lie buried (A ll. 175–190 *app. crit.*). Wordsworth now contemplates the poor by moonlight, and reflects not on their despair but on the "sweet Oblivion" of their sleep, a sleep denied the tyrannized poor of the past (A ll. 413–426 *app. crit.*). In the moving lights of a moonlight landscape he sees the "Spirits of the virtuous rove / Haunts once their pleasure," and in nighttime sounds he now hears the "low voices" of "good men" (A ll. 413–426 *app. crit.*). Time and nature selectively eradicate evil and perpetuate virtue.

The poet himself actively furthers such ends. Three times, for example, he deprecates human violence toward nature. For the lurid death of the female beggar he substitutes a tale told by shepherds, of another, less ironic tragedy in another landscape. He filters it, as it were, through several speakers, distancing it from the reader. His notebooks witness an attempt to ease the violent transition from the death of the female beggar to natural beauty: "Sweet are the sounds that mingle from afar" (A l. 301). His final substitute for this line briefly directs attention away from the concrete and painfully contrasting object toward the mind:

> The ear is lost in wonder thus to find
> Such quiet with such various sounds combined
> And wondring ever knows not if 'tis more
> Hurry or stillness, silence or uproar.[11]

(DCP)

Here presentational techniques mediate between the poetic object and the reader. Language imitates the mediation offered by the landscape it describes, and bespeaks Wordsworth's closer acquaintance with pain.

If this benign landscape is progressive in time, it is also active in space. Although Wordsworth continues to portray the changing light of sun and moon, he now looks far more closely at the surfaces or boundaries where light meets matter. In 1788, for example, he presented a deer park as a picturesque composition, and emphasized salient and characteristic lights and motions:

> In the brown park, in flocks, the troubl'd deer
> Shook the still twinkling tail and glancing ear.

(A ll. 63–64)

The line he adds in 1794 brings the eye up to the very surface of the deer's body, which becomes a generalized boundary between light and living matter:

> A spotted surface glimmering all alive.

(A ll. 70/71 *app. crit.*)

As early as the "School Exercise," he had delighted in the play of sunlight on the surface of water. Now he examines a few square feet of Derwentwater:

> Here, plots of sparkling water tremble bright
> With thousand thousand twinkling points of light;

> There, waves that, hardly weltering, die away,
> Tip their smooth ridges with a softer ray.
>
> (B ll. 120–123)

The surface of the lake actively concentrates and relaxes its energies in intimate relationship to a supervening light. A particular detail in an afternoon scene had occupied a couplet in 1788:

> Beside their sheltering cross of wall, the flock
> Feeds on in light, nor thinks of winter's shock.
>
> (A ll. 117–118)

In 1794 Wordsworth amplifies it, elaborating significant details. A shepherd now comes across the wall by moonlight, and marks

> the unchequered moonbeams fall
> Direct upon the loose rude cross of wall
> That shields from driving snow the winter flocks
> Now wandering thoughtless o'er the distant rocks.
>
> (A ll. 413–426 *app. crit.*)

Imagery again stresses the fall of light upon a naked surface, and embodies both the benignity and the physical mass of light by bringing the fall of snow into the same field of view. Landscape becomes a composite of innumerable surfaces, each an instance of exposure that is benign, and each implicitly analogous to the surface at the center of Wordsworth's attention, that of the mind:

> Yes, thou art blest, my friend, with mind awake
> To Nature's impulse like this living lake.
>
> (B ll. 86–127 *app. crit.*)

Here Wordsworth returns to the conventional theme of natural sympathy, a theme that is perhaps exalted by his recollection of the "sacred influence of light" in *Paradise Lost* (III. 1034–1035). But the empirical and indeed positivistic rigor with which he portrays the relationship between mind and nature is entirely his own;

he is gazing intently at a process that guarantees human joy and hope.

The style of such descriptions clearly develops from that of *Salisbury Plain;* it relies upon the selection and arrangement of significant images. It is clear, too, that Wordsworth continues to discipline his language on behalf of the object, attempting to clarify the relation between word and thing and in general to render the linguistic surface of his style as unobtrusive as possible. Nouns become concrete and denotative: they derive value from the object they name, and not from periphrasis. In his description of the moonlit wall, for example, the archaic "winter's shock" gives way to "driving snow." He prefers the plain and common word: the "dilated" sun of 1792 (*Descriptive Sketches,* l. 345) becomes simply "big" (B ll. 186–191 *app. crit.*), and the "bird" that had saluted the rising moon in 1788 once again becomes an "owl" (A l. 389 *app. crit.*). He deletes images in order to clarify syntactical and spatial relationship:

> 1788:   Cross the calm lakes blue shades the cliffs aspire
> (A l. 157)
>
> 1794:   Beyond the lake the opposing cliffs aspire
> (B ll. 172–174 *app. crit.*)

He corrects gratuitous inversions and eliminates the syntactical autonomy of an absolute construction:

> 1788:   Some, hardly heard their chissel's clinking sound
> Toil, small as pigmies, in the gulph profound.
> (A ll. 145–146)
>
> 1794:   Some in the gulph profound like pigmies ply
> Their clinking chissel [,] hardly heard so high
> (B ll. 162–163 *app. crit.*)

In each case he moves toward the "plain and naked" style of 1798, in response to a new understanding of the significance of the natural object, and thus of the function of language.

In numerous passages Wordsworth's celebration of nature becomes discursive as well as descriptive, and, as several commentators have pointed out, he asserts beliefs he would reassert in 1798.[12] In general, these beliefs are not new to his poetry; they recapitulate ideas he had stated in *Descriptive Sketches,* ideas that are largely conventional themes of the nature poetry of his age. But he presents these beliefs with a new and passionate sense of their personal significance, and in a language that is now self-consciously philosophic and moral. In *Descriptive Sketches* he had celebrated the charities a "doubly pitying Nature" showers on the wounded heart (l. 13); now he attributes a similar power to a concrete and familiar object, the Rydal Cascade (B ll. 53–54 *app. crit.*). In 1792 he had compared the sympathetic heart to Memnon's lyre, a simile that may derive from Akenside's *Pleasures of the Imagination* (I. 109–114); at Windy Brow he describes the responsive vibrations of the heart directly, as physiological facts: [13]

> A heart that vibrates evermore, awake
> To feeling for all forms that Life can take.
> > (B ll. 72–85 *app. crit.*)

In 1792 he borrowed images from Gray to celebrate a comprehensive taste:

> For him lost flowers their idle sweets exhale;
> He tastes the meanest note that swells the gale.
> > (*Descriptive Sketches,* ll. 19–20)

Now he praises those "favoured souls" who, "taught"

> By active Fancy or by patient thought
> See common forms prolong the endless chain
> Of joy and grief, of pleasure and of pain.[14]
> > (B ll. 86–127 *app. crit.*)

What changes in each case is not idea but language; Wordsworth restates conventional ideas in terms of empirical images or of abstract terms that derive not from poetry but from philosophical and aesthetic prose. Since Cambridge (and probably Hawkshead), he had been familiar with most of the operative terms in these and other passages—"image," "form," "object," "sense," among others. He had employed the first three in a letter of 1790 in order to describe his enthusiasm for the picturesque beauty of the Alps.[15] That they now appear in his poetry points now to a new "doctrine" of nature, but to his quest for a vocabulary that is veridical, precise, and universal, and to a developing readiness to defy a literary decorum that no longer seemed adequate to his subject. What we see here, I would suggest, is the counterpart of the changes in his descriptive style, where he remains faithful to the natural image; here he remains equally faithful to the philosophical abstraction, and refuses to embody it in the fabricated imagery prescribed by convention. In both cases he repudiates the language of poetry on behalf of a "truth" that has become sublimely significant.

If we turn from Wordsworth's developing conception of nature to his role in the poem, we find that recovery of relationship to a stable and trustworthy object-world is again accompanied, as it had been in *Descriptive Sketches,* by a forceful reassertion of subjective imperatives. Like man and nature, mind and its objects appear in active equilibrium. Style once again becomes sensitive to "thought," "sentiment" and personal feeling, and the three voices of *Salisbury Plain* effectively recombine into one, that of the poet himself. Nearly all these additions move from sensation toward thought, as Wordsworth's mind plays freely over the highly objective imagery of 1788, elaborating its moral and emotional significance. From the "blue bar" that bisects the setting sun, for example, his attention now moves to a literary analogue: the spear of Milton's Satan (B ll. 172–174 *app. crit.*). As we have seen, the objects he adds to the evening landscape shift attention toward the past and imply the benignity of nature and time. After the sun sets, attention moves into the future and beyond the sensible world entirely, as the poet claims that "triumphant Truth" will survive the "mighty arm of Time" (B ll. 186–191 *app. crit.*). From a

firmly central perspective, attention moves freely and authorita-
tively from present to past and future, and from the sensible world
to things "beyond the reign of sense" (B ll. 53–54 *app. crit.*). The
eye, in short, is no longer master of the heart.

Style, too, responds to personal feeling, as Wordsworth continues to avoid trope and to experiment with devices that imply feeling through form. He enthusiastically breaks the couplet:

> The horse's trot now faint, now loud, uneven
> As the wild road—the herd by cow-boy driven
> Afield and quickening still with cumbrous chase
> At every shout their heavy weltering pace.
> > (A ll. 311–328 *app. crit.*)

He experiments with repetition, which, as he would point out at
length in 1800, implies feeling both for words and for the objects
they represent (*PW* II, 513).

> Come with thy poet, come, my friend, to stray
> > (A ll. 195–196 *app. crit.*)

> > The sun sinks down above [,]
> Sinks slowly to a curve. . . .
> > (B ll. 186–191 *app. crit.*)

He delights in the sudden shift and bestowal of attention implied
by apostrophe, a figure which singles out a host of creatures in the
poem, including the reader, the poet's friend, the dying mother,
and the glowworm. To an audience of shepherds, frightened need-
lessly by the apparition of phantom horsemen he had painted in
1788, Wordsworth twice repeats a reassuring refrain that mingles
associations of the pastoral eclogue with his own retreat from civil
and psychological division:

> Why, shepherds, tremble thus with new alarms
> As if ye heard the din of civil arms?
> > (A ll. 175–190 *app. crit.*)

He is, in short, no longer silent; he possesses a poetic identity. His style again becomes directly sensitive to the activity of his own heart and mind, to a degree that reminds us that his first instinctive commitment, seven years before, had been to lyric poetry.

It is difficult to doubt that these changes reflect the liberating influence of the landscape and the sister that Wordsworth loved. Insofar as he had a home, he had returned to it, and to what in later years he would call a "Centre" and a "Whole without dependence or defect" (*Recluse*, ll. 148–149), a satellite world that incorporated the abiding hopes of the Revolution and yet excluded the extremity and violence he had suffered in the past year. He takes up the position that Coleridge would regard as characteristic of his genius, that of *spectator ab extra*, and does so consciously and gratefully. "Like the sun," the "love diffusive" of "favoured souls" surrounds

> The various world to life's remotest bounds,
> Yet not extinguishes the warmer fire
> Round which the close domestic train retire. . . .
>
> (B ll. 86–127 *app. crit.;* DCP)

Stationing himself on the borders of several worlds, between cottage and society, domestic and sublime, pastoral and heroic, Wordsworth refuses to commit himself to extremes and seeks above all to retain the freedom of compensating response, and an active equilibrium of opposites. And here, these fragments would suggest, he believed that a "favoured soul" armed with personal integrity and sustained by nature need not fear the loss of temporal hope.

IV   Racedown: 1795-1796

What then remained in such eclipse? what light
To guide or chear? The laws of things which lie
Beyond the reach of human will or power. . . .

The Prelude

The lyricism of 1794 was shortlived. In the poetry Wordsworth composed during the next two years, while he and Dorothy lived in frugal retirement at Racedown Lodge, Dorset, the symptoms of psychic crisis reappear and intensify: an objectivism that now totally suppresses the poet's identity; an imagery endowed with a power that is clearly symbolic and at times obsessive; and a loss of trust that extends to the fundamental premises of the age—the innate virtue of natural feeling, the ethical authority of the demonstrative reason, and the benignity of natural law itself.

Although the account of this period in *The Prelude* treats this third crisis and that of 1793 as one, there seems no reason to doubt that its principal cause was the failure of the French Revolution. The implications of this disappointment were vast. More clearly than the English declaration of war, which discredited a government Wordsworth already sought to replace, the gradual disintegration of the Revolution cast doubt on the essential goodness of man. It would seem probable, moreover, that this ambush of hope was painfully indecisive and that events repeatedly conspired to tempt and then to shatter a hope that could be prolonged indefinitely, in the absence of conclusive proof one way or the other. It is clear from Wordsworth's response to the death of

105

Robespierre in August 1794 that he had by then abjured the Terror, and that he now took up the hope of political "renovation" with renewed enthusiasm, only, as de Selincourt has pointed out, to see France embark on a "war of conquest" in the following autumn and winter (*Prelude* X. 540–557; p. 604). The Racedown poems suggest, too, that Wordsworth's perception of such political events continued to be intensified and complicated by his feelings toward Annette, and that during these years both causes betrayed him, in circumstances that rendered moral responsibility obscure, estranged him from his own deepest feelings, and cast suspicion on nature, the power to which he had looked for a "happy end of all."

The significance of this third crisis has repeatedly been framed in terms of the influence of William Godwin, but the evidence for this is conjectural, and I do not propose to consider it in any detail. There is abundant reason to suppose that many of Godwin's ideas seemed like a "greeting of the spirit" to Wordsworth, as they did to other disaffected radicals who met with the philosopher during the summers of 1795 and 1796, and it is not difficult to point to a common ground that extends late into Wordsworth's life. Both poet and philosopher shared, for example, a belief in the progressive advance of truth, a tough-minded humanitarianism, and a respect for the power and fortitude of the individual mind. But here and in nearly all other points of agreement it is difficult to show that these ideas were distinctively Godwinian or that Wordsworth was not ardently committed to them before he met Godwin. With or without the philosopher's confirmation, the Hawkshead schoolboy would very probably have continued to assert the "majesty" of truth, the friend of Beaupuy would have favored practical social reform, and the wanderer of 1793 would have returned to his native regions and embraced an individualistic quietism that drew for fortitude on the examples of Milton and Johnson. Nor are we justified in ascribing the rationalistic phase of Wordsworth's crisis to Godwin; since his schooldays he had taken for granted the assumption he would soon give up "in despair," that the demonstrative reason could resolve "moral questions" (*Prelude* X. 901). An urgent appeal from sensibility to rational principle was, as we have seen, an immediate and natural effect of the declaration of war, which at once rendered instinctive feeling relativistic and divided. Godwin's more extreme suspicions of "gratitude, conjugal fidelity, filial affection, and the belief of God"—to cite the grievance of a disillusioned Coleridge (*STCL* I, 199)—may have offered ways of rationalizing a break with Annette. But here again the philosopher's role would be instrumental only; if he forged the knife of an analytical and dissecting reason, it was Wordsworth who took this knife "in hand" for his own ends. In both the later Racedown poems and in *The Prelude* (X. 761–769; 885–889), Wordsworth presents a barren rationalism as a symptom, and not a cause, of a prior corruption of feeling brought on by events. To hold Godwin responsible for Wordsworth's crisis is therefore unjust to the philosopher's genuinely noble ends, which Wordsworth certainly perceived. But to defend Godwin against such charges on the grounds that his influence was decisive and benign would seem equally unjust to the autonomy of the poet's development.[1]

The fundamental problem confronted by all the Racedown poems is named in *The Prelude:* the "utter loss of hope itself, / And things to hope for" (XI. 6–7). At no time during the Racedown period, however, does Wordsworth's poetry assent to despair. As in the greater work to come, poetic utterance itself now becomes what he would call a "motion of hope," undertaken in the consciousness that without hope "we perish," and that the task of art is the furtherance of life.[2] In each of the Racedown poems he dramatizes despair in order to overcome it. Viewed in sequence, the poems recapitulate the earlier phases of Wordsworth's struggle for hope. Gradually, then triumphantly, they reclaim the faith of 1792 and 1794 in "nature," "truth," and "love." Intensified and focused still further by personal extremity, and applied without reservation to the purposes and the language of poetry, this triumvirate of values sustains his first great poems and molds an art that, like the cause of 1792, is at once deeply conservative and revolutionary.

I

The circumstances of Wordsworth's retirement to Racedown in September 1795 would seem to be auspicious. He had attained a modest financial independence, and was again reunited with Dorothy in a rural retreat. We look in vain, however, for any sign of the joyful liberation Wordsworth recalled in the "glad preamble" to *The Prelude,* which readers have traditionally attributed to this period.[3] His first task at Racedown took him in quite a different direction, to the narrative that dramatized the distress of 1793, *Salisbury Plain.* By November he had transformed this poem into what he could call "another work" (*EY,* p. 159), a second version that would impel Coleridge a few months later to call his new friend "the best poet of the age" (*STCL* I, 215).

Judging from the surviving manuscripts, Wordsworth now rendered this poem far more pessimistic than it had been two years before.[4] He decisively suppressed the emergent lyricism of the Windy Brow fragments, intensifying the objectivity of the poem of 1793 still further by deleting virtually all signs of the poet's existence. The militant narrator of the earlier version disappears, and attention fixes on the concrete events of the narrative with continuous intensity. The three styles of the first version are now disciplined to a uniform literalism which admits few figures expressive of subjective activity, and then only on behalf of characters. At times, furthermore, Wordsworth now begins to imitate the idiom of rural conversation.[5]

Still more decisive changes center on the anonymous traveler of 1793. He becomes a sailor, a naturally virtuous man who was goaded into murder by social injustice and who flees from the law across Salisbury Plain. Wordsworth makes few changes in the first part of the earlier version, allowing the presentational imagery of

1793 to imply the effect of landscape upon a guilt-stricken imagination. He adds a concluding section of twenty-five stanzas, however, in which the sailor continues on to the pastoral cottage viewed at the close of the first version. Here he is by chance reunited with his dying wife, confesses his crime to her, and frantically implores a forgiveness that is withheld only by her death. He then proceeds directly to the city, surrenders himself to the civil authorities, and is summarily executed. It is not surprising that Wordsworth found this version too "tragical" to publish a few year later (*PW* I, 330).

Wordsworth's explicit perspective on such a subject, and his public rationale, may be described as a bitterly objective social realism, which shares the pessimism of such contemporary protests as Godwin's *Caleb Williams* (1794) and Blake's second "Holy Thursday" (1794). He had tried his hand at Juvenalian satire a few months before, and now he attempts to "expose" vices he had already castigated discursively in 1793: the inhuman cruelty of the "penal law," and the "calamities of war as they affect individuals." [6] The function of his objective style is to unmask evil, to present, in the words of the subtitle of *Caleb Williams,* "things as they are."

The ethical effect of such a perspective is to justify the sailor, who, like the innocent Caleb Williams, becomes the victim of causes beyond his control. As he returns toward his cottage from two years at sea, "enflamed with long desire" for his wife, he is abducted by a press-gang. When he is discharged years later, the "slaves of Office" deny him his just wages. "Bearing to those he loved nor warmth nor food," enraged and humiliated, he turns homeward once again. "In sight of his own home" he robs and kills a passing traveler[7] and flees into the tortured vagrancy described by the poem (ll. 50–72 *app. crit.*). And throughout the poem he is tacitly defended, as the narrator asserts his natural benevolence and repeatedly hints the far greater guilt of those who pursue him. In one unpublished passage, for example, the sailor attempts to console the vagrant by praising the social order itself:

> Of social order's all protecting plan [,]
> Delusion fond [,] he spoke in tender [?stile]
> And of the general care man pays to man
> [Joy's] second spring, and hope's long treasured smile.
>
> (DCP)

In 1842 Wordsworth would precisely reverse the implications of this passage,[8] but here he clearly invites our sympathy for his hero, presenting him in an ironic aside as a deluded and helpless victim of political propaganda. Like the innocents of Blake's songs, he is blind to his own exploitation, and his crime exemplifies the power of social evil to corrupt human goodness. The ethic implied by such a point of view is deterministic, and its effect is to palliate the sailor's guilt. As Coleridge put it more blithely, in a letter of 1796, "*Guilt* is out of the Question—I am a Necessarian, and of course deny the possibility of it" (*STCL* I. 213).

As we approach the point of view of the characters themselves, however, such a rationale becomes less than persuasive, and indeed peripheral. For both the sailor and the vagrant guilt is appalingly real. This is the first version of the poem to justify its final title, "Guilt and Sorrow," and the first poem in which Wordsworth dramatizes that sense of personal culpability that tainted his dreams during the war years, dreams in which he delivered "long orations"

> Before unjust Tribunals, with a voice
> Labouring, a brain confounded, and a sense
> Of treachery and desertion in the place
> The holiest that I knew of, my own soul.
>
> (*Prelude* X. 377–381)

The sailor's consciousness takes us at once from an enlightened determinism to a world of nightmare. His consistent response to the visible world is paranoid; he pales at the "morning chear" of a coachman (*PW* I, 338), and is terrified by the sight of the only object Wordsworth now added to the landscape of the plain, a gibbet:

For then with scarce distinguishable clang
In the cold wind a sound of iron rang.
He looked, and saw on a bare gibbet nigh
In clanking chains a human body hang [;]
A hovering raven oft did round it fly
A grave the [re] was beneath which he could not descry.

(*PW* I, 98 *app. crit.*)

Ambushed by two images of great power, a clanking chain and a grave, the sailor's mind hallucinates. The plain rises, as if in deluge, to overwhelm him:

The stones, as if to sweep him from the day,
Rolled at his back along the living plain;
He fell and without sense or motion lay. . . .

(ll. 87–89 *app. crit.*)

Respite from psychological extremity is won only by loss of consciousness.

Later in the poem he sees a peasant beating his son and suffers a second hallucination that reenacts his own crime. Gazing down at the wounded boy, he feels the "griding iron" enter his own "brain" and is compelled into speech:

Bad is the world, and hard is the world's law [;]
Each prowls to strip his brother of his fleece;
Much need have ye that time more closely draw
The bond of nature, all unkindness cease,
And that among so few there still be peace.

(ll. 505–509 *app. crit.*)

These words, in turn, bring him a "correspondent calm" (l. 513). The ethical implications of such actions are quite incompatible with a deterministic or rationalistic ethic. This man craves atonement, and his homily appeals not to the reason for hope but to the heart: to charity, and more broadly to the domestic affection that has been violated.

Although the circumstances of the poem present the vagrant as

an entirely innocent and passive victim of the "calamities of war,"
she too suffers remorse:

> But what afflicts my peace with keenest ruth,
> Is that I have my inner self abused,
> Forgone the home delight of constant truth,
> And clear and open soul, so prized in fearless youth.
>
> (ll. 438–441)

Although several readers have found this sense of guilt incon-
gruous,[9] it is clearly justified by the vagrant's history as Wordsworth revised it in 1795. On her return to England she now suffers absolute despair, the effect of which is a wish for
self-destruction. For three days this wish remains passive: she refuses to eat or drink. It then becomes active: "in deep despair, by
frightful wishes stirred" (l. 381), she approaches the sea and is rescued from a will bent on suicide only by the loss of consciousness.
The transgression she later rues, then, is psychological: that loss of
charity toward the self that is the effect of despair. Spenser had
seen it in the movement of a hand:

> At last, resolv'd to work his finall smart,
> He lifted up his hand, that backe againe did start.
>
> (*Faerie Queene* I. IX. 51)

Wordsworth sees it in a woman's refusal to take food. The felt
ethical assumptions of both characters, in other words, are those
of *The Faerie Queene* and *Paradise Lost;* they inhabit a world of
free will, sin, and atonement.

The ethical perspective of the poem is thus deeply ambiguous.
The sailor's guilt is simultaneously palliated and intensified, rationalized and atoned for. And a further confusion blurs the
causes of this guilt. The explicit cause, of course, is the murder
of the anonymous traveler. But the sailor's feelings focus far
more strongly on a second victim, his wife, the only major character added to the poem. In the final confession scene, she takes on
the aspect of both victim and accuser. She confronts him unex-

pectedly, far from the cottage where he abandoned her, and he listens in silent anonymity as she relates the history of her sufferings, sufferings caused by his desertion of her. Her language renders her a model of patient and humble fortitude: "Oh God as I have meekly suffered, meek/Shall be my end" (l. 587–588 *app. crit.*). In appearance, however, she is anything but meek: her features mingle immense moral authority with skeletal decay:

> . . . the Woman half upraised
> Her bony visage—gaunt and deadly wan;
> No pity asking, on the group she gazed. . . .
>
> (l. 560–562)

Throwing himself on the mercy of this forbidding figure, the sailor implores forgiveness in a speech as equivocal as the character of his judge:

> "Oh bless me now! That thou shouldst live
> I do not ask nor wish—forgive me, but forgive!"
>
> (ll. 620–621 *app. crit.*)

He utters what amounts to a wish for her death, which will end the accusation she embodies. And her burial is followed by a sudden restoration of his integrity: confident, fearless, and even with "pleasure," he moves "straight" to the halls of Justice, and with self-righteous contempt delivers himself up to be destroyed (ll. 649–651 *app. crit.*).

The wife thus attracts feelings that are violently ambivalent. At the beginning of the poem she is an object of love and frank sexual desire—a combination notably absent from Wordsworth's mature poetry. In the confession scene, however, she is viewed with fear and guilt, and her death is the agency of release from both. The crime she implies is one of desertion, but the plot of the poem displaces attention to the murder of the anonymous traveler. This second crime is presented as the cause of the first and is itself, as we have seen, vigorously justified as the effect of extrinsic social causes and ultimately of necessity. The organization of this poem, then, would seem to be guided by a kind of dream-logic: guilt is displaced from its true object—a deserted and accusing wife—to a symbolic surrogate that can be contemplated and rationalized by the conscious mind. The psychological function of the poem, like a dream, would appear to be therapeutic: it permits the dramatization and the vicarious expiation of an act that is never named.

Similar constellations of guilt and fear, centering on a crime toward a wife or lover, reappear in later Racedown poems and in the tale of Vaudracour and Julia. All point to the influence on Wordsworth's imagination of Annette Vallon. It is as easy to exaggerate this influence as to ignore it,[10] and an openly autobiographical reading of this and later poems would be naïve. At the most they dramatize powerful feelings that have a distorted and at times nightmarish vision of Annette for their object, feelings Wordsworth is seeking to purge or discipline. As time passes, moreover, such symptoms tend to disappear, as Wordsworth's feelings and the symbols that embody them become representative and accessible, and as he succeeds in looking boldly on "painful things," as *The Prelude* recalls (X. 872). In the absence of other evidence, however, this poem implies decisive changes in Wordsworth's feelings toward Annette, and suggests that our understanding of their relationship at this time stands in need of correction.

From the absence of such patterns of feeling in earlier poems,[11] it would appear, first, that Wordsworth began to regard Annette with fear and guilt in 1795, and not before. It is clear, too, that he takes his relationship to her with great seriousness. He displays keen sensitivity to both the duties and the pleasures of a husband and father, and throughout the poem implies that their relationship, which he symbolizes as a marriage, is morally binding. He in no way justifies a desertion of her, in other words, by hinting that their relationship was illegitimate or casual, as his critics have sometimes done.[12] The imagery and the structure of the poem suggest, indeed, that the possibility of violating this "marriage" filled Wordsworth with horror. He buries it from view, atones for it, and rationalizes it, in a desperate struggle to avoid the conscious implications of a treacherous shift of feeling in "the holiest place" he knew of, his own soul. These implications, I suggest, would have been inconceivable to him; once recognized, the very desire for freedom that this poem dramatizes and punishes would transform him into what he had not been in 1792, a deserter of innocence and an enemy to the domestic affections he had celebrated in every poem he had written, with all the more feeling, perhaps, because he was an orphan himself. The pain of such confrontation with himself would have been sharpened by the fact that he had not intended such an act, that his motives in 1792 had been pure, and that the "Tribunals" of his own conscience were unjust. As in 1792, his inner life offered a striking analogy to the course of political events, and the disintegration of the glorious cause of that year may have seemed an ironic reflection of the history of his own feelings and the decay of love into fear, guilt, and hate. In both inner and outer worlds the passage of time forced Wordsworth toward a deliberate repudiation of what he had been and loved, and induced a shattering repetition of earlier crises of hope. It would appear equally mistaken, therefore, to ignore Annette's role in this crisis, or to sentimentalize Wordsworth's response by attributing it to remorse. What we see in the Racedown poems is the anguish of a man who is trapped, by forces he had trusted, into betraying and destroying what he loved.

The immediate effects of such feelings on Wordsworth's practice of poetry recapitulate and intensify those of earlier crises. The objectivity of the poem's style is clearly protective, erecting a transparent but impenetrable barrier between the self and the emotions dramatized by the narrative. These emotions, however, are now invested in an object-world that works with intense and threatening symbolic meaning. The image of the grave now takes on immense but unexplored meaning, as a focal point of guilt and fear. The sound or sight of iron fetters reappears in nearly all of the Racedown poems as an instrument of punishment, a metaphor for an imprisoning and delusive hope, or the slavery of a humanity that was born free but is in chains. Intense significance continues to attach as well to images of the domestic affections, and particularly to the skeletal features of the accusing wife who refuses to die. Chief among these symbols, however, is the compulsive wanderer, whose freedom is the result of crime against the domestic affections and whose guilt and isolation sanction utterance that is authoritative and universal. This figure reappears, in various guises and at various stages of his life cycle, in all the Racedown poems, and clearly provides one model for the Ancient Mariner. In a broader perspective he is a prototype of a host of romantic and modern characters who symbolize violent but liberating alienation from society.

These symbols would contribute immensely to the power of later poems, but in *Salisbury Plain* their power is so great as to disorganize Wordsworth's art. The sailor utters a wish for his wife's death, for example, not because it is appropriate to his character—it is not—but because of the poet's need to utter, and then to punish, these words. Similarly compulsive breaches of dramatic propriety occur in later poems. An infamous example ends *Vaudracour and Julia,* for example, where the hero, by some "mistake / Or indiscretion," allows his son to die (*Prelude* IX. 906–907). In both cases Wordsworth responds to an image that accuses him—the image of a deserted wife, or of the child of a deserted wife—by seeking to destroy it in a violent and desperate attempt to recover integrity. The apparent effect of such lapses is a sudden failure of feeling, as the poet erects what he would call in later years an "unfeeling armour" against pain. In all the Racedown poems a "mind beset / With images, and haunted by itself" (*Prelude* VI. 179–180) struggles to reestablish its authority over an imagery that threatens to destroy it.

The effects of guilt upon the major themes of Wordsworth's earlier poems are equally profound. Like the traveler of *Salisbury Plain,* the sailor is isolated from both man and nature, but he now has no hope of redemption from either source. The goal of hope in 1793, the cottage, effectively vanishes from the poem and becomes an invisible center around which the sailor circles, in an orbit that measures fear and desire. Wordsworth's alienation from the domestic order is apparent in the final scene of the poem, as the sailor's body is hung in chains before the indifferent stares of a holiday crowd:

> And dissolute men unthinking and untaught,
> Planted their festive [booths] beneath his face;
> And to that spot, which idle numbers sought,
> Women and children were by Fathers brought.
>
> (ll. 659–662 *app. crit.; DCP*)

He indicts the callousness of the crowd and at the same time dramatizes a grotesque and humiliating atonement, which exposes the sailor's "face" to the family groups that embody the order he has violated. Hate focuses on both society and self.

If the glad humanism of 1794 disappears, so does the possibility of a redemptive relationship to nature. In 1793 the traveler had called the vagrant to the window to view the cheering sunrise. Now it is the vagrant who sees "the dawn salute the silvery east / With rays of promise" (ll. 313–314). An unpublished passage makes the sailor's psychological and epistemological isolation explicit:

> His withered cheek was tinged with ashy hue
> He stood, and trembled both with grief and fear [;]
> But she felt new delight and solace new. . . .
>
> (DCP)

Elsewhere Wordsworth renders the transaction between mind and nature far more enigmatic than it had been in 1793. Then, for example, the vagrant had described the calm and sunlit ocean in language that specified the immanence of Divine consolation:

> With wings which did the world of waves invest
> The Spirit of God diffused through balmy air
> Quiet that might have healed, if aught could heal, Despair.
>
> (ll. 340–342 *app. crit.*)

In 1795 she simply looks:

> A heavenly silence did the waves invest;
> I looked and looked along the silent air
> Until it seemed to bring a joy to my despair.
>
> (ll. 340–342 *app. crit.*)

He emphasizes the subjective energies of the vagrant's mind ("I looked and looked") and the impression that resulted ("seemed to bring"). But the external world becomes a vast and enigmatic vacancy in which only a hint of divinity ("heavenly") survives amid silence and extension ("along").

In every respect, then, the crisis of 1795 appears more violent than those of earlier years. This poem may indeed be regarded as a bitterly ironic comment on the first version, which had presumed the possibility of reconciliation with nature and man. As the two travelers walk into the morning landscape that had offered them hope in 1793, their attention is abruptly distracted from the "silver gleam" of rising mist—an image Wordsworth had celebrated since his schooldays:

> To them the sight was pleasant, but a scream
> Thence bursting shrill did all remark prevent.
>
> (*PW* I, 338; ll. 460–465)

Like the sunset cannon of 1793, this scream implies the division of man from nature. But it now implies, further, that there is no escape from evil, that guilt has invaded not only the pastoral landscape but the virtuous soul itself. Within the dream language of this poem, personal integrity and hope are compatible only with the deliberate and conscious destruction of the self.

II

In the spring of 1796 Wordsworth read Coleridge's latest poem, *Religious Musings,* and chose two passages as his favorites, "worth all the rest" (*STCL* I, 215–216): a lurid portrait of the "black-visaged, red-eyed Fiend," the final Destruction, and a description of the "ambrosial gales" that offer the "favoured good man" a portent of the millennium (ll. 377–401, 345–354). Both measure the distance Wordsworth had come since he composed such visionary tableaux at Hawkshead, and suggest that he admired an apocalyptic optimism he could not share. His "business," he recalled in *The Prelude,* "was upon the barren sea" (XI. 55), and in the few fragments that survive from the spring of 1796 he continued his rigorously objective studies of human sorrow and guilt. Two fragments appear to begin another version of *Salisbury Plain,* set in a Dorset landscape and with a woman in the role of the traveler. In one, perhaps the later, Wordsworth returns for the first time since his Cambridge years to the meter that most closely resembles prose, blank verse, and takes particular pains to imitate the rhythms and syntactical cadences of speech in a style that stands at the opposite extreme from Coleridge's.[13]

In a third fragment he returned to the study of guilt and its effects on the imagination. The twenty-five pseudo-Spenserian stanzas that survive describe the approach of two travelers, a blind man and his youthful guide, to a ruined castle—a setting modeled on the Gothic fragments of the Cambridge years. After revealing that the youth plans to murder his helpless companion, Wordsworth focuses the reader's attention upon the psychological interaction between the youth's mind and the sensible world. The youth seeks justification from his senses:

> And all the man had said but served to nurse
> Purpose most foul with most unnatural food;
> Each kindred object which, that night, had braced
> His fluctuating mind, he busily retraced.
>
> (*PW* I, 290; ll. 139–142)

But his unnatural purpose is repeatedly thwarted by sights and sounds he does not expect: a disembodied hand, a star twinkling through a crevice in a dungeon, a scream. Though terrifying, each appearance is duly revealed to have a natural cause; a later fragment suggests that the blind man was to be rescued by a band of smugglers.[14]

Although de Selincourt called this a "Gothic Tale," it clearly seeks to transcend Gothic sensation, and dramatizes what can be called the epistemology of criminal action, the struggle between human will and natural influence for hegemony over the imagination and the soul. In the dungeon where he isolates the blind man, the youth instinctively seeks the enclosure that guilt had imposed on the sailor's mind; but external power, acting through the senses, seeks to invade that enclosure and to reclaim a mind that has "strayed out of the course of nature." What we see here, in work that predates close association with Coleridge by several years, is a first portrait of the "ministry of fear" and a first version of *Peter Bell.* Placed beside the revision of *Salisbury Plain* Wordsworth had just completed, the *Gothic Tale* tentatively reaffirms the moral power of natural influence.

Wordsworth echoed *Hamlet* in this portrait of a "foul" and "unnatural" crime, and in the fall of 1796 he began to transform it into the far more ambitious form of a Shakespearian tragedy, which he entitled *The Borderers.*[15] Although the action of the play is set in the time of the Crusades, it too centers on the unnatural murder of a venerable blind man, a dispossessed nobleman, the Baron Herbert. His murderer now becomes a man of equal virtue: Mortimer, who loves Herbert's daughter, Matilda, and who leads a band of just and benevolent outlaws. Like Othello, Mortimer is goaded into the crime by a malevolent subordinate, Rivers, who convinces him that Herbert is not Matilda's true father and that he plans to sacrifice her to the wicked voluptuary, Clifford. After several attempts to kill Herbert are frustrated by psychological interventions similar to those in the *Gothic Tale,* Mortimer abandons him on a wind-swept heath. Rivers is exposed and killed, but not before the blind man dies of exposure. Repulsing all consolation, Mortimer seeks death in morbid solitude.

That *The Borderers* embodies a critical transition in the history of Wordsworth's thought has long been recognized, but for more than four decades after Legouis detected the language of *Political Justice* in the monologues of Rivers, and linked these to the moral crisis recalled by *The Prelude,* critics concerned themselves principally with the question of Godwin's influence on the play. Several recent studies have explored other frames of reference; Rivers, in particular, has been compared to the modern ideological criminal, the existentialist hero, or the Nietzchean superman.[16] Other aspects of the play, however, deserve notice. That Wordsworth should now begin a spirited imitation of Shakespearean tragedy, for example, witnesses a decisive recovery of artistic confidence and involves an ambitious and not unsophisticated attempt to reproduce a wide variety of spoken idioms, ranging from the dialect of the Dorset peasantry to a highly metaphorical language of passionate philosophical meditation. Like the second version of *Salisbury Plain, The Borderers* dramatizes psychological trauma, but in a less compulsive form that argues psychological recovery. Finally, it represents Wordsworth's first comprehensive assessment of his experience during the previous five years and a tentative reconstruction of hope that looks forward to the achievements of 1798.

As Wordsworth's first and only play, *The Borderers* carries the objectivism of earlier poems to its logical conclusion: a form that denies the existence of the poet altogether, and theoretically guarantees the psychological autonomy of his characters. A similar attempt to prescind and objectify guided the choice of the play's setting, which procured "the absence of established Law and Government; so that the agents might be at liberty to act on their own impulses" (*PW* I, 342). Virtually no responsibility, in other words, is assigned to social evils; the action of the play takes place in an "interregnum" similar to that which followed the death of Robespierre:

> To Nature then,
> Power had reverted: habit, custom, law,

> Had left an interregnum's open space
> For her to stir about in, uncontrol'd.
>
> (X. 610–613)

Form and setting exclude the adventitious intervention of both poet and society, and thus permit the heuristic isolation of "Nature" in both its aspects, human and external. The play in effect tests both kinds of nature; it recreates the conditions Wordsworth had posited in 1794 but had believed since his Hawkshead days: "Let the field be open and unencumbered, and truth must be victorious" (*EY*, p. 125).

Human nature is represented in the play by two symmetrical life histories, both of them dramatizations of Wordsworth's own past. Like the sailor of *Salisbury Plain*, Mortimer is an innocent man who is inexorably forced to destroy what he loves. Falsely informed by Rivers, he struggles to kill Herbert in the name of "truth," "justice," and "nature." With an eloquence that profits from *Macbeth, Lear,* and *Othello,* he observes and articulates the stages of his own psychic disintegration: he ceases to trust his moral instincts, his reason, and ultimately his will. "Cut off from man," he suffers ultimate moral solitude. His response to traumatic disorientation is a compulsive but vain search for "proof" and "evidence"; he scrutinizes his own heart, questions his fellow outlaws, and looks to nature for confirmatory signs. Unable to murder the old man, he finally commits him to an "ordeal" that relies upon the justice of a "judge above," abandoning him to the elements. His power as a moral agent is thus effectively paralyzed by psychic conflict; he gives up moral questions in despair and relinquishes all moral authority to nature. When nature kills the innocent Herbert, his betrayal is complete.

Considered as a psychological history, this clearly parallels Wordsworth's own in *The Prelude,* and suggests that by late 1796 he had begun to understand his past in terms he would recall and reapply in 1804. As a more objective and searching exploration of images and actions that Wordsworth had repressed a year earlier in *Salisbury Plain,* Mortimer's history also points to the healing effects of time. His crime, for example, is now openly identified as desertion, and his victim, Herbert, embodies the domestic virtues and affections far more openly than did the anonymous traveler of 1795. Violence now focuses on the heroine as well, who is at one point visually identified with her father and who will be reduced by the crime to the "skeleton" the sailor's wife became (l. 581; cf. 1764–71 *app. crit.*). Like the sailor, Mortimer confesses to her without affection and then seeks atonement (and freedom) in morbid solitude. As in *Salisbury Plain,* the feeling dramatized sometimes seems less relevant to character and plot than to the psychological needs of the author. Wordsworth's attempts to exculpate Mortimer are urgent and artistically disastrous: the crime is blamed on nearly everyone but the hero, and on nature as well. Like that of Vaudracour's child, Herbert's death results from a "mistake"—Mortimer simply forgets to leave him food. Other actions embody the violence of Wordsworth's hostility toward the domestic affections and duties. Quite gratuitously and with pulse "calm as a sleeping child" (l. 1405 *app. crit.*), Mortimer points a sword at Herbert's heart, miming feelings Wordsworth could not openly dramatize, feelings he may have recalled (and disguised) as the deliberate yet horrified dissection of the "living body of society" (*Prelude* X. 876). At such times, when Mortimer becomes a paralyzed shadow of such tragic prototypes as Othello and Karl Moor, both he and his creator seem to exemplify a single truth: that guilt deranges the imagination.

To the other central character in the play, Rivers, Wordsworth gives a life history that parallels Mortimer's, and again dramatizes his own past, from a more distant and more analytic perspective. Rivers too was tricked into the merciless desertion of an innocent man, and thereby destroyed the daughter of that man. Like Mortimer, he suffered "loss of power" and "hope," and "sank into despair" (ll. 1761–1763 *app. crit.*). At this point, however, the histories of the two characters diverge: Rivers refuses to repent. Drawing on a subjective "energy" that astonished him (ll. 1788), he immersed himself in action and thought. Contemplation of nature—"the moonlight desert, and the moonlight sea"—taught him

> What mighty objects do impress their forms
> To build up this our intellectual being
>   (ll. 1809–1810 *app. crit.; DCP*)

and confirmed his refusal to bow to a self-abnegating remorse that seemed "a slavery compared to which the dungeon / And clanking chains are perfect liberty" (ll. 1777–1778). He turned to his intellect for self-justification, and perceived that society, its fame and its law, were selfish and corrupt: "a great mind / Contemns its age" (ll. 1823–1856 *app. crit.*). He concludes by welcoming Mortimer into the fellowship of free and enlightened minds, who are saved from "the curse / Of living without knowledge that you live" (ll. 1870–1871 *app. crit.*).

A far more complex and sophisticated character than his victim, Rivers' numerous literary prototypes include Iago, Edmund, and the free-thinking villain of Gothic fiction, and it was clearly his "metaphysical obscurity" that resulted in the rejection of the play by Covent Garden (*EY,* p. 197, n1). In its essentials, however, his role is straightforward enough: as Wordsworth pointed out in a prefatory essay, he demonstrates the "dangerous use which may be made of reason when a man has committed a great crime" (*PW* I, 348). Despite his repeated claims to a private vision of the truth— "I saw unveiled the genuine shapes of things" (ll. 1823–1856 *app. crit.*)—Rivers is, in the words of the essay, "perpetually imposing on himself." "Something of the forms of objects he takes from objects, but their colour is exclusively what he gives them; it is one, and it is his own" (*PW* I, 346). As he describes the solipsism of his victim's crazed daughter, he is also describing himself:

> She neither saw nor heard as others do
> But in a fearful world of her own making

> She lived—cut off from the society
> Of every rational thing. . . .
>
> (ll. 1764–1771 *app. crit.*)

His philosophy, in other words, is compulsive. The actions of his mind, like his actions on stage, are directed to one end: self-justification, and escape from remorse. He is a study not in rationalism, but rationalization.

Wordsworth attempts to make this point throughout the play. Rivers' characteristic language is irony; he subverts ideas with an aesthetic precision that is apparent to him alone. As the shaken Mortimer emerges from the dungeon, where he unsuccessfully attempts to murder Herbert, Rivers presents himself as a man who has to struggle against his nature *not* to murder the old man:

> do you think
> I would so long have struggled with my Nature,
> And smothered all that's man in me?
>
> (ll. 871–873)

He knows and enjoys the precision with which these words describe Mortimer's agony and invert the truth: that "Nature" forbids this crime. In the light of the prefatory essay, however, Wordsworth here attempts and fails to convey a further irony: although Rivers claims to have vanquished remorse, and to enjoy absolute freedom, the very act he is engaged in—the subversion of Mortimer—is a compulsive attempt to justify himself. More truly than he knows, he too is struggling against his nature and is a slave to his own guilt. His freedom is an illusion.[17]

Rivers' actions, therefore, continually belie his words. A brilliant man, he nevertheless cites whatever principle serves his immediate end and characteristically ignores or inverts its relation to the truth. As Legouis first pointed out, several of these principles derive from Godwin, such as the appeal to the "law / Flashed from the light of circumstances / Upon an independent Intellect" (ll. 1494–1496 *app. crit.*). This is precisely what Rivers, whose intellect is enslaved, does not do: he is citing Godwin ironically, and when alone he mocks "the dull particulars whose intrusion mars/The dignity of demonstration" (ll. 1155–1158 *app. crit.*). Nor is his repertoire of ideas drawn entirely from Godwin. Repeatedly he cites principles that Wordsworth himself would exalt in later works. He upholds a justice based not on intellect, but feeling: "There is no justice when we do not feel/For man as man" (ll. 868/869 *app. crit.*). He appeals to the formative power of nature's "mighty objects" to justify his refusal to repent, subverting beliefs that would inform *The Prelude*. Elsewhere he advances his ambition to "enlarge/The intellectual empire of mankind" (ll. 1823–1856 *app. crit.*), in language that Wordsworth would recall in 1798, when he sought to present the hope of an exemplary and comprehensive mind to "raise to loftier heights/Our intellectual soul" (*PW* V, 403). In each case Rivers bends a valid principle to a purpose that mocks it: the murder of an innocent man and the moral destruction of another. He is no more a Godwinian than a Wordsworthian. His only relevance to Godwin is methodological: rational demonstration is clearly powerless to reform a mind that so habitually bends reason to its own purposes. As Wordsworth wrote little over a year later in his only explicit discussion of Godwin's philosophy, "lifeless words, & abstract propositions will not be destitute of power to lay asleep the spirit of self-accusation & exclude the uneasiness of repentance." [18]

The point of the contrast between Mortimer and Rivers, and the essence of Wordsworth's judgment on human nature, centers on pride and "repentance." Both men are betrayed into violating the moral law, and both suffer a shattering blow to their moral integrity. But Rivers' pride keeps him from remorse, and by enslaving his reason to this end isolates him within a shadowy world of abstractions that justify the repetition of his crime and thus perpetuate his guilt. In these two characters, therefore, Wordsworth juxtaposes the two responses to guilt he had perhaps unconsciously dramatized in *Salisbury Plain,* a year earlier: atonement and rationalization. And now he deliberately exposes the futility of the latter, and with it the Enlightenment's faith in the moral veracity of the demonstrative reason. He does so, moreover, by further elaborating the symbolic life cycle that first appeared in 1795. A crime of desertion and its effects, guilt and despair, now become a *rite de passage* beyond which the soul can progress only through humility and atonement. The effect of Rivers' pride is psychological fixation; he reenacts the same obsessive ritual over and over again, denying himself the freedom and the hope symbolized by Mortimer's agonized and yet unconstrained pilgrimage of atonement.[19]

In an early version of the play Wordsworth dramatized a still later phase in this symbolic history. Matilda meets a wandering pilgrim modeled on the crazed yet awesome woman of the prose "Tale" of the Cambridge years.[20] Like the sailor of *Salisbury Plain* and like Mortimer, this pilgrim atones for a crime against the domestic affections; he refers ambiguously to a dead child. Although he is invited to make his home in a nearby cottage, he refuses, citing what he calls the "dreadful contrariety" of his feelings. Although he has been a shepherd, he can now watch a lamb "spring to meet its mother's call" and feel "no pleasure in the sight" (*PW* I, 355). In a speech which offers an idea of what Dorothy meant to Wordsworth at the time, Matilda urges him to reconsider:

> there is a power,
> Even in the common offices of love
> And friendly ministration, to revive
> Nature within thee, bid thee smile again
> With those that smile, and weep with those that weep.
>
> (*PW* I, 355)

For a moment he is "beguiled," but he returns to himself and continues on his way.

We see here a clear if sentimental sign of psychological

recovery; what awaits the repentant wanderer is the pastoral cottage and reunion with nature and man. But this character also exemplifies the realism of Wordsworth's assessment of human nature in the play. Though intrinsically good, all the faculties of the human soul—reason, feeling, imagination and will—are vulnerable to perversion, or what in Rivers' case he calls "a universal insurrection of every depraved feeling of the heart" (*PW* I, 348). If Wordsworth does not charge mankind with radical evil, therefore, he nevertheless demonstrates that man has no subjective guarantee against sin. He rejects both an arrogant and self-justifying rationalism and an epicurean and introverted sentimentalism. Both, he implies, mask an isolating pride.

Urgent emphasis therefore falls throughout the play on the moral bearing of the natural object-world. And here, too, the results of Wordsworth's experiment are equivocal and indeed contradictory. When conceived as a system of laws, of temporal causes and effects, the physical world is presented as indifferent and potentially treacherous to man.[21] Both of the central characters expect moral response from nature, and both are disappointed. Rivers drops his contemptuous facade only once, to recall that nature might have altered his history:

> I brooded o'er my injuries, deserted
> By man and nature;—if a breeze had blown
> It might have found its way into my heart,
> And I had been—no matter.

> (ll. 1699–1702)

Both men entrust their victims to the elements, which in both cases remorselessly destroy the innocent, inverting the vengeance Wordsworth had expected from them in 1793.

Imagery and action stress nature's indifference to man. The rock on which Rivers marooned his victim "swarmed" with tiny living things, "Not one of which could give him any aid/Living or dead" (ll. 1725–1727 *app. crit;* DCP). The elements prolong an innocent man's agony:

> 'Twas an island
> But by permission of the winds and waves.
> I know not how he perished; but the calm,
> The same dead calm, continued many days.
>
> (ll. 1740–1744)

Nature's "permission" is not revoked on behalf of man. The circumstances of Herbert's death are more pointedly ironic. Before abandoning him, Mortimer reads the inscription on his staff:

> I am eyes to the blind, saith the Lord.
> He that puts his trust in me shall not fail!
>
> (ll. 1413–1414)

We next see Herbert struggling toward the sound of a church-bell —one recalls the "church-going bell" of the vagrant's childhood. But this bell hangs in a ruined chapel, is rung by the wind, and leads Herbert to his death. The last visible effect of natural justice is a crow rising from the "spot" where his body lies (ll. 1983, 2073).

No reader of this play can wonder at ambivalence in Wordsworth's later attitudes toward nature, or can support the view that he naïvely accepted the optimistic naturalism he inherited from the eighteenth century. That he goes out of his way to hint natural treachery suggests his own sense that the covenant of 1792 had been broken, not only by man, but by a nature that here resembles that of Malthus, Darwin, or Thomas Henry Huxley. More clearly than a later Huxley,[22] he perceives that the moral indifference of nature to man does not vary with latitude, and that a crow in an English field can indict the universe. Nor would he forget this vision, although he would struggle urgently to ameliorate it.

The pessimism of this view is implicitly contradicted, however, by a simultaneous appeal to the potentially benign psychological influence of nature, considered as epistemological object. Throughout the play Wordsworth invests value, truth, and hope in an order of being that is ontologically independent of the human mind and yet available to it through the senses, in what he would call in retrospect "the laws of things which lie / Beyond the reach of human will or power" (*Prelude* XI. 97–98). The effect of guilt on both major characters, for example, remains what it was in the second version of *Salisbury Plain:* psychic estrangement from the sensible world. Rivers repeatedly scoffs at the senses; he celebrates the mind's power to "look / Beyond the present object of the sense" (l. 654 *app. crit.*) and "to clothe the shapes of things" with accidental meanings (ll. 644–646 *app. crit.*). But Mortimer clings instinctively to the senses. His love for Herbert is incorporated in an "image" he received in early childhood (l. 97 *app. crit.*); an image of Matilda keeps him from the murder in the dungeon (ll. 955–990 *app. crit.*). The excursive tendencies of his mind are particularly evident in the dialogue that precedes his descent into the dungeon. As he reviews their journey to the castle, pointing to facts that seem to contradict Rivers, he recalls that at Herbert's protestations of innocence "the spirit of vengeance seemed to ride the air,"

> Yet nothing came of it. I listened, but
> The echoes of the thunder died away
> Along the distant hills.

(ll. 794–795 app. crit.)

Mortimer looks for a confirmatory revelation, much as Wordsworth expected a sign of natural vengeance against the English fleet in 1793. Rivers, on the other hand, ignores the world of sense: "What then?" he asks, "great souls / Look to the world within" (ll. 794–795 *app. crit.*).

Like that of the "Gothic Tale," the setting of the play works to prevent such introversion. Both crimes take place in landscapes that recall Salisbury Plain and the Isle of Wight, and strip human evil of all equivocation and ambiguity. "All is naked" on the heath where Herbert dies (ll. 1658–1666 *app. crit.*). In ironic contrast to the abstraction of his philosophy, and his mockery of the "dull particulars" that would expose him, the concrete circumstances of Rivers' crime are burned into his memory.

> One day at noon we drifted silently
> By a bare rock, narrow, and white, and bare;
> No food was there, no drink, no grass, no shade,
> No tree, nor jutting eminence, nor form
> Inanimate large as the body of man,
> Nor any living thing whose span of life
> Might stretch beyond the measure of one moon.
>
> (ll. 1705–1711 *app. crit.*)

To the query—"And was he famished?"—Rivers replies with further images:

> 'Twas a spot—
> Methinks I see it now—how in the sun
> Its stony surface glittered like a shield.
>
> (ll. 1721–1727 *app. crit.;* DCP)

Perhaps the most powerful evocation of unmediated exposure in Wordsworth's poetry, this scene compresses effects we have noticed in earlier poems into a few lines. Negation strips away all mediation, emphasizing the confrontation of irreducible and elemental opposites: rock, sea, and sky. At the center of the landscape, but left entirely to the imagination, is the unspeakable suffering of an innocent man and the guilt Rivers vainly strives to suppress. An analogue to the image of Herbert that sustains Mortimer's innocence, this scene mocks Rivers' own attempts to escape beyond "the present object of the sense."

Other patterns of imagery make the same point, that the object-world offers truth when the mind does not. In the second version of *Salisbury Plain,* Wordsworth had described the effect of guilt and despair in terms of nourishment; at the focus of the sailor's guilt lay the spectacle of his wife's slow starvation, and the vagrant's despair took the form of a refusal to eat or drink. In *The*

Borderers such imagery becomes insistent. Both Mortimer and Rivers starve their victims. Herbert is found "near the brink/Of a small pool . . ./His face close to the water" (ll. 2033–2034 *app. crit.*). Rivers' victim is "famish'd" on a barren rock in the sea (l. 1721). Both of the deserters, moreover, reenact this starvation. The solipsist Rivers consumes himself; he lived for "many days," he reports proudly, "without meat or drink" (ll. 1790–1791). Mortimer's final atonement is to seal off his body and his mind from all intercourse with the external world:

> No human ear shall ever hear my voice
> No human dwelling ever give me food.
> <div align="right">(ll. 2287–2321 <i>app. crit.;</i> DCP)</div>

In the most literal sense, he neither gives nor receives.

Elsewhere Wordsworth employs categories that are more explicitly philosophical and that reproduce the implications of his experience, years earlier, of the "abyss of idealism." He vests truth and redemptive power in a solid and palpable substance that lies beyond the mind, and resists all human efforts to deny its existence. Rivers, for example, seeks to reduce Mortimer to the shadow of a single substance, Rivers himself (l. 2009); pride takes the philosophic form of monism. As the erring Mortimer plumbs the "abyss of vengeance," he touches a solid substance that indicts him: "Something . . . that turns my thoughts/Back on myself" (ll. 782–784 *app. crit.;* DCP). When he finally resolves to murder Herbert, all external substance vanishes:

> I did believe all things were shadows—yea,
> Living or dead all things were bodiless,
> Till that same star summoned me back again.
> <div align="right">(ll. 1214–1217 <i>app. crit.</i>)</div>

Later, after his suspicions of Herbert have been confirmed by new falsehoods, he bitterly retracts what now seems to be a superstitious naturalism:

> Oh Fool!
> To let a creed, built in the heart of things,
> Dissolve before a twinkling atom's eye.
>
> (ll. 1218–1220 *app. crit.*)

The effect of Rivers' "creed" is to reduce a living star into the "atom" of a reductive materialism. Even as Mortimer's intellect strives to deny the autonomous life of the star, however, his language affirms it: the atom remains an "eye," a watching presence, able to judge and redeem. Later, after his crime, Mortimer again disembodies a "substance" that accuses him, Herbert's body (ll. 2245–2278 *app. crit.*). His final atonement takes the form of an existence that is purely subjective, a flight from external substance: he will become a "shadowy thing" that is "compelled to live" by "pain and thought" (ll. 2287–2321 *app. crit.*).

Here, I would suggest, we see the single positive result of the moral experiment performed in *The Borderers*. Emerging from a crisis that discredited not only subjective guarantees of integrity and truth—feeling, and the demonstrative reason—but the benignity of the "certain course" of natural law, Wordsworth turns once again to the sole remaining support available to the mind, nature in its role as epistemological and emotional object. The personal significance of this traditional view, which Wordsworth first began to affirm in response to the disappointments of his Cambridge years, is now immense. To a mind struggling toward proof and certainty, the "common range of visible things" becomes the locus of abiding and normative values, a bedrock of truth in a void of psychic division and moral relativism. To a Protestant conscience shattered by the revelation of personal as well as collective human guilt, the Cartesian distinction between subjective and objective substance circumscribes the depravity of fallen man and thus preserves the possibility of redemption and grace: it is to the sheer existence of something beyond the mind that this play looks for hope. The border of its title is therefore not merely political, but epistemological and theological,[23] a crucial interface that separates and yet connects man and nature, subject and object, the soul and grace. The powers on each side of this border are highly equivocal; in the words that mark Rivers' entrance and exit, both are "strong to destroy, . . . also strong to heal" (ll. 46–47; 2245–2278 *app. crit.*). But the hope remains that authentic relationship may be restored, a relationship Wordsworth would within a few months once again describe as love.

Placed in the perspective of the earlier development, this play may be regarded as a second, still tentative reconsolidation of the hopes of 1792 and 1794, and another repetition of the schoolboy's instinctive appeal to a substantial object-world. To both Coleridge and Blake this appeal would be tainted by materialism, a "clinging to the palpable," or an insurrection of the natural against the spiritual man. Neither poet, however, had been forced by psychological extremity to a sweeping distrust of the mind and its powers, and neither could fully understand the spiritual urgency of Wordsworth's appeal to the natural object. Blake's confident idealism—

> Nor is it possible to Thought
> A greater than itself to know [24]

would, in particular, have seemed a counsel of despair to the author of *The Borderers,* as it will to any man who senses his isolation within a "fearful world" of his own making and perceives hope only in the possibility that the mind can know a "greater than itself." In this and other respects, the tendency of Wordsworth's development at this time is not at all commensurate with the cluster of attitudes commonly regarded as "romantic." It was with Johnson and the elder Milton that he had allied himself in 1794, and now he grounds his hopes far more urgently in the few traditional premises that remain trustworthy. He adopts an ethic of humility and contrition that recognizes the fact if not the necessity of human depravity and man's consequent dependence upon grace. If he continues to affirm the innate goodness of natural feeling, any sentimental complacency is thoroughly chastened by the knowledge that the passions are treacherous and that they may rise to destroy the mind. In no sense does he regard the "spontaneous overflow of powerful feelings" as its own guarantee, but rather seeks to subject feeling to the discipline of powers external to the mind. If he now recognizes, with Blake, that the demonstrative reason can guarantee neither truth nor integrity, he turns for hope not to the visionary imagination but to the senses, and the common experience of man. It is true that in this play Wordsworth crosses the moral frontier between the modern world and the eighteenth century; but he takes with him the essential values that had molded his spirit at Hawkshead.

V   Racedown: 1797

And lastly, Nature's Self, by human love
Assisted, through the weary labyrinth
Conducted me again to open day.

The Prelude

In the poems of spring 1797 the Racedown crisis comes to an end. Most are experimental in form and style, but in none is Wordsworth's art disordered by compelling personal feeling. In each of the surviving poems, furthermore, he seems to be searching for ways of articulating a spiritual regeneration that may have become a fact in his life at this time.

I

Only two short fragments of *A Somersetshire Tragedy* survive, but reports of its plot make clear that this Spenserian narrative brought the Racedown cycle of symbolic life-histories to a decisive climax. Like his predecessors, the hero of the *Tragedy,* a Quantock charcoal-maker, is naturally good and pious. Despite his love for a local girl, however, he is trapped by circumstance and the malice of a stepmother into marriage with a semi-idiot, a creature of "weak and witless soul," as a fragment puts it. In a sudden fit of despair and rage he murders her, is arrested and hanged. His last words (as reported by Thomas Poole) could summarize the moral dilemma of any of the Racedown heroes: "I am guilty of the crime I am going to die for, but I did it without foreintending it, and I hope God and the world have forgiven me." [1] Here the crime that first appeared in *Salisbury Plain* two years earlier is named, reenacted, and again atoned for. Judging from the ten lines that survive, the style of the poem was objective and realistic —perhaps Wordsworth's boldest look at painful and accusing things.

In a second narrative the poet turned to a subject with equal personal significance: the desertion of an innocent and helpless wife. In less than two hundred lines of blank verse [2] he tells a straightforward story: the poet happens on a ruined cottage, where he meets a stranger, a wandering pedlar. After a few lines describing the "cheerless spot," the poet lapses into silence as the pedlar relates the history of "poor Margaret," the woman who lived and died in the cottage. Constantly directing attention to the ruin, he recalls her charity and industry, laments her death, and then traces the gradual decay of her happiness: the effects of economic depression on her husband, his sudden enlistment, and a wait for his return that ends in death. This is the first poem Wordsworth included among the works of his maturity; entitled *The Ruined Cottage* in 1797, it ultimately became the first book of *The Excursion*. As Legouis surmised from that book, and as later critics have confirmed from a study of the early manuscripts,[3] it is not only Wordsworth's first great poem, but one of the great elegiac meditations in the English language. As Coleridge wrote in June 1797, in introduction to its last lines, "This is a lovely country— & Wordsworth is a great man" (*STCL* I. 327).

Given the poems that lead up to it, this achievement may seem anomalous. But it is in most respects the fruit of the entire development, a victory over past adversaries that is won with the aid of techniques elaborated in the past. Like its predecessors, *The Ruined Cottage* embodies a struggle to master overwhelming and potentially destructive emotions in art. Unlike them, it succeeds. With great honesty, Wordsworth confronts a subject that had inspired guilt, fear, and despair, the desertion of a wife, and does so with dignity, strength, and compassion. And this psychological and moral victory is facilitated by a technical apparatus that braces and supports the observing mind, allowing the contempla-

tion of painful objects without loss of control. The pedlar's opening lament for Margaret offers an impressive example of such mediation:

> Many a passenger
> Has blest poor Margaret for her gentle looks
> When she upheld the cool refreshment drawn
> From that forsaken well, and no one came
> But he was welcome [;] no one went away
> But that it seemed she loved him—She is dead
> And nettles rot and adders sun themselves
> Upon the floor where I have seen [her] sit
> And rock her baby in its cradle. She
> Is dead and in her grave and this poor hut
> Stripp'd of its outward garb of household flowers [,]
> Of rose and jasmine [,] offers to the winds
> A cold bare wall whose earthy top is trick [d]
> With weeds and the rank spear grass.

(DCP)

Like the feudal castles of 1794, Margaret's suffering is placed at a
distance in time and space, as she is introduced and contemplated
through the relics of her suffering in the landscape of present
time.

These relics, in turn, are invested with powerful significance,
public and private. In this ruin, usurped by beasts, Wordsworth
taps a haunting fear of social and cultural decay that extends back
through the ruin poems of Augustan and Renaissance tradition to
Ecclesiastes. Nor is there need to emphasize its personal meaning.
Since his Hawkshead poems he had employed the cottage as the
visible "seat of Peace and Love" (*PW* I, 262, l. 45), of hope (*An
Evening Walk,* A ll. 415–416), and of freedom (*Descriptive
Sketches,* l. 724). During the Racedown years the cottage had become the "seat" of guilt and accusation and a touchstone of redemption. Here, then, it may be viewed as a powerfully suggestive
image of the loss of hope, an image that transcends its particular

causes in Wordsworth's past, the failure of the Revolution and the ruin of his love for Annette. The cottage, furthermore, bears a significant and familiar relationship to its natural surroundings. Like landscapes in *Salisbury Plain* and *The Borderers,* its naked walls offer a focal point of exposure and extremity. The weeds and speargrass of an overgrowing nature slowly repossess and variegate the ruin, manifesting a power that is at once both purgative and destructive.

Such images are contemplated through a second line of defense, the pedlar's consciousness.[4] His language testifies to and embodies his strength and self-control. Diction and attention fix rigorously on the object, not on the self; he names the thing, not the feeling, or directs feeling toward the thing with a single adjective ("poor"). The human protest against decay that we feel in his speech is a product of form: the violence with which he juxtaposes images of past and present, life and death. His characteristic idiom, here and elsewhere, is a controlled understatement that clearly profits from Wordsworth's experiments in *The Borderers* and other early Racedown poems. When he expresses feeling directly, his language assimilates his response to that of common man. A sound is "a melancholy thing/To any man who has a heart to feel" (DCP). Of Margaret's request that he ask for news of her husband, he simply adds that "any heart had ached to hear her" (l. 691).[5] His references to feeling are regularly adjectival in form; they qualify concrete objects and in effect confirm and discipline the unstated feelings elicited by the objects themselves. Such a style is morally functional; it embodies a host of virtues—fortitude, compassion, and humility among them—and purifies the reader's response to the scene. The pedlar is thus the antithesis of earlier personae. Exemplary and normative, he seems a first product of the quest for objective truth that informed *The Borderers.* Like the abiding "substance" of the external world, he represents what is essential and eternal in the human heart, the best of human nature.

The greatness of this poem proceeds not only from such discipline, however, but from the power of emotions that test and at

times threaten to overwhelm it. In the first draft the pedlar continued his lament, citing images that build in emotional intensity and
regress in significance toward the symbols of earlier Racedown
poems. He recalls a stormy night:

> But two nights gone [I crossed]
> This dreary common. Driv'n by wind and rain
> The poor man's horse that feeds along the lanes
> Had hither come within these roofless walls
> To weather out the night, and as I passed
> While restlessly he turn'd from the beating wind
> And from the open sky within I heard
> The iron links with which his feet were clogg'd
> Mix their dull clanking with the heavy sound
> Of falling rain.
>
> (DCP)

He hears the sound of iron chains that terrified earlier characters,
but his response is not recorded. The power of the image to evoke
morbid or fearful surmise is disciplined, furthermore, by the structure of the passage, which begins by assigning a naturalistic cause
to the sound: the restless turnings of an animal. But it is not difficult to detect other implications. Given a slight change of structure, the pedlar would be startled by an unexplained sound ema-
nating from the cottage of a supposedly dead woman, a sound that
suggests an inhabitant bound in chains. An analogy to "poor
Margaret," who is "rooted" to her cottage by hope, is clear, as is a
repetition of the situation of *Salisbury Plain,* where a husband is
ambushed by a wife who lives to accuse him.

In a second scene the pedlar again detects an anomalous life
within the cottage:

> But two nights gone I cross'd this dreary moor
> In the still moonlight. When I reach'd the hut
> I look'd within but all was still and dark.
> Only within the ruin I beheld
> At a small distance on the dusky ground

> A broken pane which glitter'd to the moon
> And seem'd akin to life.
>
> (DCP)

Moved by a fascination he does not name, the speaker looks in the darkened cottage. The moving, glittering point of light that he sees recalls the star that rescued Mortimer from himself. But this "life" is spurious, projected on a broken shard of the past by emotions that, though unnamed, are clearly compulsive and related to the human life this cottage had once sheltered. The verb "glitter" takes on the function it displays in later poems, that of presaging radical and preternatural dislocations of reality, in a context that suggests the abandonment of the observing mind to obsession. In both passages imagery exerts a power that recalls work of 1795, and may reflect the derangement of Wordsworth's imagination in that year, when he first arrived at Racedown and observed the ruined huts of the Dorset peasantry. But both nevertheless dramatize a fear and solipsism that the pedlar functions elsewhere to overcome, and Wordsworth properly transferred them to another fragment in which the speaker's psychological disintegration is made explicit.[6]

If the structure of this poem is molded by the premise that confrontation of subject and object is painful, its style renders any withdrawal into a protective subjectivism impossible. In *The Borderers,* Wordsworth had identified introversion with pride, and in *The Ruined Cottage* he employs a language that rivets attention and emotion to concrete objects, in a sustained triumph of the presentational techniques he had elaborated in passages of earlier poems. In 1793, for example, the vagrant of *Salisbury Plain* had described the effects of economic blight in a style that moved abruptly from literal statement:

> My happy father died
> Just as the children's meal began to fail
> And round the silent loom for bread they cried
>
> (ll. 266–268 *app. crit.*)

to decorative personification:

> How changed at once! for Labour's thoughtless [hum]
> Long suppliant looks and Fear's distracted train.
>
> <div align="right">(ll. 271–272 <i>app. crit.</i>)</div>

In 1797 such oscillation disappears; an analogous scene is unremittingly literal and concrete. The pedlar sees

> the idle loom
> Still in its place. His Sunday garments hung
> Upon the self-same nail—his very staff
> Stood undisturbed behind the door. . . .
>
> (ll. 681–684)

The skill with which Wordsworth selects and arranges images has grown immensely. The "silent loom" of 1793 functions as a general sign of economic depression; its pathos is intensified by the children's cries, but it offers a tableau that is essentially self-contained. The loom of 1797 is "idle," however, because the activity it invites no longer seems significant to Margaret. The image records the decay of her industry, and, more broadly, of the excursive and self-preserving energies of her mind. That it, together with objects intimately associated with her husband, "stood undisturbed" suggests her refusal to surrender hope of his return, and gives visible form to a fixation that is psychological. These images are presented as concrete effects—in this case negative ones—of human actions and thus of human feelings, selected and organized by the insight into the psychology of despair that Wordsworth won from the suffering of the Racedown years.

This passage clearly announces the style Wordsworth would defend in the Preface to the *Lyrical Ballads,* three years later. It would appear to have been "composed under the persuasion, that all which is usually included under the name of action bears the same pro[por]tion (in respect of worth) to the affections, as a language to the thing signified." [7] Action takes on importance as the "language" of feeling, or, to put it in the words of the Preface, "the feeling therein developed gives importance to the action and situation, and not the action and situation to the feeling" (*PW* II, 388–389). Such an understanding of the visible world had been implied by the presentational style of 1793, which traced the "action" of the traveler's eye; it is presumed by *The Borderers,* in which Rivers' outward "action" is presented as a sign of inward guilt. Here, however, every rift is for the first time loaded with ore. Like a leaf that betrays the existence of the wind that drives it, every action, physical or psychological, and every image, are visible and outward signs of feeling. In a particular or quite limited sense, we may describe such images as "symbols," in that their effect is to prompt passionate surmise. But they are in no sense literary artifacts or transcendental emblems; they proceed from a vision of organic correspondences between mind, body, and object that is rigorously literal. The effect of such images is theoretically limitless because it proceeds from the excursive power of the reader's affections. It depends, that is, on the reader's "nature," and exerts what Wordsworth would call "a power like one of Nature's" (*Prelude* XII. 312).

Such a style shifts attention to the senses and renders the abstract language of reason unnecessary. As several critics have pointed out, Wordsworth was familiar with Cowper's portrait of Kate in *The Task:*

> A serving maid was she, and fell in love
> With one who left her, went to sea, and died.
> Her fancy follow'd him through foaming waves
> To distant shores; and she would sit and weep
> At what a sailor suffers; fancy, too,
> Delusive most where warmest wishes are,
> Would oft anticipate his glad return,
> And dream of transports she was not to know.
>
> (I. 537–546) [8]

In several respects this tender and sympathetic portrait of hopeless expectancy exemplifies the best of the tradition Wordsworth transcends. Cowper's attention moves directly into Kate's mind, which he describes in terms of a personified "fancy" that reaches out toward the "foaming waves" associated with her lover, the only concrete image in the passage. Syntax and diction become objective and plain in response to the simple pathos of the subject ("She would sit and weep"), but the ironic and painful contrast between Kate's expectation and the reality is couched in an informed aside, which raises her plight to the level of a general human predicament by employing an abstract language of psychological description: "fancy, too,/Delusive most where warmest wishes are,/Would oft anticipate his glad return. . . ."

Now this is precisely the general truth exemplified by Wordsworth's Margaret, and the pedlar draws a similarly ironic contrast between desire and reality toward the end of his tale:

> Master, I have heard
> That in that broken arbour she would sit
> The idle length of half a sabbath day
> There—where you see the toadstool's lazy head,
> And when a dog passed by she still would quit
> The shade and look abroad. On this old Bench
> For hours she sate, and evermore her eye
> Was busy in the distance, shaping things
> That made her heart beat quick.
>
> (ll. 699–707 *app. crit.*)

Wordsworth's style reveals a different world, in which all meaning, including that which for Cowper demanded explicit abstractions, resides in concrete images. Forcefully directing attention to "that" arbour, the pedlar reconstructs the Margaret of past time, sitting there "the idle length of half a sabbath day"—a line in which prepositional phrases unfold the significance of a single noun and mark syntactical time, imitating the idleness they describe and preparing for the covert ambush of the next line. The pedlar's sudden "there" wrests attention from the past to a present in which Margaret's place has been usurped by the "toadstool's lazy head," an image that implies the ironic difference between the pathetically vulnerable idleness of human despair and the "lazy" and patient processes of an inexorably encroaching nature.

In the next lines Wordsworth makes Cowper's point, that Margaret's "fancy" is "delusive," by allowing us to see her rise and "look abroad," in the knowledge that what has stirred her into activity is a dog, an object that embodies the desperation of her hope and its crushing disappointment. In the final sentence Wordsworth, like Cowper, moves into the mind, but his language remains concrete. Instead of a personified "fancy" he names the "eye" and "heart," and allows clustered consonants and spondaic emphasis to suggest the excitement heart craves from eye ("heart beat quick"). Two homely and unobtrusive metaphors, "busy" and "shaping," render the compulsive energies of her "fancy" concrete, and remind us that the industry of her "busy" eye has been expropriated from a hand that had once shaped and domesticated the landscape about it with excursive love. In a few lines Wordsworth enacts the total introversion of psychic power. But he does not name it in abstractions that would divert attention and passion from Margaret, the true object of concern.

To the degree that it is successful, such a style directs attention beyond itself, concealing the artifice that produced it. That it requires great insight and skill is clear, however, when we look at a style that seeks similar ends with similar means. As Jonathan Wordsworth has pointed out,[9] in *Hannah: A Plaintive Tale,* Robert Southey addresses a pathetic subject in as plain a style:

> So she pin'd, and pin'd away,
> And for herself and baby toil'd and toil'd,
> Till she sunk from very weakness. Her old mother
> Omitted no kind office, and she work'd
> Most hard, and with hard working, barely earn'd
> Enough to make life struggle. Thus she lay
> On the sick bed of poverty, so worn
> That she could make no effort to express

Affection for her infant: and the child
Whose lisping love, perhaps, had solac'd her,
With strangest infantine ingratitude,
Shunn'd her as one indifferent. She was past
That anguish—for she felt her hour draw on;
And 'twas her only comfort now to think
Upon the grave.

(ll. 32–46)

Placed beside any passage from *The Ruined Cottage,* these lines suggest that Wordsworth's originality did not lie so much in a theoretical departure from the ideas of his contemporaries as in the profundity with which he experienced, and the intensity with which he applied, common principles and aspirations. Like Wordsworth, Southey was a disaffected radical, and here he employs a style that is leveling in political significance; in the name of the human heart he seeks to dissolve the distinction between prose and poetry. It is apparent, too, that the decision to use a plain style forces Southey, like Wordsworth, to rely upon formal devices, such as repetition, sound effects, and metrical variation.

What he produces, however, is not poetry but something close to prose. Formal devices direct feeling toward objects that are vague or stereotyped. Repetition, for example, emphasizes clichés (Hannah "pined" and her work was "hard"), as do spondees ("old mother," "kind offices"). Other spondees stress actions in the poet's mind, sudden leaps from literal to figurative language ("sick bed of poverty") or from particular to general ("enough to make life struggle"); Southey cannot keep his eye on the object. Alliteration is nakedly sentimental ("lisping love"). What feeling is developed is stereotyped; Southey seeks undiluted pity for Hannah, a victim of undeserved misery, and takes pains to explain that she was in no way responsible for her child's suffering. And this feeling lacks clear and concrete objects; Hannah remains a vague, semi-abstract figure.

In an analogous passage from *The Ruined Cottage,* Wordsworth

at once directs feeling toward concrete images that function, as we
have seen, as signs:

> Meanwhile her poor hut
> Sank to decay, for he was gone, whose hand
> At the first nippings of October frost
> Closed up each chink, and with fresh bands of straw
> Chequered the green-grown thatch. And so she lived
> Through the long winter, reckless and alone;
> Till this reft house, by frost, and thaw, and rain
> Was sapped, and, when she slept, the nightly damps
> Did chill her breast, and in the stormy day
> Her tattered clothes were ruffled by the wind
> Even at the side of her own fire. Yet still
> She loved this wretched spot, nor would for worlds
> Have parted hence, and still that length of road
> And this rude bench one torturing hope endeared,
> Fast rooted at her heart; and, Stranger, here
> In sickness she remained, and here she died,
> Last human tenant of these ruined walls.
>
> (ll. 726–742 *app. crit.*)

The initial shift of attention from Margaret to her cottage is psychologically significant; it expresses a sympathy profound enough
to impel passionate personification. And it enables Wordsworth to
describe the invisible and painful decline of the human being by
means of the analogous, visible, and mediating decline of the object; where it was Hannah who "sunk from very weakness" it is the
cottage that "sank into decay." Formal devices direct attention
and feeling toward the inexorable advance of the elements, and
imply the pedlar's compassion for Margaret. The spondee in "first
nippings," for example, adds a shade of portent to a metaphor
that hints at predation even as it domesticates nature, a hint that is
kept alive by the unobtrusive alliteration with "frost" in the same
line and confirmed by the spondee on "long winter" a few lines
later. Mention of the absent husband brings vitality and decision

to rhythm and sound; massed spondees and clustered consonants embody the energy that would have protected Margaret from the elements:

> whose hand
> Closed up eách chínk, and with frésh bánds of straw
> Chequered the green-grówn thátch.

The slower rhythms and long vowels of the following lines—

> And so she lived
> Through the long winter, reckless and alone;
> Till this reft house, by frost, and thaw, and rain
> Was sapped

imply a relinquishment of fond surmise, and a submission to the inevitable end to come. The pedlar's eye then traces the sudden advance of the elements to the surface of Margaret's "breast," and to the living center of the cottage, the hearth. The repetitions of the final cadences ("yet still . . . and still"; "and here . . . and here") emphasize the complementary power of the human heart and the force of the "one torturing hope" that bound Margaret to her cottage and to her own destruction.

These passages bring Wordsworth's stylistic development to one of its logical conclusions. Deeply humanitarian in spirit, applying as it does formal devices of Miltonic grandeur to common subjects, this style also succeeds in resolving the epistemological dilemma that had constrained the age of sensibility. Rigorously literal in assertion and yet sensitive to the most delicate nuances of feeling, it buckles the senses and the heart to substantial things, correcting the introversion of the poetry of sensibility without suppressing its claim to emotional intensity. It can be described accurately in Milton's terms as a poetry "simple, sensuous, and passionate," or in those of an arch-critic of romantic sentimentality, T. E. Hulme: it makes "you continuously see a physical thing," prevents "you from gliding through an abstract process." [10] From Wordsworth's point of view, however, the function of such a literal style is also moral; stripping away the fabrications of the reflective intellect or the excited imagination, it reforms the mind and heart by exposing them to the moral discipline of substantial things.

Such discipline molds Margaret's story as well as the style in which it is told. As Wordsworth traces the effect of desertion upon her mind, he shows her to be the victim of her own desires, which isolate her from the external world and ultimately destroy her. Unlike earlier characters, however, she is driven not by guilt but by hope, a life-giving and yet "torturing" hope that imprisons her within a world of delusive expectation. Implied in the poem, such isolation becomes explicit in contemporary fragments: denied "the common food of hope," the mind rebels, and "fastening on all things / That promise food, doth like a sucking babe / Create it where it is not" (*PW* I, 315–316, ll. 9–11, 60). The motif of starvation, which in *The Borderers* was literal, here becomes metaphorical; starved of objects of hope, Margaret's mind creates them, binding her ever more inexorably to the "wretched spot" that offers the sole promise of her husband's return, and rendering her pathetically vulnerable to the encroachment of an alien but innocent nature.

This perspective is terrible as well as pathetic. Unlike such victims of undeserved misery as Southey's Hannah, Margaret is an active and responsible agent in her own destruction. In her struggle to avoid the truth, she turns away from the substantial world; if Rivers had retreated into the shadows of abstraction, she escapes into the visions of imagination. Both characters suffer what Rivers called "a slavery compared to which the dungeon / And clanking chains are perfect liberty." Neither can confront the *rite de passage* of despair, and both are consequently halted at a particular point in time, where they endlessly repeat the same psychological action. The pedlar's last memory of Margaret—

> by yon gate
> Which bars the traveller's road she often stood
> And when a stranger horseman came, the latch
> Would lift, and in his face look wistfully . . .

precisely formulates the pathos of her fixation, and silhouettes her against the wanderers who have passed through and beyond despair to new life and hope.

In the pedlar we see such a wanderer, a man who preserves the freedom and vision earlier wanderers had won from exile, and who yet has returned to man. As is implied by his wares, clothes for the poor, he is a rock of defense for humanity, a representative of the best in human nature, and a prototype of the poet as Wordsworth would portray him in the Preface of 1802. Constantly in motion, free of compulsive involvements, profoundly sane, his consciousness is guaranteed against the fixation that destroys Margaret. He thus offers a stable and trustworthy perspective from which Wordsworth can contemplate once again a narrative that reenacts the critical task of the Racedown years: the repudiation of a false but beloved hope. Margaret fails this test, and the pedlar's attitude toward her failure is delicately balanced. His language is shaped by a compassion that seeks to shield and protect her, and as a whole the poem renders a profound tribute to a love that, refusing to acknowledge time and change, bears it out to the edge of doom. For himself, for Annette, and for an enslaved humanity that had been betrayed by the French Revolution—the starving peasants of Savoy, or the "hunger-bitten Girl" of the Loire—Wordsworth pays what he had called ten years before "the mighty debt of grief," with an intensity and in a form that for the first time merits the Virgilian epigraph he had quoted then: *sunt lacrimae rerum, et mentem mortalia tangunt.*

But this deep sympathy with the desires of the human heart is disciplined and tempered by an equally profound realism, which insists on the necessity of renunciation. As the poem draws to a close, the pedlar rebukes Margaret more sharply for her "reckless" and willful self-destruction, and withdraws to the position of a survivor who is implicitly aligned with the natural order that exposed the illusions of her heart as inexorably as it exposed the naked walls of her cottage. Wordsworth emerges from this greatest ambush of his hopes in the spirit he had imitated at the close of

The Vale of Esthwaite, the spirit of Johnson's *Vanity of Human Wishes.* He relinquishes a hope that has been exposed as illusion, however painful that relinquishment may be, and turns to what remains. The curve of feeling in the poem thus follows that of the traditional pastoral elegy, from involvement with the dead to alliance with the living, the moving, and the free. The accents of a final farewell would become explicit in a later version, but they are audible in the pedlar's last words:

> and, Stranger, here
> In sickness she remained, and here she died,
> Last human tenant of these ruined walls.

In the silence that follows we may hear the Virgilian coda: *surgamus,* let us rise.

II

In other works of the spring of 1797, themes developed in *The Borderers* and *The Ruined Cottage* are applied in new, and prophetic, directions. In two fragments, for example, Wordsworth described a living analogue to the ruined cottage, an aged beggar:

> He travels on, a solitary Man;
> His age has no companion. On the ground
> His eyes are turned, and, as he moves along,
> They move along the ground; and, evermore,
> Instead of Nature's fair variety
> Her ample scope of hill and dale, of clouds
> And the blue sky, the same short span of earth
> Is all his prospect.[11]

Here the symbolic wanderer reaches another destination: an existence that has passed beyond human trauma and survives into a region where hope and fear have no meaning. He has been stripped of sensation; like the blind Herbert, his eyes are fixed.

"Seeing still, and never knowing that he sees," he traverses a landscape that is unchanging, "in the same line, at distance still the same." He is passed and ignored by all travelers; even "the miller's dog / Is tired of barking at him." The effect of such purgation is a tranquillity that is imperturbable and absolute: he is "by nature led"

> To peace so perfect that the young behold
> With envy what the old man hardly feels.
>
> (*Old Man Travelling*, ll. 12–14)

Nowhere in the two fragments does Wordsworth seek to evoke a conventionally condescending pity for this wanderer, who is viewed as an awesome instance of what the poet would in later years call the "sublime of duration." [12]

A second group of passages focuses more explicitly on the redemption of the wanderer. Entitled "Incipient Madness" by de Selincourt, they form the personal recollection of a speaker who recalls the occasions of the clanking irons and the glittering speck of glass. Unlike the pedlar, however, this speaker acknowledges the obsessive power of these scenes. He flees from the sound of irons: "I started from the spot / And heard the sound still following in the wind" (*PW* I, 315). And he conceives an unnatural affection for the moonlit cottage and the speck of glass:

> Many long months
> Confirmed this strange incontinence; my eye
> Did every evening measure the moon's height [,]
> And forth I went before her yellow beams
> Could overtop the elmtrees o [']er the heath [;]
> I went, I reach'd the cottage, and I found
> Still undisturb'd and glittering in its place
> That speck of glass more precious to my soul
> Than was the moon in heaven.
>
> (*PW* I, 315 *app. crit.*)

In a second part of the same fragment the speaker describes his recovery. Like Margaret, he stays by the cottage he loves through a length of time that is measured by a procession of passersby. Now, however, these are natural events. For three weeks "a glow worm hung its light / And then was seen no more." The passage of time accelerates, and he remains: "Three seasons did a blackbird build his nest / And then he disappear'd." A linnet sings "two summers, and then vanished." And so he lingers until all accident is stripped away:

> I alone
> Remained: the winds of heaven remained: with them
> My heart claimed fellowship and with the beams
> Of dawn and of the setting sun that seemed
> To live and linger on the mouldering walls.
>
> (*PW* I, 315; ll. 34–38)

He passes into another region of being in which only elemental forces—wind, sun, and the cottage—survive. Purged of terror and despair, his heart now asserts the excursive power of love: it *claims* fellowship with the elements, as Wordsworth had claimed fellowship with these same primordial forces in *Descriptive Sketches* and the Windy Brow fragments. The final image, of living sunlight touching the surface of ruined stone, signals a return to the imagery of hope and relationship, and taps feelings that extend back to the analogy that summarized his love for the Vale of Esthwaite ten years before. This fragment more openly affirms the spiritual redemption offered by nature than any of the major Racedown poems and offers our only contemporary dramatization of the transition that was to produce the *Lyrical Ballads* a year later.

Another passage from this period moves in a second direction, toward a personal confession of gratitude to nature:

> Yet once again do I behold the forms
> Of these huge mountains, and yet once again,

> Standing beneath these elms, I hear thy voice,
> Beloved Derwent, that peculiar voice
> Heard in the stillness of the evening air,
> Half-heard and half-created.
>
> (*PW* V, 340)

Both point of view and theme are prophetic. Wordsworth sets aside the impersonal and dramatic mode of the Racedown poems and speaks in his own character. Like Rivers, he presents the landscape of his youth as a locus of implicitly powerful "forms." [13] For the first time he echoes Edward Young's tribute to the creative power of the senses and the "primary imagination" in order to describe the dynamic alliance between the active powers of the mind and those of nature, the alliance that is in various ways perverted or denied in all the Racedown narratives. What we see here, in other words, is a first version of *Tintern Abbey,* which suggests that both the form and the theme of that great and auto-biographically central poem were latent, waiting to be released by an actual return to a landscape that summarized Wordsworth's restoration.

In one of his last works at Racedown, the poet composed an in-scription for another object recalled from his early years, a yew tree near the shore of Esthwaite Water, and a stopping-place on a "favourite walk in the evenings" during his schooldays (*PW* I, 329). In this poem, the "Lines left upon a Seat in a Yew-tree," he summarizes the moral lesson of *The Borderers* and a central text of Christian and deistic humanism, that human pride is unlawful. But he does so in a form that suggests a decisive reorientation of purpose, and represents still another permutation of the techniques proven in *The Ruined Cottage.*

The attack on pride is tacit in the poem's opening lines, which constitute a brilliant and novel experiment with the presentational style:

> Here, Traveller, rest! This lonely Yew-tree stands
> Far from all human dwelling: what if here

No sparkling rivulet spread the verdant herb?
What if these barren boughs the bee not loves?

(ll. 1–4 *app. crit.*)

The initial command to halt, conventional in both inscription and epitaph, begins a contest of wills between the poet and a passerby who is presumed to condescend to the desolate landscape of the poem. Moreover, by stating what is not present in this landscape, Wordsworth implies what is in the mind of the disappointed observer. He had first employed negation, in 1793, to express the desperate quest of an isolated mind for images of hope, but here he uses it for precisely the opposite purpose, to imply the subjectivism and pride of the observing mind. Even as the poet concedes what this landscape lacks, he names what the reader desires: a conventionally picturesque landscape that is humanized by man or by the diminutive society of Virgilian bees. For the first time in Wordsworth's poetry, style becomes openly parodic, as he mimics and exaggerates vices that embody contempt for both the natural world and the audience. Three times, for example, he attaches a single qualifying adjective to a generic noun in order to suggest that the reader cannot understand or value concrete particulars without referring them to larger abstract classes. A pompous and euphemistic Latinism, "verdant herb," condescends to what it names by adorning it. The personifying verb "spread" hints at nature's gracious obeisance before the fastidious human eye. Syntax and sound call attention to the speaker's poetic skill and to his willful distortion of the language of men; even in blank verse he conforms to the rhythmical constraints of the pentameter line and of the couplet. The alliterating b's of the last line witness a delight in artifice that parades itself before the audience, rearranging the order of words at the expense of the objects they denote. The target of this parody is not only the style of Wordsworth's contemporaries; these are devices he had himself assiduously cultivated in 1788 and 1792.[14] That he now resurrects and mocks them suggests again that he had formulated the principles he would enunciate in the Preface to the *Lyrical Ballads* three years later.

In the following lines this veil of subjectivism and pride drops away:

> Yet, if the wind breathe soft, the curling waves,
> That break against the shore, shall lull thy mind
> By one soft impulse saved from vacancy.

(ll. 5–7)

Diction becomes plain and literal. Syntax and rhythm develop the ampler cadences of spontaneous feeling. The line-ending, in particular, becomes a point of delicate equilibrium between process and stasis. Sound effects cease to advertise the poet's skill and exert their power covertly through an intricate patterning of long vowels and alliterating fricatives, as in *soft* and *saved from vacancy*.

If Wordsworth parodied the vices of his contemporaries in the opening lines, he here corrects them. In form these lines resemble an inscription Southey composed a year earlier for a "Tablet on the Banks of a Stream":

> If the sun rides high, the breeze
> That loves to ripple o'er the rivulet
> Will play upon thy brow, and the cool sound
> Of running waters soothe thee.

(ll. 2–5)

Despite Southey's enthusiastic naturalism, his language is by Wordsworthian standards quite impure. Three of his four finite verbs tend to personify their objects, and the second, *loves,* sentimentalizes and humanizes the relation between wind and water. The following infinitive, *to ripple,* subserves art rather than nature; if it alliterates with *rivulet,* it nevertheless transfers the properties of the stream to the wind, blurring the distinction between elements. Southey trifles with nature even as he celebrates it. In Wordsworth's lines, on the other hand, the distinction between wind and water is kept perfectly clear, and attention focuses on the motion and power communicated across this elemental boundary:

> Yet, if the wind breathe soft, the curling waves,
> That break against the shore, shall lull thy mind . . . .

He implies the transfer of power from wind to wave, and in the next line arranges a richly significant parallel between the forceful impact of these waves on the shore and the "soft" impact of their "impulse" on the mind, which it saves from complete sensory deprivation, or "vacancy."

In this opening passage Wordsworth in effect places the reader in the role of the traveler of *Salisbury Plain,* compelling him to undergo a miniature crisis of exposure to a landscape that strips his mind of purpose and will, of a host of conventional expectations, and of pride. He is humbled before an external power that is benignly responsive to his need: unlike the nature that had failed to rescue Rivers from his crime, this gives itself freely to "save" the mind that is opened to it. The manner in which this exposure is accomplished, furthermore, is equally benign; the speaker's force is delicately adjusted to the moral resistance expected. The violence of the opening command at once gives way to the gentler suasion of concession ("what if") and then vanishes, as the reader is handed over, so to speak, to an external landscape that is then itself reduced to a single, exquisitely delicate impulse. Such an art unites unrelenting moral purpose with a snailhorn intensity of effect seldom recognized in Wordsworth's poetry.

The second part of the poem places a similar meeting of mind and the external world in dramatic form. Like the ruined cottage, the yew tree memorializes a human history, that of a "favour'd youth" who "own'd no common soul," but was rebuffed by the world's neglect. Alienated from both society and self, he retired to this desolate spot, in which he found an "emblem" of his "own unfruitful life." This solitary mingles the pride of Rivers with Margaret's morbid fixation to a particular landscape, but unlike both characters his mind is open to the redeeming power of natural influence. As he raises his eyes from the desolate foreground to the beauty of a distant prospect, and to an emblem of what might have been, his pride is overwhelmed:

> And, lifting up his head, he then would gaze
> On the more distant scene,—how lovely 'tis
> Thou seest,—and he would gaze till it became
> Far lovelier, and his heart could not sustain
> The beauty, still more beauteous!
>
> (ll. 33–37)

Here we see a second dramatization of exposure, in which nature again humbles human pride and initiates a rapprochement with man:

>   Nor, that time,
> At the return of thought would he forget
> Those kindred beings to whose favoured minds
> Warm from the labours of Benevolence
> The world and man himself as lovely shewed.
>
> (ll. 37–41 *app. crit.*)

Wordsworth had described this psychological process in 1794, when natural influence poured "balm" on the "morbid passions," and "love of nature" led to "virtue." But these truths are now implied by dramatic presentation.

In the third and concluding part of the poem he presumes an openly didactic authority:

> Stranger! henceforth be warned; and know that pride,
> Howe'er disguised in its own majesty,
> Is littleness; that he who feels contempt
> For any living thing, hath faculties
> Which he has never used; that thought with him
> Is in its infancy.
>
> (ll. 50–55)

What has been dramatized is here named, in a language that is for the first time in the poem continuously discursive. The reader has been compelled to experience "contempt," for example, in the role of arrogant passerby assigned to him at the poem's beginning, and has then witnessed its social and psychological effects in the history of the solitary. The word itself thus carries an unusual weight of significance and precision, as the language of reflection is redeemed by the experience of substantial things given us earlier in the poem.

This discursive language then bends in response to powerful emotions:

> The man whose eye
> Is ever on himself doth look on one,
> The least of Nature's works, one who might move
> The wise man to that scorn which wisdom holds
> Unlawful, ever.
>
> (ll. 55–59)

The curve of thought in these lines is circular; it dips impulsively toward self-contempt, but then enacts the discipline it exhorts, and regains self-esteem in obedience to a "wisdom" that holds both extremes, self-abnegation and pride, "unlawful." This "wisdom" consists in a dynamic equilibrium of thought and feeling, powers that in earlier poems had paralyzed each other but that here are reconciled in the excursive actions of love and speech. As the poem moves to its conclusion, equilibrium is restated in terms that grow more and more condensed:

> O be wiser, Thou!
> Instructed that true knowledge leads to love;
> True dignity abides with him alone
> Who, in the silent hour of inward thought
> Can still suspect, and still revere himself,
> In lowliness of heart.
>
> (ll. 59–64)

The static balance of the penultimate line, which itself summarizes the lesson of the poem, is rendered dynamic by the concluding phrase, into the last word of which the moral urgency of the entire poem is condensed. This "intensity" is not sensuous but intellectual; it renders the language of thought incandescent with feeling.

In the three parts of the poem, then, a single lesson is given three distinct forms, descriptive, dramatic, and discursive. These parts in effect rearrange and purify the three voices of *Salisbury Plain* and the psychological states they had implied. In the opening description human experience is stripped to its fundamental Lockean elements: a meeting between an otherwise vacant mind and a single simple idea of sensation. Other and higher faculties, memory and the private and social affections, appear in part two, where they are once again reconciled to a central confrontation between mind and nature. In the third part, finally, we hear a voice that like the narrator of 1793 relies on the nominal but universal abstractions generated by the reason. After erasing Locke's tablet of the mind, Wordsworth subjects it to a controlled and therapeutic reconstruction, ensuring that the language of reason is solidly grounded in sensation and feeling. Although the poem has been viewed as an attack on Godwinian rationalism,[15] it is therefore antirational in neither spirit nor effect. Wordsworth seeks to validate, and not to supplant, the reason, and he does so by locating its authority not in the power of demonstration, which sanctions departure from sensation and feeling, but in intuition. Recalling the world of Gray's Eton College Ode, in which reflective "thought" was incompatible with hope, we see that this poem in fact tends to reconstruct the "right reason" of pre-Enlightenment culture, the reason that in *Paradise Lost* guided the fallen Adam to humility and love. The result of this systematic psychological reconstruction is to produce a poetic voice that is fully human, a voice that in Coleridge's words brings "the whole soul of man into activity, with the subordination of its faculties to each other, according to their relative worth and dignity" (*BL,* II, 12).

This poem offers a convincing demonstration of Wordsworth's recovery from the personal crisis of the Racedown years and his mastery of the poetic techniques evolved during that crisis. The values of 1792 and 1794 reappear, tested and reconfirmed: a chastened humanism that finds man's dignity in loving humility and a hope that looks not to the invisible heaven of an orthodox Christian dualism but to a substantial order of truth and grace, nature. An even more striking symptom of recovery, however, is the systematic way in which Wordsworth now applies these values to the redemption of his audience. This poem seeks to master not the self but the reader, whom it compels to undergo a purgative crisis of exposure to truth and nature. Like the pedlar, the speaker presides over this crisis, reclothing the reader's mind, as it were, in new garments of humility and love. Wordsworth's attention now shifts from the idols of the cave to those of the marketplace and the theater, from private trauma to the solipsism and pride that are the effects of public convention, of language, false doctrines, and what he would call a year later "our pre-established codes of decision." His art thus becomes an instrument that actively seeks to attain the end of the revolution that had failed, the regeneration of human nature.

VI   Alfoxden: 1798

> . . . thence may I select
> Sorrow that is not sorrow, but delight,
> And miserable love that is not pain
> To hear of, for the glory that redounds
> Therefrom to human kind and what we are.
>
> *The Prelude*

In July 1797 a fast-ripening affection for Coleridge brought the Wordsworths to Alfoxden Park, a manor house on the wooded slopes of the Quantock Hills, a few miles from Coleridge's cottage in Nether Stowey. Here, during the fall, *The Borderers* was revised, and here, in late January 1798, Wordsworth began to compose the poems that bring his poetic apprenticeship to a triumphant end.

The consummation of 1798 has been viewed as a sudden emergence into the sunlight of romantic joy, or a regression into the mists of romantic subjectivism. It has been ascribed to the mystery of poetic inspiration or to the philosophical influence of Hartley or Coleridge.[1] But its most striking characteristic, when viewed in the light of Wordsworth's earlier work, is the inevitability with which it fulfills and completes the promise of the past. His psychological, philosophical, and stylistic development during the spring quite precisely reenacts earlier consummations of hope, but does so for the first time in a language that is adequate to its subject. In February and March, as in 1792 and 1794, style becomes openly responsive to personal feeling and thought, and again subjects remembered imagery to discursive and meliorative reinterpretation. Wordsworth again affirms the beneficence of natural influence, in a language that is again explicitly philosophical. Pain, violence, and extremity again disappear before a passionate tide of joy and optimism. The promise of the Windy Brow fragments is openly fulfilled in March, when Wordsworth returns to the lyric mode, and sings, for the first time since his adolescence, in his own character. In the following months his attention shifts to the reformation of society, as he composes a series of experimental ballads in new and brilliant permutations of the presentational style. And in June he condenses both lyric and discursive modes into a single odal meditation, *Tintern Abbey,* in which he surveys and affirms the course of his own life since youth.

One cannot doubt Coleridge's immense contribution to these achievements. A brilliant and profoundly generous man, he offered a philosophic and poetic comradeship Wordsworth had not known since his headmaster encouraged him with "kind hope," and John Fleming joined him in "repeating favourite verses with one voice." Coleridge furthermore was probably the only man in England who recognized the achievement of the Racedown poems and could articulate its philosophical and historical significance. He was, finally, a great poet, whose work throughout this year quite literally interbraids with Wordsworth's. Themes, motifs, and technical innovations pass from one mind to the other and back again, enriched and transformed at each passage. But at all times the work of each poet remains fully his own, and Coleridge's influence in no way deflects or distorts the flowering of Wordsworth's genius, which proceeds with awesome independence to the consummation implied by the work of 1794. Coleridge's gift to his friend at the time was not a philosophy, but recognition, encouragement, and love, and it is above all a tribute to the quality of his influence that Wordsworth so completely became himself.

I

The accomplishments of 1798 began on or shortly after the night of January 25, when Wordsworth was inspired to composition by an object that had been dear to him since Hawkshead, the moon:

> The sky is overspread
> With a close veil of one continuous cloud
> All whitened by the moon that just appears
> A dim seen orb, yet chequers not the ground
> With any shadow—plant or tower or tree.
> At last a pleasant instantaneous light
> Startles the musing man whose eyes are bent
> To earth; he looks around—the clouds are split
> Asunder,—and above his head he views
> The clear moon, and the glory of the heavens.
>
>   (*A Night-piece,* ll. 1–13 *app. crit.;* DCP)

Throughout *A Night-piece* Wordsworth employs the present tense. The poem is framed not as the product of "emotion recollected in tranquillity," but as an immediate response to the event it describes. Like the Windy Brow fragments and nearly all of the poems of this historic springtime, it is shaped by a sense of the worth and joy of present existence.[2]

As these opening lines make clear, moreover, Wordsworth's attention has returned to the "common range of visible things": a natural landscape that is contemplated for its own sake, as were the landscapes of *An Evening Walk, Descriptive Sketches,* and the Windy Brow fragments. Style, however, is now continuously presentational, as it imitates the sudden reorganization of attention and feeling by the moon and encourages the reader to join the "musing" pedestrian in gazing upward:

> There, in a black-blue vault she sails along,
> Followed by multitudes of stars, that small,
> And bright and sharp along the gloomy vault
> Drive as she drives: how fast they wheel away,
> Yet vanish not!
>
> (ll. 14–18)

Architectonic devices that in *The Ruined Cottage* directed attention to concrete signs of human feeling are here employed to suggest the impressiveness of the natural object and the intensity with which the observer views that object. Rhythm, imagery, and repetition lay great stress, in particular, on the passionate fixity with which the eye dwells on the fixed moon, which is set into apparent motion by wind-blown clouds. Both eye and object are endowed with a dynamic stasis that intimates power. As feeling builds to a climax, however, diction remains stubbornly literal. The only semantic aberration introduced by the excited and creative imagination is the personifying pronoun "she." Powerful emphasis falls instead on the verbs that denote the motion and power of the moon: "sails," "drives," "wheel." As the spectacle comes to an end, attention returns to earth and to self, imitating the onset of tranquillity described by the closing lines:

> At length the Vision closes; and the mind,
> Not undisturbed by the deep joy it feels,
> Which slowly settles into peaceful calm,
> Is left to muse upon the solemn scene.
>
> (ll. 23–26)

A final verb of motion, "settles," ends the communication of power from nature to the observing mind, which now decays into calm in a cycle of excitation and relaxation that harmoniously comprehends man and the natural universe.

This poem, then, is clearly and forcefully presentational. It seeks to reenact the presentation of phenomena to the mind in experience. But here, as in many poems to come, Wordsworth puts this style to a new use. The movement of attention in the poem is not determined by character—by the fears or hopes of an individual mind. Imagery does not function primarily as a sign of human feeling, as it had, for example, in *The Ruined Cottage,* where an "idle loom" implied both the selective compassion and insight of the pedlar and the decay of Margaret. Here the observing mind, like the "musing" pedestrian, is uncharacterized by any predominant interest of its own, and its attention is forcibly captured during the course of the poem by the emergent moon. The natural image itself now performs the role of the narrator in the *Lines* on the yew tree, as it ambushes an unconcerned passerby for purposes that are implicitly redemptive. *A Night-piece* thus argues renewed trust in the autonomous power of the natural image, a trust Wordsworth would justify in later years by citing an analogous passage from *Paradise Lost:*

> Now glowed the firmament
> With living sapphires; Hesperus that led
> The starry host, rode brightest, till the Moon,
> Rising in clouded majesty, at length
> Apparent Queen unveiled her peerless light,
> And o'er the dark her silver mantle threw.
>
> (IV. 604–609)

Hesperus, he wrote to Lady Beaumont, is an intrinsically "poetical" object, because the "glory of his own Nature gives him the pre-eminence the moment he appears" (*MY* I, 148). Here, too, the moon is a "glory," a revelation that recalls the millennial landscapes of 1792 and witnesses a renewed ability to perceive the visible world as what Coleridge would describe as "the art of God." If this revelation no longer presages a political revolution, it nevertheless testifies, as did the Alpine scenes of *Descriptive Sketches,* to a covenant of love that links man, nature, and God. The image of the moon functions as a sign of natural "feeling," and embodies the benevolent purpose that offers visible phenomena to the human mind, thereby elevating and redeeming it.

The role of the artist in this poem is virtually invisible, because he dedicates his art to the accurate imitation of the presentational activity of nature. In later years Wordsworth would recall the question prompted in March 1798 by the sight of a common thorn on a stormy day: "Cannot I by some invention do as much to make this Thorn permanently an impressive object as the storm has made it to my eyes at this moment?" (*PW* II, 511). The poet seeks to accomplish in art what the storm accomplished in experience: the transfiguration of a common object, and the permanent renewal of its power to "impress," to touch and alter, the human mind. This implied analogy between the energies of a natural tempest and the artist's mind would reappear in several poems of 1798, and here it led to the composition of *The Thorn,* a poem that seeks to elevate response to its object by employing the "invention" of a tragic human narrative. In *A Night-piece,* on the other hand, Wordsworth imitates the presentation of an intrinsically sublime object, the moon, and therefore eschews "invention." In both poems, however, he offers us a glimpse into the exalted conception of the power of his art that was granted him in this spring of 1798. Poetry is truly a "power like one of Nature's" (*Prelude* XII. 312), embodied by the poet in the permanent form of art. Like the scientist, the natural magician, or the priest, the poet wields a power that is not his own. His capacities and his responsibilities are immense.

Within a few weeks, Wordsworth would begin to articulate this conception of the poet discursively, but it is in the practice of *A Night-piece* that we sense, for the first time, that his poetic technique is completely reconciled with his conception of "nature." In the work of 1797 he had once again aligned himself morally and emotionally with this power, but here he dedicates his art to its ends. He displays that lofty conception of the philosophical sanctions of art that was a condition of the greatest romantic poetry, and effectively recovers the confidence that had inspired the great Renaissance poets. In this poem, in particular, the classical conception of art as an imitation of nature recovers a meaning it had largely lost during the Enlightenment, that of a human action that completes the activity of nature, or, in W. J. Bate's phrase, "an active rival or duplication of the ordered process of nature itself." [3] To adopt the terms used by Coleridge in later years, this poem succeeds in transposing nature's "language"—a configuration of images ordered significantly in time and space—into the human language of words, where it is given permanent form. Placed in the perspective of Wordsworth's psychological history during the preceding decade, *A Night-piece* looks forward to Coleridge's observation that the "artist must first eloign himself from nature in order to return to her with full effect."

> Why this? because if he were to begin by mere painful copying, he would produce masks only, not forms breathing life . . . He merely absents himself for a season from her, that his own spirit, which has the same ground with nature, may learn her unspoken language in its main radicals, before he approaches to her endless compositions of them.
>
> (*BL* II, 258)

Although Coleridge's subject is a psychological process, he illuminates the function in Wordsworth's history of the estrangement from nature and man suffered during the Racedown years. To know and imitate a nature that has the "same ground" with the human spirit, man must know himself. And this is what Wordsworth came to know, slowly and painfully, during the years after 1793. Although it is cast in a conventional genre, which extends back to Lady Winchelsea, *A Night-piece* could only have been written by a man who had learned, through personal experience, that the "unspoken language" of nature is love.

Within a few days, Wordsworth explored other and equally impressive configurations of imagery. In a celebrated passage he later transferred to *The Prelude,* but which originated as a companion to *A Night-piece,* he described another ambush of the mind by redemptive power, his meeting with a discharged soldier during the summer vacation of 1788 or 1789. In the first part of this episode he recalls a solitary walk homeward through a moonlit landscape. His imagery suggests specious illusion, and unnatural transpositions of elements:

> I slowly mounted up a steep ascent
> Where the road's watry surface, to the ridge
> Of that sharp rising, glitter'd in the moon,
> And seem'd before my eyes another stream
> Stealing with silent lapse to join the brook
> That murmur'd in the valley.
>
> (*Prelude* IV. 370–375 *app. crit.*)

He then shifts attention to the boy's consciousness, employing a psychological diction that is virtually opaque to the visible world:

> On I went
> Tranquil, receiving in my own despite
> Amusement, as I slowly pass'd along,
> From such near objects as from time to time,
> Perforce intruded on the listless sense
> Quiescent. . . .
>
> (IV. 375–380)

Like the opening of the yew-tree inscription, succeeding lines name what the boy is *not* looking at—the "dark blue vault, and universe of stars" (IV. 384)—and imply the absence of the authentic communion exemplified by *A Night-piece*. The boy's mood then alters from "listless" passivity to a pleasurable complacency, as "beauteous pictures" rose

> As from some distant region of my soul
> And came along like dreams.
>
> (IV. 392–395)

Mind expands to encompass nature, relationship with which becomes entirely conjectural.

In such a hedonistic reverie the boy meets the soldier:

> While thus I wander'd, step by step led on,
> It chanced a sudden turning of the road
> Presented to my view an uncouth shape
> So near, that, slipping back into the shade
> Of a thick hawthorn, I could mark him well,
> Myself unseen.
>
> (IV. 400–405)

For the opening lines of this great passage Wordsworth chose a dialogue from an early version of *The Borderers,* in which a "sudden turning of the road" presents the tormented Mortimer to the eyes of a peasant.[4] Here it suggests the boy's utter passivity; he is "led on" by unnamed powers, into an ultimately beneficent ambush. As in *A Night-piece,* style imitates the sudden reorganization of visual attention by an external object. It becomes rigorously objective, and subjective events are implied, not described. The emotion implied, furthermore, is fear, which the narrator refuses to name, and indeed conceals by subordinating the boy's frightened retreat in a clause: "slipping back into the shade/Of a thick hawthorn." In following lines this "shape" is given a succession of names that enact recognition: it gains humanity and masculinity ("him") and ultimately receives a social identity ("military garb," l. 414). Imagery traces the slow movement of attention across the soldier's body to his face:

> He was tall
> A foot above man's common measure tall
> And lank and upright. There was in his form
> A meagre stiffness. You might almost think
> That his bones wounded him; his hands were bare,
> His cheeks and eyes were sunken, and his mouth
> Shewed ghastly in the moonlight.
>
> (DCP)

Overcoming a "specious cowardice," the boy emerges from the thicket, approaches this awesome figure, and converses with him.

Discovering he is ill, the boy sees the soldier to a nearby cottage, receives his blessing, and parts from him.

The power of this episode has its roots deep in Wordsworth's past. Like *A Night-piece* and earlier poems, it traces a psychological ambush that is benign; external power intrudes forcibly into the boy's mind, disciplining an egocentric and isolating subjectivity. But the motif of ambush has also become literal; it is now accessible simply as an archetypal situation in romance. The significance of this ambush is intensified and complicated, furthermore, by images and feelings that derive from the Racedown period, the central conflicts of which this episode reenacts and resolves in brief and symbolic compass. The soldier evokes both fear and pity, and he resembles both victim and criminal in earlier poems. His skeletal features recall those of the accusing wife in *Salisbury Plain,* and like Herbert he is "lank as a ghost and tall" (*The Borderers,* l. 461). As the soldier receives a human identity, however, he comes to resemble the exiled wanderers of earlier poems, such as Mortimer or the crazed pilgrim of *The Borderers.* His initial effect on the boy recalls the confession scene in *Salisbury Plain,* during which the sailor watched his accuser in silent anonymity. And the boy's struggle to emerge from enclosure, to confront and humanize this specter, reenacts the central psychological action of the Racedown period and in particular the role of the pedlar in *The Ruined Cottage.* His successful attempt to initiate a human relationship issues in an act of charity that recalls the parable of the Samaritan; in terms of the symbolic life cycle of earlier poems, he ushers the exiled wanderer to a cottage-home, and in so doing exorcises his own guilt and isolation. In a later version he too returns home, with "quiet heart." Such echoes of earlier work may be multiplied, but they suffice to reveal the psychological complexity of such retrospects as *Nutting,* or the great "pictures" of the past Wordsworth painted in *The Prelude.* Symbols that are highly private in significance coalesce with others drawn from the Bible, romance, or epic, and are projected upon commonplace incidents from Wordsworth's childhood and youth. The result is a highly literal poetry that reverberates with rich, varied, and often uncanny symbolic implications.

In two other poems that date from the early spring, Wordsworth returned again to work composed at Racedown, subjecting it to openly optimistic reinterpretation that has the effect of exorcising the fears suffered then. In each, moreover, he accomplishes this by surrounding the haunting imagery of the Racedown poems with a discursive commentary that mitigates or belies its original effect. He now divided the "Description of a Beggar" into two parts, in each of which he humanized the awesome solitary of 1797. In the *Old Man Travelling,* published among the *Lyrical Ballads,* he transformed the beggar into an example of stoic fortitude: a father on his way to take a "last leave" of his dying son (l. 18 *app. crit.*). The remainder of the poem he reworked into *The Old Cumberland Beggar,* in which the beggar becomes the exemplum of an attack on the poor law. Placed at the center of a network of social relationships of which he is hardly aware, the old man functions like a natural object, exerting a beneficent psychological influence on those around him. He provides a "living record" that binds together past "offices of charity" (ll. 89–90 *app. crit.*) and an insensible stimulus to immediate and spontaneous benevolence (ll. 96–108). More broadly, he becomes an illustration of the workings of a beneficent necessity, an "intricate machine of things" (*PW* IV, 447) in which nothing is "divorced from good—a spirit and pulse of good, / A life and soul to every mode of being / Inseparably linked" (ll. 77–79).

Such optimistic necessitarianism becomes still more explicit in the final and most ambitious project of the early spring, an extensive revision of *The Ruined Cottage.* Begun shortly after the composition of *A Night-piece,* this task lasted throughout February and early March, as the poem of 1797 grew from less than two hundred to nearly nine hundred lines in length. Wordsworth's additions to the greatest of the Racedown poems move in two essentially contradictory directions. He now added nearly two hundred lines that describe the pedlar's repeated returns to the cottage, and sustain and deepen the pathos of Margaret's decline. On February 4, for example, Dorothy observed "moss rubbed from the pailings by the sheep, that leave locks of wool, and the red marks with which they are spotted, upon the wood (*DWJ,* I, 7). In the revised version of *The Ruined Cottage,* a month later, this image appears as one of the signs of decay the pedlar notices on his second return, "towards the wane of summer." He finds Margaret absent, and as he waits he notices

> the corner stones
> Till then unmarked, on either side the door
> With dull red stains discoloured, and stuck o'er
> With tufts and hairs of wool as if the sheep
> That feed upon the commons thither came
> As to a couching-place and rubbed their sides
> Even at her threshold.
>
> (ll. 585–591) [5]

Like other additions, this meshes perfectly with the symbolic pattern of the earlier poem, focusing attention on the gradual usurpation of Margaret's place by nature, and the gradual decay of her will to live. Its effect is anything but meliorative.

Most of Wordsworth's additions, however, concern the pedlar of 1797, who becomes a spokesman for the optimistic "creed" of natural piety that Wordsworth would announce in several of the *Lyrical Ballads.* An introductory biography identifies him as a good friend of the poet, and emphasizes the discipline imposed by a continuously loving and reverent relationship to nature. The pedlar is now a "chosen son" of nature, whose personal history begins with the reception of "precious" images that mold his feelings and provide a lifelong standard of value and truth. In one passage Wordsworth describes the "ecstasy" of a boyhood vision of "unutterable love" in the morning sky (ll. 122–155). In another great passage, which he later transferred to *The Prelude,* he celebrates the young man's vision of the "one life" of joy that works beneath all created things. Impelled by such love, the pedlar

leaves home and takes up his wandering profession, which offers
him a broad and comprehensive experience of men,

> Their manners, their enjoyments and pursuits,
> Their passions and their feelings, chiefly those
> Essential and eternal in the heart
> Which mid the simpler forms of rural life
> Exist more simple in their elements
> And speak a plainer language.

(ll. 61–66)

The mature man is "sublime and comprehensive" of mind
(l. 157). His eye flashes "poetic fire" (l. 267). In an Alfoxden
draft he becomes a "prophet," to whom

> solitary thought had given
> The power miraculous by which the soul
> Walks through the world that lives in future things.

(PW V, 413)

This impressive figure interrupts his tale repeatedly to comment
on more general subjects, and at its end delivers a lengthy monologue in which he celebrates the power of natural influence to
evoke human love, and upholds it as the agent of the redemption
of the human mind.

Such transformation of the humble countryman of 1797 into
poet, prophet, and philosopher clearly reflects the encouragement
of Coleridge, whose own plan for a comprehensive philosophical
poem, "The Brook," Wordsworth may have appropriated at this
time. It was in the first weeks of March, when he was working on
the Pedlar's final orations, that Wordsworth announced his conception of a poem entitled *The Recluse or views of Nature, Man,
and Society* (*EY*, p. 214). The burden of the Pedlar's creed, furthermore, is consistent with Coleridge's memory of the "grand didactic swell" that was to conclude *The Recluse* as it was first conceived (*STCL,* IV, 575): a poem in which Wordsworth would
"infer and reveal the proof of, and necessity for, the whole state of

man and society being subject to, and illustrative of, a redemptive process in operation, showing how this idea reconciled all the anomalies, and promised future glory and restoration" (*PW* V, 364).

It is equally apparent, however, that the operative ideas in the new poem are the product of Wordsworth's own experience. The redemptive agency it defines is natural influence, which Wordsworth had celebrated poetically in 1792 and philosophically in 1794. The pedlar's mind and heart are disciplined by the external "substance" predicated in *The Borderers.* If the Racedown characters had in various ways been "chained" by perverted and compulsive feelings to "dead things," the pedlar's eye binds his feelings to natural objects "even as in a chain" (l. 300), and it is a "chain of good," he asserts, that shall "link us to our kind" (*PW* V, 401; ll. 40–41). He combines the intellect of Rivers with the heart and senses of Mortimer, and represents an idealization of Wordsworth's own life as it might have become in different "circumstances" (*PW* V, 373). These circumstances, we may note, quite precisely exclude the reversals of hope Wordsworth had suffered since 1793; the pedlar is driven to wandering not by guilt but by nature; he suffers no "piteous revolutions," "no wild varieties of joy or grief," and his mind rests serenely in a "just equipoise of love" (*PW* V, 386 *app. crit.*; DCP). In his history, then, we see a further transformation of the symbolic wanderer of 1795 into a character who now clearly resembles the hero of the first two books of *The Prelude.*

The pedlar furthermore defines the role of the poet, as Wordsworth would define it in the *Preface* of 1800. Guaranteed against relativism and subjectivism by a firm and habitual perception of universal norms of value, his claim to moral (and poetic) authority is grounded on a theory that is not expressionistic but mimetic. He finds these norms both in natural images and in "essential" and "eternal" human nature, as it is revealed by the manners and the language of "rural life." He also defines the presentational style, which allows us to "read" in all things a "lesson" of human significance. Above all, he seeks to redeem what Wordsworth would in the *Preface* call the "beauty" and "dignity" of the human mind (*PW* II, 389). Such changes suggest that another epoch in Wordsworth's career has reached its end. He again articulates the recovery of hope, and in effect becomes what he had been in 1792, a "joint-labourer" in the "redemption" of the age (*Prelude* XIII. 439–441). His art assumes an authority that is not only didactic but prophetic, and it claims immediate and practical utility.

These ideas are not presented *in vacuo,* however, but in the context of the decline and death of an innocent woman, a history that implicitly belies the pedlar's optimism. His concluding discourse, for example, is highly generalized; in terms that Coleridge used in a letter of early March, it turns from "immediate" to "fundamental & general causes—the 'causae causarum' " (*STCL* I, 397). But unlike the equally discursive conclusion to the *Lines* on the yew tree, it is not at all compatible with the concrete facts of the preceding narrative. Margaret's decline is simply not consistent with an optimistic faith in man's inevitable progress along the path of "order and of good," and to proclaim such truths precludes the generosity with which a year earlier Wordsworth had presented her suffering to "any man who has a heart to feel."

In his dramatic role as narrator of her tale, the pedlar is caught in a similar dilemma, between human sympathy for Margaret and the reverent obedience demanded by nature. He is conscious, for example, that the mere narration of her story is a willful violation of natural sympathy. "Why," he asks, "when all things which are not at rest / Are chearful,"

> should we thus with an untoward mind,
> And in the weakness of humanity,
> From natural wisdom turn our hearts away,
> To natural comfort shut our eyes and ears,
> And, feeding on disquiet, thus disturb
> The tone of Nature with our restless thoughts?
> (ll. 447–452 app. crit.)

Natural influence not only comforts man, as it had in earlier poems; it offers him a mode of existence that is free from pain and weakness, a serenity that reduces grief to the status of a subjective aberration.

Similar implications appear in the lines Wordsworth now added to the pedlar's great lament before the cottage, in which he had implicitly protested against the forces of ruin and change. Now he corrects himself:

> But I have spoken thus
> With an ungrateful temper and have read
> The forms of things with an unworthy eye.
>
> (ll. 366–367 *app. crit.*)

A "chosen son" of nature, he is "ungrateful" in deploring the effects of natural process, and has therefore seen wrongly and unworthily. He then relates an experience that ascribes benign and redemptive power to the very forms he has reproached, the "weeds and the rank speargrass" on the naked wall:

> I well remember that those very plumes,
> Those weeds and the high spear-grass on that wall,
> By mist and silent rain-drops silvered o'er,
> As once I passed, did to my heart convey
> So still an image of tranquillity,
> So calm and still, and looked so beautiful,
> Amid the uneasy thoughts which filled my mind,
> That what we feel of sorrow and despair
> From ruin and from change, and all the grief
> The passing shews of being leave behind
> Appeared an idle dream that could not live
> Where meditation was. I turned away
> And walked along the road in happiness.
> You will forgive me, Sir. I feel I play
> The truant with my tale.
>
> (ll. 366–367 *app. crit.; DCP*)

A superlative example of the presentational style, this passage traces the progress of an "image" into the pedlar's mind, where it calms, restores, and redeems.[6] Epistemological implications are finely balanced; if Wordsworth's language recalls the Berkeleian idealism Coleridge had advanced in *Religious Musings,* where "life is a vision shadowy of truth," and

> vice, and anguish, and the wormy grave,
> Shapes of a dream
>
> (ll. 396–398)

this vision is nevertheless offered by a substantial nature and is a means of healing grace like that Wordsworth had attributed to the Rydal Cascade in 1794. An active nature intervenes, as it were, to restore the living "equipoise" of the pedlar's mind.

Here too, however, we sense that the pedlar's reverent naturalism does not permit a full and generous response to Margaret's plight, or, more broadly, to the plight of man.[7] He is forced to choose between relationship to man and relationship to nature, between a shared consciousness of grief and mortality and a psychological identification with nature that offers timeless joy. In another portrait of the pedlar Wordsworth described this latter relationship more fully:

> Some men there are who like insects
> . . . dart and dart against the mighty stream
> Of tendency . . . others with no vulgar sense
> Of their existence, to no vulgar end
> Float calmly down . . .
> They rest upon their oars,
> Float down the mighty stream of tendency
> In a calm mood of holy indolence
> A most wise passiveness in which the heart
> Lies open and is well content to feel
> As nature feels and to receive her shapes
> As she has made them.
>
> (*PW* V, 413; *Prelude,* p. 566)

Whether we frame this experience in psychological or religious terms—and it invites both—it clearly suggests that naturalism is now inconsistent with humanism, as it had been in *An Evening Walk* ten years before. Nature no longer presides over a specifically human consummation, as in 1792, nor is it the instrument of a chastening truth, as in the Racedown poems. It now offers escape from the human condition into an elevation of spirit that, though guaranteed by the senses, invites the charge of subjectivism and of spiritual pride, or *hubris,* and is implicitly vulnerable to the intrusion of painful truth.

It is significant, therefore, that Wordsworth attempted to compensate for this disequilibrium in early March, when he attempted to frame a conclusion to the revised poem. Four drafts survive, in all of which another character comes to life, the silent poet of 1797. This figure now develops an identity that resembles that of the Wedding Guest in *The Ancient Mariner;* he becomes a humble initiate and a "better and a wiser man" (*PW* V, 400). He also displays, however, a human compassion for Margaret that implicitly compensates for the "chearful" necessitarianism of the pedlar, and prophesies the dignified pessimism of the Solitary in *The Excursion.* In the final version of the conclusion he acknowledges the power of the pedlar's oration, and yet, as if unconvinced that all things move along the path of "order and of good," turns back toward the cottage:

> Yet still towards the cottage did I turn
> Fondly, and trace with nearer interest
> That secret spirit of humanity
> Which, 'mid the calm oblivious tendencies
> Of nature, 'mid her plants, her weeds and flowers,
> And silent overgrowings, still survived.
>
> (PW V, 403, ll. 111–116)

The compassionate humanism of the original pedlar, whose task it was to render homage to the greatness of Margaret's spirit, is here transferred to the poet, a figure more openly representative of Wordsworth himself. And his view of natural law is far more ambivalent than the pedlar's. In these "silent overgrowings" we see the nature of *The Borderers,* a force that if tranquil is nevertheless profoundly alien to the "secret spirit of humanity" that it slowly obliterates.

At this point the pedlar intervenes, cutting the poet's last ties to the cottage by citing the vision of the speargrass, which in this new position becomes a means of disciplining the poet's grief. Both characters then enact the disengagement of feeling proper to the pastoral elegy. The sun's "mellow radiance" shoots through the trees; birds sing, admonishing their grief; and they "chearfully" pursue their "evening way" (*PW* V, 404, ll. 137–147). Modern readers have interpreted *The Ruined Cottage* primarily in terms of this version, and not that of 1797, and some have therefore inferred from the role of the pedlar that Wordsworth himself was now a "chearful" necessitarian.[8] This final shift in roles would suggest, however, that even as he sought to complete the poem, the poet sensed the vulnerability and the paradoxical inhumanity of the pedlar's optimism, and sought, as always, to compensate for it.

It is not as the pedlar, furthermore, but as the humble and chastened poet, that in his third draft for a conclusion Wordsworth's personal feeling builds to an intensity that threatens the formal integrity of his blank verse:

> How sweetly breathes the air—it breathes most sweet
> And my heart feels it, how divinely fair
> Are yon huge clouds, how lovely are these elms
> That shew themselves with all their verdant leaves
> And all the myriad veins of those green leaves
> A luminous prospect fashioned by the sun
> The very sunshine spread upon the dust
> Is beautiful.
>
> (*PW* V, 400)

Here the architecture of the presentational style disintegrates before an overwhelming pressure of joy. Wordsworth's preferred syntactical unit, the paragraph, breaks down into a series of short, bald statements. Attention darts from object to object, seeking to comprehend and condense. Metrical variation and patterned sound effects become the norm, as if to attain an intensity beyond the scope of blank verse:

How sweetly breathes the air—it breathes most sweet
And my heart feels it.

Here, in short, Wordsworth moves toward the form as well as the theme of another poem he composed in early March:

It is the first mild day of March:
Each minute sweeter than before,
The red-breast sings from the tall larch
That stands beside our door.

There is a blessing in the air,
Which seems a sense of joy to yield
To the bare trees, and mountains bare,
And grass in the green field.

My Sister! ('tis a wish of mine)
Now that our morning meal is done,
Make haste, your morning task resign;
Come forth and feel the sun.

(*To My Sister,* ll. 1–12)

The paradoxical issue of Wordsworth's attempt to begin a great and universal philosophical poem and to elaborate the character of the ideal poet, is a lyric poem in his own person, set in a domestic situation and in the humblest measure known to him, that of the ballad.

Without examining this first lyric of the spring in detail, we may observe that it, too, marks an epoch in Wordsworth's career. In it he recovers the lyric voice of the Hawkshead poems. If we seek a comparably open statement of personal feeling, indeed, we must return to the close of *The Vale of Esthwaite,* where he had declared his love for Dorothy, for Fleming, and for his "native regions." He furthermore regains a perspective that offers the moral and psychological equilibrium the pedlar lacked, and that unites thought, feeling, and sensation. "At a small distance" from his house, the speaker stands, quite literally, on the borderline between cottage and landscape, man and nature, the domestic and the sublime, binding his love for both into a single utterance. His very posture embodies the dynamic equilibrium of forces that in earlier poems had threatened disproportion or paralysis. The outward vector of his exhortation, toward nature ("come forth and feel the sun"), is precisely balanced by the desire that has stopped him, his love for his sister, and by extension his refusal to relinquish relationship to man. Like a figure in classical sculpture, his forward motion is disciplined by his backward glance, and the poem as a whole embodies a moment of stasis that will spontaneously dissolve into action, an action that participates in the mounting intensity of the season and yet does so in communion with man. Attention moves from the bare and chaste landscape to the humblest ritual of domestic life, a communal meal that takes on openly spiritual significance when set against the imagery of starvation in earlier poems. In later stanzas the poem builds toward the sublime, a perception of the "blessed" power that frames the human soul to love. It is quintessentially Wordsworth's, an affirmation of recovery from despair and a joyful repossession of personal and cosmic integrity.

The implications of the poem are epochal in a broader sense as well. Wordsworth here returns to the mode of personal utterance that would dominate his own later work and the work of his age, a mode that locates the function and the excellence of poetry in the expression of personal feeling rather than the imitation of extrapersonal norms. It is therefore appropriate, as he takes a decisive step toward a seemingly expressionistic and "romantic" art, to remind ourselves that for ten years he had been unwilling or unable to speak in his own voice, and that he now does so only under conditions that guarantee that voice against subjective aberration. In this lyric his feelings are bound, "as in a chain," by the two supports that had survived a decade of reversal, despair, and guilt: his sister and "nature." In the Preface to the *Lyrical Ballads,* two years later, he mentions the "spontaneous overflow of powerful feelings" as a truism that his readers will take for granted, and goes on to qualify it: "For all good poetry is the spontaneous overflow of powerful feelings: and though this be true, Poems to which any value can be attached were never produced on any variety of subjects but by a man who, being possessed of more than usual organic sensibility, had also thought long and deeply" (*PW* II, 387–388). In later years he continued to justify a poetry that to his audience grew ever more idiosyncratic by appealing to psychological and moral laws that were universal, and by continuing to insist that the presence of emotion itself guarantees neither good poetry nor good sense. From a theoretical point of view, therefore, he never committed himself to a view of poetry that was fully "expressionistic." From a practical point of view, we cannot take Wordsworth's personal voice as the naïve effusion of a child of nature, or the devouring egotism of an idiosyncratic individualist. In 1798, as in later years, the very act of saying "I" in a poem was of immense moral and psychological significance to the poet: it implied that the self was fit to represent man before man and God and that it was disciplined by forces that though subjective in agency were neither private, idiosyncratic, nor relativistic. This is egotism, but it is the egotism of a "dedicated Spirit," a Dante or a Milton. It springs from humility before a lofty conception of poetry, and, in Wordsworth's case, before an equally lofty conception of human nature.

II

The lyrical impulse dominated Wordsworth's poetry for the rest of the spring. After seeing Coleridge "half-way home" from a ten-day stay at Alfoxden on March 18, he composed a literal description of a landscape, *A Whirlblast from Behind the Hill,* but he did so not in the blank verse of *A Night-piece,* but in the meter of the Hawkshead poems, the octosyllabic couplet. A day later he began the attempt to render a "stunted thorn" impressive in the same meter, and in a poetic voice that is by no means that of an exemplary philosophic poet. Throughout April and May he continued to compose the rest of the experimental lyrics he would publish in the late summer under the title of *Lyrical Ballads.*

As Francis Wrangham would point out in his review of the second edition of this volume, this title is redundant: "What *Ballads,*" he asked, "are not *lyrical?*" To Wordsworth as to his audience the ballad was a lyrical poem because it was assumed to be sung to a musical accompaniment.[9] Nor was its purpose the expression of private emotion; whether we take as our model the medieval folk ballad or the modern literary ballads of Percy, Goldsmith, and Bürger, its task was felt to be the presentation of a story of intrinsic and universal interest to an audience that (as Wordsworth said of *Goody Blake and Harry Gill*) consisted of "many hundreds of people" (*PW* II, 401 *app. crit.*). It is not misleading to think of these poems, then, as songs, in which Wordsworth sheds his role of philosophic poet and becomes a minstrel who sings to the people on behalf of the people. All are songs of triumph which celebrate what Wordsworth would call in the *Preface* the "indestructible qualities of the human mind" (*PW* II, 389). They are sung, however, not in the presence of the sympathetic and understanding community that greeted the medieval minstrel,

> Opening from land to land an easy way
> By melody, and by the charm of verse.
>
> (*The Excursion* II, 17–18)

Wordsworth's audience is the England of Pitt, Lord Lonsdale, and "Spy Nozy," the society from which he had in spirit exiled himself for five years. His use of the ballad form therefore becomes covertly ironic, a deliberate invitation to single combat with the reader that is compounded by a deliberately plain style and by audaciously humble subjects. Each of these poems conceals a presentational structure that, like the *Lines* on the yew tree, ambushes the reader for ends that are ultimately benign: the elevation of his perception of the object, and the restoration of the bond between men that is presumed by the ballad form.

As I have suggested, Wordsworth called these ballads "lyrical" not to stress their romantic subjectivity, but to alert the reader to their music. The function of the title is intensive; it emphasizes an aspect of the poems that the reader was likely to take for granted, their meter, and encourages him to yield to its influence and to give these poems the "animated or impassioned recitation" that Wordsworth requested in 1815 and that Hazlitt witnessed in 1798.[10] The function of meter in these poems, as Wordsworth explained it in the *Preface* of 1800, is indeed analogous to a musical accompaniment. It is, he pointed out, essentially adventitious, a source of pleasure and regularity that the poet employs to modulate and discipline the feelings evoked by his subject. As the sound of a harp transfigures the pain of a tragic history, so, he implies, the pleasure that we blindly associate with meter, or the sound effects that cluster with far greater intensity in stanzaic forms, mitigate and transfigure the pain evoked by the poet's imagery and provide a kind of contract or covenant of order upon which both poet and reader can rely. He looks to meter, in other words, for the psychological discipline that in experience he attributes to natural influence. It guarantees the mind against extremity, offers equipoise, and permits a direct contemplation of painful things that would be impossible in prose or blank verse.

Wordsworth's meaning may be illuminated by recalling a passage added to *The Ruined Cottage* in February or early March. There Margaret speaks:

> "I am changed,
> And to myself," said she, "have done much wrong,
> And to this helpless infant. I have slept

> Weeping, and weeping have I waked; my tears
> Have flowed as if my body were not such
> As others are, and I could never die."
>
> (PW V, 396; ll. 602–607)

Given the relative freedom of blank verse, feeling tends to generate form. Building in long cadences to peaks of intensity, it controls and threatens to fix the movement of attention and molds variations in the iambic rhythm. When condensed into a stanzaic form, however, a similar sentiment yields an entirely different effect:

> In sleep did I behold the skies,
> I saw the crackling flashes drive;
> And yet they are upon my eyes,
> And yet I am alive.
> Before I see another day,
> Oh let my body die away!
>
> (The Complaint of a forsaken Indian
Woman, ll. 5–10)

Both voices utter a despairing wish for death, but the Indian Woman's voice is far less painful in effect. It is braced and stiffened by marching rhythms that yield to the claims of feeling only once ("Oh lét"), and seek not to intensify response but to discipline it. Syntax at once sets up a pattern of couplets ("I did behold . . . I saw") and stays with it to the end. Feeling, in other words, is not allowed to generate form. The poet is guaranteed against fixation by the commitment to regular progression implied by meter; like the pedlar's regular rounds, which prevented too near an approach to the cottage, the ballad stanza keeps the poet in motion. Pain is tempered, furthermore, by purely aural effects, such as the ample and energetic chiasmus of assonance and alliteration in "crackling flashes," and the powerful rhyme of "drive"/"alive," which also underscores the power with which the speaker struggles for life. In the presence of such implied strength, the devices used to mitigate pain in the blank verse, such as understatement and indirection, no longer become necessary. Margaret's pathetic negatives, which imply both her wish to die and her inability to utter that wish, become flat statements: "Oh let my body die away!" The effect is paradoxical. Wordsworth presents an action that is far more obviously painful than that of *The Ruined Cottage*, the deliberate abandonment of a helpless woman by her people, and yet through the use of meter renders her voice implicitly triumphant over despair.

It follows from such effects that in 1798, and after, Wordsworth's choice of meters has profound psychological implications. Throughout the great decade he employs lyric forms not to indulge personal feeling, as we might expect from a "romantic" poet, but to discipline it. He consistently approaches the most painful and threatening truths in his life through the lyric, and speaks in blank verse only from positions of relative safety, of subjects that can be mastered without the aid of extrinsic guarantees. At any given time in the great decade, therefore, he commands two voices, and in the lyric may confront fears that in contemporary blank verse he represses, rationalizes, or denies. Such differences are obvious in the *Lyrical Ballads* themselves, which as a group correct and chasten the naturalistic optimism of the philosophic blank verse written earlier in the spring. Four lyrics advance the pedlar's "creed," but others implicitly contradict it, presenting a vision of natural law as grim as that in *The Borderers*, or confronting images and situations that had haunted and accused Wordsworth at Racedown. In most, Wordsworth's "music" liberates his art from fear.

The primary task undertaken by these ballads, however, is the liberation of the reader from his own "pre-established codes of decision." With the exception of two poems that to all intents and purposes are written in Wordsworth's own character, *To My Sister* and *Lines Written in Early Spring*, they are presentational structures that subject the reader to a redemptive experience. Of these the simplest are the two dramatic monologues, *The Mad Mother* and *The Complaint of a forsaken Indian Woman,* which dramatize the powers of the mind to survive extremity. In *Expostulation and Reply* and *The Tables Turned* we are presented with a debate between two speakers who represent a formal opposition of types, such as *L'Allegro* and *Il Penseroso,* and who together generate a stable and comprehensive equilibrium. "William" advances the pedlar's naturalistic creed, but in a form that is highly condensed and gaily provocative. Matthew's humanism is eloquent and complementary, and by no means supplies the target for the more serious attack on the "meddling intellect" in the second poem, *The Tables Turned.* If Matthew is denied the last word, his praise of the "spirit / Breath'd from dead men to their kind" is nevertheless an eloquent assertion of Wordsworth's own commitment to his art. He sought to transfigure "those barren leaves," not to deride them.

In all the other ballads Wordsworth employs a narrative persona, who, like the speaker of the *Lines* on the yew tree, enters into direct relationship with the reader and molds his response to a shared object. In *Goody Blake and Harry Gill,* for example, this speaker plays a relatively straightforward role: like characters in the Racedown poems, his language represents a purified selection of common speech and his tone assumes a perfect unity of interest between his audience of "farmers," himself, and his subject. He directs attention not only to the power of the imagination, under the influence of a curse, to "produce such changes even in our physical nature as might almost appear miraculous" (*PW* II, 401 *app. crit.*), but to the subjection of the imagination to the moral law of charity.

In other ballads the relationship between narrator, reader, and object grows more complex. As Robert Mayo has pointed out, the subjects of most are quite conventional.[11] In the magazine poetry of the day a reader would have found many sympathetic studies of such impoverished beggars as Simon Lee, rural tragedies like Martha Ray's, and even, perhaps, benevolent treatments of an idiot boy. But Wordsworth's use of such stock subjects is anything but conventional. He relies upon their power to elicit a stock response, to fit the taste of his audience like a glove, and then, by deft and brilliant manipulations of tone, imagery, and point of view, subjects such responses to redemptive discipline. He conducts the emotions of his reader like a symphony, isolating pride, contempt, or disgust, and calling forth other powers of the mind to transmute and obliterate them.

Many readers, for example, have deprecated the banality of Simon Lee's swelling ankles, without noting that their dissatisfaction with the image is presumed and exploited by the poem itself. As John Danby has pointed out in his penetrating study of the poem,[12] it gradually unfolds a vision of a world in which all living things are subject to decay. At the same time, however, Wordsworth's tone delicately balances between earnest and game, and suspends a solemn response to what would otherwise be an object of conventional pity. It is in the course of a conventional list of Simon's ills that the offending image first appears:

> He has no son, he has no child,
> His wife, an aged woman,
> Lives with him, near the waterfall,
> Upon the village common.
>
> And he is lean and he is sick,
> His little body's half awry
> His ancles they are swoln and thick
> His legs are thin and dry.
> When he was young he little knew
> Of husbandry or tillage. . . .

(ll. 29–38)

The image is introduced casually, and no notice whatever is taken of the discomfiture it might produce in a reader who reserves his pity for tidier objects, such as the speaker of the popular *Beggar's Petition,* which Wordsworth knew as a schoolboy:

These tatter'd clothes my poverty bespeak,
These hoary locks proclaim my lengthen'd years;
And many a furrow in my grief-worn cheek
Has been a channel to a flood of tears.[13]

As the first part of the poem ends, however, attention suddenly returns to this image:

Few months of life has he in store,
As he to you will tell,
For still, the more he works, the more
His poor old ancles swell.

(ll. 65–68)

Although the tone of these lines remains that of a homespun chronicle of rural woes, diction again veers toward the particular, as the reader's attention is led by a simple but ineluctable logic back to Simon's ankles, a concrete fact that, like the intrusive truths of the Racedown poems—the scene of Rivers' crime, for example—cannot be veiled in abstraction or generality. The tale told by these lines is universal and portentous: the hopeless struggle of a decaying organism to survive. Their very form, indeed, stresses the irony with which this struggle brings on its own defeat: the formerly excursive energy of Simon's "work" is now also "working" within and destroying him, with a power realized by the ugliness of the final verb.

The speaker then drops the subject of Simon Lee altogether, and without warning, in the center of a stanza, turns on the reader:

My gentle reader, I perceive
How patiently you've waited,
And I'm afraid that you expect
Some tale will be related.

(ll. 69–72)

Each word is edged with an irony that owes much to the position of this address immediately following the indecorous image of Simon's ankles. Even as it acknowledges the social gulf between the old huntsman and the reader, the adjective "gentle" reminds us that mortality does not respect class boundaries, and that the pride that finds organic decay offensive is no defense against an identical fate.[14] The cool scrutiny of "I perceive" is sharpened by the fact that the reader has by no means waited "patiently" for the tale he expects, as the rambling structure of the first part has insured. Implied, too, is the reader's blindness to the "tale" already told by Simon's ankles, a tale that concerns him more than he knows.

Wordsworth's speaker thus sets a trap for the reader's pride, using the image of Simon's ankles as bait. By suddenly revealing his insight into the reader's reactions, furthermore, he establishes his authority. Casting off the mask of humble balladeer, he assumes a role not unlike that of the pedlar, and establishes what Wordsworth would call "that dominion over the spirits of readers by which they are to be humbled and humanised, in order that they may be purified and exalted" (*PW* II, 426). In the following stanza this implicitly hostile confrontation suddenly dissolves, as the speaker's voice undergoes a further transformation into that of a redeemer, bent on the reader's salvation:

> O reader! had you in your mind
> Such stores as silent thought can bring,
> O gentle reader! you would find
> A tale in every thing.

(ll. 73–76)

Suffused by such enthusiasm, the epithet "gentle" comes to mean "generous" or "charitable," a meaning at once dramatized by the speaker's gift of the tale the reader expects.

The concluding anecdote presents another act of charity, in a form that elaborates the "tale" told by Simon's ankles. The speaker recalls the old man's vain struggle to uproot a stump, and his own easy and hearty response:

> "You're overtasked, good Simon Lee,
> Give me your tool" to him I said;

> And at the word right gladly he
> Received my proferr'd aid.
> I struck, and with a single blow
> The tangled root I sever'd,
> At which the poor old man so long
> And vainly had endeavour'd.
>
> (ll. 89–96)

At the conclusion of a poem in which the only action has been the slow decay of life, this "single blow" becomes more than a particular act of charity. It is a powerful and liberating release of protective energy, a gesture of defense, and even revenge, on behalf of a humanity caught in the inexorable processes of natural law.

The narrator's tone suggests, however, that he speaks in the pride of his youth and strength, and Simon's response comes to him as a revelation:

> The tears into his eyes were brought,
> And thanks and praises seemed to run
> So fast out of his heart, I thought
> They never would have done.
> —I've heard of hearts unkind, kind deeds
> With coldness still returning.
> Alas! the gratitude of men
> Has oftner left me mourning.
>
> (ll. 97–104)

The first four lines of this final stanza alter our perspective once again. Attention shifts from Simon's outward decay to the undiminished activity of his heart. The unobtrusive metaphor "to run," which constitutes the poem's only "run-on" ending at this point in the stanza, recalls the physical activity of Simon's youth, when he was a "*running* huntsman merry." It suggests his spiritual survival, identifies it with the physical vigor of the youthful speaker, and precludes a condescending pity for the "poor old man," as Simon was described at the close of the preceding stanza.

To the uninitiated reader, who expects from the poet some sign of pleasure won from benevolence, some complacent hint that self-love and social concern are the same, the final lines will come as a paradox and an anticlimax. But the initiated reader has been taught to resolve this paradox. He understands that this "gratitude" is extorted from Simon's heart by a decay that is the common fate of man, and that it is ampler cause for "mourning" than the "unkindness" that he himself has been asked to surrender during the course of the poem. He is thus invited to compare what he was with what he has become during his experience of the poem, and to join the speaker and Simon Lee in an act of charity that springs from a shared understanding of what it is to be a man.

The Idiot Boy asks still more of the reader, and again does so through a narrator who transforms a condescending pity and indeed disgust into an affirmation of the dignity and the autonomy of the boy's existence. The plot of the poem not only traces the "more subtle windings" of the "maternal passion," as Wordsworth explained (*PW* II, 388 *app. crit.*); it renders Betty Foy a means of elevating our response to her son, who is from the beginning of the poem presented as an object of her love. The narrator himself elevates our response still further, encouraging us to apprehend and to participate in the boy's feelings for their own sake. The first fourth of the poem, for example, describes an episode that is mock-heroic: the mounting of a steed. But the narrator manipulates attention and molds response to protect Johnny against ridicule, and to suggest that he possesses a dignity that rises above the bustling solicitude of his mother. At the climactic moment of his departure she becomes quiet:

> She gently pats the pony's side,
> On which her idiot boy must ride,
> And seems no longer in a hurry.

> (ll. 79–81)

Gesture renders Betty's conflicting feelings visible: her love and fear for her son and her dependence on the saner of the two travelers, the pony. In the next stanza attention moves, via the body of

the pony, to another image of touch: Johnny's sensation, for the
first time in his life, of the movement of a living steed beneath
him.

> But when the pony moved his legs,
> Oh! then for the poor idiot boy!
> For joy he cannot hold the bridle,
> For joy his head and heels are idle,
> He's idle all for very joy.

(ll. 82–86)

We are lured into an act of empathic identification, first with the
boy's senses, and then, carried on the tide of the narrator's enthusiasm, with his heart.

Even as the narrator's syntax breaks down before his feelings,

> Oh! then for the poor idiot boy!

his diction mimes a conventional pity for the "poor" idiot, a stock
pity that is belied by the shared joy of both boy and narrator, and
in the following lines is obliterated. Repetition, patterned syntax,
and clustered sound effects such as alliteration, consonance, and
the feminine rhyme, all condense, intensify, and purify the power
of "very joy," with a force that in Wordsworth's later phrase
"bears down before it, like a deluge, every feeble sensation of disgust and aversion" (*EY,* p. 357). Calling on the power of the
human heart as he had called on a "deluge" of divine, natural, and
human power in 1792, he forces the condescending reader to a
spiritual crisis: he must assent to and participate in this celebration of joy, or deliberately and actively resist it. He must commit
himself.

Nor does Wordsworth allow this act of affirmation, if undertaken, to proceed on the reader's own terms; he refuses to encourage the pretense that the idiot is a normal child, as his readers, including Coleridge, advised him to do.[15] At the poem's end he
reverts to the mock-heroic mode and allows us to listen to Johnny's recitation of his adventure:

And thus to Betty's question, he
Made answer, like a traveller bold,
(His very words I give to you,)
"The cocks did crow to-whoo, to-whoo,
"And the sun did shine so cold."
—Thus answered Johnny in his glory,
And that was all his travel's story.

(ll. 457–463)

We are given his "very words" with a precision that calls attention to this supreme violation of the "language of the higher and more cultivated orders," as Francis Jeffrey called it,[16] and to the fact that we have been brought into sympathy with a creature whose vision of the world is utterly alien to ours.

Wordsworth thus confirms the gulf we have bridged if we have read his poem with feeling; and in the penultimate line he suggests the significance of this act with the word he had applied to the moon in the *Night-piece*—"glory." Both the moon and the idiot are indeed "glories," or revelations, and both merit the "sublime expression of scripture" that Wordsworth would apply to the idiot in 1802: "their life is hidden with God" (*EY,* p. 357). Both visions, furthermore, extend back to 1792, when he read in Ramond of the *cretin* of the Rhone Valley, and the reverence paid him by the Swiss,[17] a race that to the author of *Descriptive Sketches* seemed a type of human excellence, and an "image" of man's "glorious sire" (l. 527). In *The Idiot Boy,* therefore, he invites an English audience to regain this state by participating in an act of affirmation and charity that, as he wrote to John Wilson, is the "great triumph of the human heart," and a manifestation of "the strength, disinterestedness, and grandeur of love" (*EY,* p. 357). He seeks to accomplish the "glorious renovation" promised by the Revolution, and the "glory" he names at the end of his poem is intended not only for his putative hero, but for the far greater triumph of the reader himself.

In both *Simon Lee* and *The Idiot Boy* the narrator functions in the same way as the pedlar; he ministers to the reader, conducting him through an experience of purgation that issues in a final transfiguration. In a final group of ballads, however, Wordsworth inverts this pattern in a direction that prophesies the narrative techniques of *Emma* or *The Turn of the Screw:* he constructs a dramatic context that exposes the limitations of the narrator's mind. The narrator himself becomes an object of criticism and a butt of irony, and the reader is invited to rise above him. In the *Anecdote for Fathers* and *We Are Seven,* for example, adult narrators enter into seriocomic debates with children, and seek violently to impose demonstrative categories of thought and value on their seemingly helpless but truly invulnerable victims.

A comic antitype to the voice who spoke from the yew tree, the father of the first poem forces his son not only to choose between two landscapes and to exalt one at the price of contempt for the other, but to justify that choice: "Why? Edward, tell me why?" (l. 48). He thus coerces the boy into a palpable lie, which is occasioned by an impulse (the image of the weathercock) from the very landscape the boy demeans. Perceiving what he has done, the speaker then recovers his humility before the landscape and his own son.

The narrator of *We Are Seven* comes upon a scene that survives from the Racedown poems: a fixed, dedicated vigil by a grave. And he responds as Mortimer, or Wordsworth, had responded to a similar accusation, by appealing to rational categories of thought that dissect the living being of their victim. But this victim is now a little girl, and the criminal is an obtuse commonsensical adult who is quite helpless before the obdurate integrity of her vision of death. He is, furthermore, quite precisely at the "cross-purposes" Max Beerbohm satirized in his well-known cartoon. He is capable of an intuitive response to her beauty and power, as the daring simplicity of his language makes clear:

> Her eyes were fair, and very fair,
> —Her beauty made me glad.
>
> (ll. 11–12)

But before her vision, which cannot distinguish between physical
and spiritual, he retreats, grasping at the categories of demonstrative reason for certainty and order. Unlike the speaker of the previous poem, he remains unregenerate, and his final words ironically indict him:

> 'Twas throwing words away; for still
> The little Maid would have her will,
> And said, "Nay, we are seven!"
>
> (ll. 67–69)

He confidently assumes the support of his reader, who
nevertheless perceives that he has been "throwing words away" in
a sense far deeper than he can understand, and that it is his will,
and not the girl's, that these categories subserve.

Perhaps the greatest personal triumph among the ballads is the
third poem in this group, *The Thorn*. Here Wordsworth confronts
the most threatening images of the Racedown years, clustering together in a single "spot" a gibbet, a pool, a grave, and the figure
of a deserted woman who is rooted to her place by love and grief.[18]
And he approaches these objects through a narrator who again
burlesques the division of sensibility he had himself suffered and
provides a living foil to what he sees. This speaker, whose function and character have been debated since the poem appeared,[19]
is Wordsworth's third depiction of a mind incapable of reconciling
intuitive and demonstrative modes of perception. Haunted by the
central images, he responds to their mystery and power with an
insistent, implicitly obsessive and at times violent struggle to be
relieved of uncertainty, and to reduce it to mathematical order or
positive fact.

Such conflict is implied entirely by style in the opening stanzas
of the poem, even before the reader has been introduced to Martha Ray or her story:

> There is a thorn; it looks so old,
> In truth you'd find it hard to say,

> How it could ever have been young,
> It looks so old and gray.

(ll. 1–4)

The narrator begins with a brute fact—"There is a thorn"—and evinces a concern for "truth" that is at once ironically qualified by an uncritical imputation of this truth to the reader, and an easy assumption of agreement. His is a repetitive mind which circles back to a given fact, moving at great speed but going nowhere. And, despite its positivism, it is an imaginative mind which at once begins to elaborate the concrete fact and to personify it: the thorn becomes "old," and finally, like a human being, "old and gray."

The next stanza witnesses another characteristic act, as the speaker measures the thorn:

> Not higher than a two-years' child,
> It stands erect this aged thorn. . . .

(ll. 5–6)

That his "measuring-rod" is a child not only prepares the reader for the revelations that follow, but assesses the quality of the speaker's mind: he is haunted by the image of Martha's child and the living mystery of her passion, which he will seek to measure and dissect throughout the poem. A final and more grotesque implication is that he has literally measured the thorn to determine whether an infant could be hanged on it.

In the second stanza he personifies the moss, endowing it with an active desire to "bury" the implicitly evil presence of the thorn. As his attention moves toward the second of the four central objects, the pond, his concern with measurement becomes obsessive. He fixes each object in precise relationship to its neighbors, noting details that suggest his struggle to control and stabilize haunting and powerful images. The thorn is "five yards" from the path, to the left, and "three yards beyond" is the pond, which he has observed long enough to know that it is "never dry," and which he has measured from "side to side": " 'Tis three feet long, and two feet wide" (l. 33). Since Coleridge singled out this line as evidence of the point that Southey and others had made before him, that a dull narrator cannot tell an interesting tale, it has repeatedly been cited as an example of Wordsworth's own banality.[20] But it proceeds from an attempt to expose a banality that is not Wordsworth's but the modern world's: an insensitivity that measures but cannot feel. The passage demonstrates, furthermore, that any act may be rendered significant (and theoretically poetic) by the mind that performs it. This speaker has measured the pond, as well as the thorn, to determine whether it is the proper size. A man who can "peep and botanize" on a grave, he is blind to the moral and emotional implications of his actions.

The speaker proceeds to describe the remaining empirical facts —the hill of moss and the figure of Martha Ray herself—and then lays bare the rest of his evidence in the manner of an amateur detective reporting on a private inquest into a village mystery. He repeats the local gossip, and then moves to the more authoritative evidence of his own confrontation with Martha Ray on the summit of the mountain. His presentation constantly and repetitiously distinguishes between fact and surmise, between what he "knows"—a word that becomes the leitmotif of his discourse— and what he "cannot tell." [21] He is clearly fascinated and frightened by the mystery and seeks to probe it to its heart. His emblem is the telescope he carries to the mountaintop, an instrument that suggests a refusal to trust the eye, and the strained but frightened curiosity of the voyeur.[22] When Martha suddenly appears close before him, in an ambush that recalls the sailor's meeting with his wife in *Salisbury Plain,* he flees:

> I did not speak—I saw her face,
> Her face it was enough for me.
>
> (ll. 199–200)

In her absence, however, he speculates with an intensity that takes visible form in the "spades" that slice toward the "little infant's bones" (ll. 234–235). Throughout this excited, hurrying, huddled colloquy, he draws the reader into his confidence, offering help, and imputing the questions of "what" and "wherefore" that obsess him. He is, in short, a precise antithesis to the pedlar: he cannot "read" the "moral properties and scopes of things"; he cannot move from fact to surmise; he cannot see with the "watchful eye of love." He is a study in busy, unselfconscious littleness.

He is, however, a faithful observer of the central image in the poem, that of Martha Ray. Five times his attention circles back to her fixed, unchanging figure, to the grand and permanent natural images that surround her—wind, mountain and stars—and to her unchanging cry: "Oh woe is me! Oh misery!" And each time he does so the reader's perception of these images enlarges, as a result of the gradual addition of fact and circumstance, and of the emerging contrasts between Martha Ray and the speaker himself. These contrasts range from obvious antitheses, between plain and mountain, town and landscape, society and solitude, to "modes of being" that verge on the ineffable. The hyperactivity of his mind, for example, renders Martha's fixity increasingly majestic. His fear implies her power. His earnest but banal sympathy—

> Oh me! ten thousand times I'd rather
> That he had died, that cruel father!
>
> (ll. 142–143)

purifies her complaint of sentimentality. His garrulity renders her single cry supremely eloquent. His refusal to move from fact to surmise becomes petty before her unceasing pain, and his preoccupation with causation and lurid detail (was it the pond or the thorn?) stresses the terrible simplicity of effect: "misery." Throughout the poem, then, the narrator's incessant activity pumps significance into the repeated images and the words of Martha Ray. The result is technically miraculous, and it fully justifies Wordsworth's defense of "repetition and apparent tautology" in his note to the poem (PW II, 513). Purely through the manipulation of context, Wordsworth transfigures the meaning of what is repeated, words that themselves remain utterly literal and commonplace. And he thus initiates the reader into a vision that rises far above the voice that speaks to him.

The ultimate effect of the poem is to exalt Martha Ray, and, by extension, the symbolic victims that had haunted Wordsworth's imagination since 1795. Placed beside Margaret, whose refusal to surrender hope had been rendered pathetic and terrible by her vulnerability—

>   and in the stormy day
> Her tattered clothes were ruffled by the wind
> Even at the side of her own fire—
>
> (PW V, 399; ll. 734–736)

Martha Ray becomes heroic and indeed exultant, an aristocrat of pain. Her power is implied simply by the defiant integrity of her "scarlet cloak," or her indifference to the elements that had killed Margaret:

> And she is known to every star,
> And every wind that blows.
>
> (ll. 69–70)

She is as obdurate and permanent as the crag the narrator takes her for, and yet she remains fully human in her pain. At the end of the poem the narrator affirms, for the last time, that this is all he knows, and leaves us with a scene from which horror, pity, and littleness have been purged: [23]

> And this I know, full many a time,
> When she was on the mountain high,
> By day, and in the silent night,
> When all the stars shone clear and bright,
> That I have heard her cry,
> "Oh misery! oh misery!
> "Oh woe is me! oh misery!"
>
> (ll. 247–253)

Attention moves from the "grand and permanent forms of nature" to a single human cry. Refusing all consolation, and uttering its agony in the face of time, of necessity, and of silence, this tragic cry becomes triumphant.

Even such summary notice of the structure of these ballads suggests that they make immense demands on the reader. They resemble the "yellow primrose" that remained itself and "nothing more" to the hardened sensibility of Peter Bell, or the hero of *A Poet's Epitaph,* whom we must love before he will seem worthy of our love. They are predicated, that is, upon a reading that is at once close and responsive, and they quite obviously confounded the "pre-established codes of decision" that Wordsworth asked his audience to suspend when introducing them in 1798 (*PW* II, 383). To simple readers, as Coleridge pointed out, they could seem simple effusions and nothing more, the work of a *"Sweet, simple poet!* and *so* natural, that little master Charles and his younger sister are *so* charmed with them, that they play at 'Goody Blake,' or at 'Johnny and Betty Foy' " (*BL* II, 131). To a sentimentally inclined reviewer like Charles Burney, *The Idiot Boy* could seem a tale of terror and not joy, and *Simon Lee* a touching genre-piece: "the portrait, admirably painted, of every huntsman who, by toil, age, and infirmities, is rendered unable to guide and govern his canine family." [24]

Neoclassical standards of decorum were of course equally opaque to the purposes of these poems, but if attacks based upon vulgarity of language and subject sometimes came from unexpected quarters, as when Southey compared the idiot boy to a "Dutch boor," [25] Wordsworth had presumed and indeed provoked such criticism in his poems, and enemies such as Francis Jeffrey were perhaps less unsettling than friends who debased as they praised. But Jeffrey could see these poems no more clearly than Master Charles. In his earliest reply to the *Preface* he pointed out that the emotions of a "clown, a tradesman, or a market-wench" were intrinsically unpoetic, and that "arts that aim at exciting admiration and delight, do not take their models from what is ordinary, but from what is excellent; and that our interest in the representation of any event does not depend upon our familiarity with the original, but upon its intrinsic importance, and the celebrity of the parties it concerns." [26] He at once exemplifies the pride of class that is Wordsworth's target in the ballads, and illustrates the poet's paradoxical relationship to the neoclassical tradition. With the exception of his reference to "celebrity," Jeffrey's understanding of the purpose of art in no way differs from that which produced *The Idiot Boy*. Wordsworth by no means regards the idiot as "ordinary," but as a divine revelation. Nor does he hold up the idiot as an exemplary model of human nature; the "excellence" he imitates in the poem is an action, an ideal response to the idiot that is itself molded by a conception of human nature that is neither idiosyncratic nor primitivistic. As we have seen, we may trace it to Wordsworth's experience of the French Revolution, to a Miltonic conception of the nobility of man, and to an understanding of charity that is ultimately rooted in the New Testament. His attack on a neoclassical decorum that perpetuates human pride is itself classical in form, in that it appeals to objective and universal norms that are not only excellent but sublime. To Jeffrey, however, and to many readers since, Wordsworth appears to be degrading human nature: a precise inversion of his purpose that we must ascribe not only to a failure to read with the "watchful eye of love," but to a poetry that relies, to perhaps an impossible degree, on implication and indirection, and thus on the reader's heart.

For all the controversy they have inspired, these poems are nevertheless technical triumphs, which transcend received stereotypes of Wordsworth's genius. The unassuming form of the ballad conceals an architectonic skill that recalls the lapidary art of Jonson or Horace, and that is paralleled in his own age only by the novels of Jane Austen. In the greatest of these poems he displays a mastery of tone and irony, and a delight in reducing the differences between him and his age to the focal point of a single word, that looks back to the metaphysical lyric and forward to the deliber-

ately difficult and often ironic styles of the disaffected poets of
later generations, Baudelaire, Eliot, and Joyce. These poems are
not romantic effusions, but complex, sophisticated, and deliberately pragmatic presentational structures, in which the poet himself does not appear, and of all Wordsworth's great poems, least
deserve to be described as the product of the "egotistical sublime."
They present a moral vision that is profoundly and comprehen-
sively charitable, a vision in which the swelling ankles of an old
man are reconciled with what Yeats called the "soul's magnificence." And this vision is offered to the reader, not imposed upon
him; Wordsworth insists that it be our own, and that we see what
he cannot tell us. These poems thus argue a trust in the capacities
of the reader that is itself an act of charity, and what they offer is
the sense that an exalted vision can be shared. They create the
"commonalty" of human feeling that Wordsworth would describe
as his subject in *The Recluse*. If their music rises toward planes of
feeling and thought more appropriate to the ode, the hymn, or the
tragedy than the ballad, it nevertheless remains a music of humanity, which is sung in unison.

VII   Return to the Wye: 1798

In a number of poems written during the spring of 1798—the additions to *The Ruined Cottage,* several fragments of blank verse, the four credal lyrics, and *Tintern Abbey*—Wordsworth presents his philosophy of nature in a mature form. Although his attitudes toward nature were no more settled in 1798 than in earlier years, these texts have provided a traditional starting-point for the study of his philosophy, and we may pause to consider the bearing of earlier poems upon the problem of defining and assessing this philosophy. As a glance at the voluminous literature devoted to this end will suggest, precise definition is not easy, and the philosophical and poetic value of Wordsworth's creed remains controversial. Some readers follow Arnold in an attempt to resurrect the man and the poetry by rescuing both from the philosophy, often on grounds Arnold would hardly have approved of, such as the influence of Annette Vallon. Of those critics who stress the importance of the philosophy, some, like G. M. Harper, identify it with the "great positive, naturalistic movement" of the Enlightenment.[1] A second group emphasizes the "romantic" characteristics of the naturalism, its status as a private, mystical, or religious vision.[2] Each point of view is reflected by the quest for Wordsworth's sources, which have been found in or compared to Jacob Boehme or David Hartley, Aristotle or Plato. Sophisticated and comprehensive attempts have been made to reconcile such contradictions within a specifically philosophical nomenclature,[3] and to recapitulate these here would be redundant. But it is pertinent to remind ourselves of the place the creed of 1798 holds in the larger development, to note that many of Wordsworth's philosophical ambiguities arise from the form of his poetry rather than the nature of his ideas, and finally to point out a few of the dangers attendant on an uncritical application of romantic or idealistic points of view.

I

We may recall, firstly, that 1798 is the third occasion on which psychological recovery was heralded by a poetry that openly celebrated nature and that did so in a language that was "philosophical," in that it moved from sensation to reflection and from the particular to the general. In 1792 Wordsworth had affirmed the covenant between man, nature, and God, in a discursive language that was largely conventional. Two years later he portrayed the beneficent effects of natural influence in an early form of the presentational style and celebrated this influence in a language that had become deliberately philosophical. In 1798 he does so again, with an intensity of feeling and attention that is heightened still further by the crisis of psychological, moral, and spiritual isolation dramatized in the Racedown poems. At the heart of his joy and gratitude in 1798, indeed, is the awareness that he has repossessed a relationship to nature that he knew before, and that he is "still / A lover" of the visible world.

It is furthermore apparent from the history we have traced that Wordsworth's naturalism was not a systematic doctrine which assumed a particular and coherent form and kept that form through time. From 1788 onward, his attitude toward the natural order oscillates rapidly, in response to the changing evidence of his own experience. Even in 1798, as we have seen, he struggles to correct and humanize a relationship to nature that threatens to exalt itself above the human condition, and in such ballads as *Simon Lee* presents a "nature" that is difficult to reconcile with that celebrated by the pedlar. If, for the sake of analysis, we isolate a discursive affirmation of nature, such as the pedlar's concluding monologue, a further difficulty arises. None of the identifiable tenets of Wordsworth's creed are esoteric, and most are what we would describe as commonplaces if we met them in philosophic prose. The pedlar rests his faith in the inevitable amelioration of the human condition, for example, on the premise that love of natural objects will conduce to love of man. This promise is peculiar neither to 1798 nor to Wordsworth; he had first stated it in 1794— "From love of nature love of virtue flows"—when he was forced by experience to substitute a psychological for a political hope of human redemption, and a similar hope was expressed by Mark Akenside in 1744. Throughout the philosophical verse of 1798, to take another example, Wordsworth conceives of the transaction between mind and nature in terms that are Lockean. Nature presents images to the mind, where they are stored, contemplated, and compared. His passionate interpretation of the process, of course, is anything but Lockean; the penetration of redemptive images into the mind becomes the focus of powerful feelings of gratitude and can be described as the "very nerve" of his poetic greatness.[4] If the effect is unique, however, the fact itself remains something of a commonplace, which is transformed by its poetic context. What we see in 1798 is the consummation of a personal history that has endowed such commonplaces with immense personal significance, a history that bears out Coleridge's observation that "in poems, equally as in philosophic disquisitions, genius produces the strongest impressions of novelty, while it rescues the most admitted truths from the impotence caused by the very circumstance of their universal admission" (*BL* I, 60).

The most formidable problem Wordsworth places in the way of students of his philosophy, however, is his style. In both the blank verse and the lyrics, his philosophical language is largely presentational, consistently shaped by feeling as well as thought, and therefore subject to the conditions we have noted in the *Lyrical Ballads*. The principal effect of such a style is to suspend the acts of abstraction and classification necessary to analysis; as Whitehead pointed out, Wordsworth renders the "concrete facts of our apprehension." [5] His greatest descriptive poetry tends to exhibit the irreducible ambiguity of nature itself; it tempts and justifies interpretations that mirror and confirm the predispositions of the critic, who may infer pantheism or theism, sensationalism or transcendentalism, from a single passage. I do not mean to suggest that such inquiry is vain, but to point out that the very act of applying a philosophical nomenclature to Wordsworth's poetry constitutes a radical departure from the realm of discourse in which his poetry claims authority. The point of his philosophical poetry, like *The Ruined Cottage* or the *Lines* on the yew tree, is to secure an apprehension of reality that transcends abstraction.

As a first example of the practical problems that follow from such a style one may take the fact that Wordsworth's speakers vary in philosophical authority, and that the form of their discourse is shaped by the decorum of the poem in which they speak. In a celebrated and eminently quotable stanza from *The Tables Turned,* for example, "William" declares that

> One impulse from a vernal wood
> May teach you more of man;
> Of moral evil and of good,
> Than all the sages can.
>
> (ll. 21–24)

To quote these lines as a sober summary of Wordsworth's doctrine of nature is to ignore the fact that the speaker of this poem and its companion-piece, *Expostulation and Reply,* is a dramatic character, and that his language is appropriate to the debate, a genre that sanctions hyperbole, ellipsis, and condensation, all tacitly understood as the product of the contest dramatized. "William's" language, then, is deliberately and gaily provocative, particularly in its sweeping contrast between the "one" impulse and "all" the sages of the past. If read literally, without allowances for the form of the poem, it can lead to the assumption that this vernal wood read audible moral lessons to the poet, who was afflicted by an uncritical animism, and who expounded a "confused anti-intellectualism." [6] Placed within its poetic context, however, "William's" enthusiasm is acknowledged and corrected by the form of the poem, which balances it against the antithetical sentiments of the opposing speaker, Matthew. Although Wordsworth gives his namesake the last word, neither of the two speakers can be regarded as his philosophical spokesman. His views are embodied in the dramatic conflict between human and natural wisdom, and he refuses to dismiss either. The final effect of this poem, indeed, is to moderate, discipline, and humanize the solitary and egotistical naturalism of the additions to *The Ruined Cottage,* where "William's" sentiments were first clearly articulated.

Such a passage is thus extremely vulnerable to misinterpretation. In the heat of argument, "William" condenses an idea that in other contexts takes quite different verbal forms. When it is advanced by a speaker of comprehensive and sober mind, for example, all hints of animism and hyperbole disappear. At the outset of his discourse, the pedlar affirms the value of such impulses as that sent by the "vernal wood."

> . . . by contemplating these forms
> In the relations which they bear to man
> We shall discover what a power is theirs
> To stimulate our minds. . . .
>
> *(PW* V, 401; l. 24–27)

When Wordsworth himself addresses a similar subject in prose, before a strange and possibly hostile audience, his language becomes pointedly and stiltedly technical:

> For our continued influxes of feeling are modified and directed by our thoughts, which are indeed the representatives of

all our past feelings; and . . . by contemplating the relation of these general representatives to each other, we discover what is really important to man. (*PW* II, 388)

When he records a similar experience in blank verse, however, poetic form again introduces a weight of feeling that modifies our perception of his meaning.

> In many a walk
> At evening or by moonlight, or reclined
> At midday upon beds of forest moss,
> Have we to Nature and her impulses
> Of our whole being made free gift, and when
> Our trance had left us, oft have we, by aid
> Of the impressions which it left behind,
> Looked inward on ourselves, and learned, perhaps,
> Something of what we are.
>
> (*PW* V, 343–344)

In each of these passages, I would suggest, Wordsworth makes substantially the same point. He notes the self-evident and yet mysterious bond of feeling that links our minds and hearts to the external world, and states that by reflecting on this fact we shall grow in self-knowledge and dignity. In *The Tables Turned* he suggests further that by doing so we shall learn more than by perusing the "barren leaves" of such systematic moralists as Godwin and Paley, who secure conviction by appealing to the categories of the demonstrative reason. Although its form is exaggerated, the point made by "William" is not, then, anti-intellectual. Wordsworth is not seeking to substitute an unthinking and instinctive communion with nature for the life of reason proper to man, but is rather pointing to the proper use of reason. The impulse of this vernal wood will teach us only if we reflect upon its spiritual and cosmological implications. Wordsworth's ultimate injunction in each of these passages, as in the *Lines* on the yew tree, is the Delphic aphorism cherished by Coleridge, "know thyself."

The question of Wordsworth's religious beliefs offers a second example of the difficulty of deducing a systematic doctrine from a poetry that seeks to transcend system. The poet of 1798 is frequently described as a "pantheist," a term that, at the lowest level of interpretation, calls up an uncritical primitivist, who not only animated but deified material things, rocks and stones and trees. The term suggests, as well, that he was self-consciously heterodox and that he regarded the Christian revelation as false. And it implies that he subscribed to the logical corollaries of a systematic pantheism: that he rejected the distinction between God as creator and nature as created, and denied the possibility or the necessity of grace. If we examine the evidence for such beliefs, we find again that they must be inferred from a poetry that is guided to its objects by feeling, and not by the methods of systematic exposition; the edifice of Wordsworth's philosophy is illuminated by a spotlight of passionate attention, which leaves much in permanent obscurity. That he very seldom names God in 1798 can be adduced, for example, as evidence that he worshipped nature as God; but it can also be ascribed to the conditions of a poetry that sought above all to direct attention and feeling to images, and thus refused to personify a God who was in truth invisible. The principal evidence for Wordsworth's pantheism, however, is a number of passages in which he directs religious feeling— gratitude, reverence, and love—toward nature, and asserts the existence in the temporal world of a "spirit," "mind," or "life" that he never explicitly identifies with God or with matter. Such passages are of course compatible with a systematic pantheism, but they are also compatible with beliefs far more orthodox: a conception of a Trinitarian God that is both immanent and transcendent, and a created world that is the visible handiwork and instrument of its creator. This is the universe promised Milton's Adam by Michael; implied in the Hawkshead poems, it is explicit in *Descriptive Sketches;* and there is no reason to assume that Wordsworth had rejected it in 1798. To assert that a "spirit . . . rolls through all things" is, strictly speaking, no more or less pantheistic than to assert that the "spirit of God moved upon the face of the waters." In both cases a human language constrained to categories of time and space struggles to express the mystery of a God whose presence is indubitable, who has not deserted his creation, and who yet remains unquestionably transcendent.

On the few occasions when Wordsworth places the created world in express relation to God, furthermore, his language is quite orthodox. Even at the height of a "visitation from the living God," as he perceives an "unutterable love" in the morning clouds, the young pedlar "did not feel the God; he felt his works" (*PW* V, 382, ll. 134–136). God is invisible, but his love can be seen and felt in his works—a distinction that is quite impossible to a pantheist. In the first draft of the poem that would become *The Prelude,* in the late fall of 1798, Wordsworth drew a similar distinction, citing as matter for a "loftier song" than his the "breeze" of feeling sent into the infant mind by an "eternal spirit" whose life is in "unimaginable things," and who paints "what he is in all / The visible imagery of all the world" (*Prelude,* p. 636). Here he echoes St. Paul: "For the invisible things of him from the creation of the world are clearly seen, being understood by the things that are made, even his eternal power and Godhead" (*Romans* I.20). In both passages Wordsworth conceives of the phenomenal world as the visible language of an invisible God. His religious celebration of nature is not, therefore, *prima facie* evidence of pantheism. The very literalism of his descriptive style in 1798 is a tacit acknowledgment that the "visible imagery" of the natural world is sanctioned by divine power. Never, furthermore, does he render the "unimaginable" visible by employing the divine analogy or by manufacturing images for God. In a spirit that he would in later years identify as Hebraic, he refuses to impose the "bondage of definite form" upon what is literally invisible (*PW* II, 439). His lack of alarm before the spectacle of "Jehovah—with his thunder, and the choir / Of shouting Angels"(*PW* V, 4, ll. 33–34) does not imply a lack of piety, as Blake thought, but a devout refusal to bow before idols manufactured by the human imagination. He rejects an anthropomorphic image of God on the grounds that justified Blake's own rejection of "Nobodaddy." On behalf of both truth and piety, therefore, his poetry employs the images given by God through nature and scrupulously respects the autonomy of their being.

Rendered equally ambiguous by the form in which it is presented is the epistomology assumed by Wordsworth in 1798. That he places great emphasis on the "language of the sense" has long been recognized, as has the further possibility that he therefore conceived of the mind as essentially passive, as in the Lockean psychology. Although Arthur Beatty has argued this position forcefully, other critics have perceived quite different emphases. René Wellek finds, for example, that the poet "disconcertingly vacillates" between rival theories of perception, and Melvin Rader states that this question is the "great paradox" of the philosophical poetry.[7] We may recall that this paradox was assumed by Wordsworth as a schoolboy, and that his earliest conception of poetry was molded by poets who stressed the active powers of the mind as opposed to its objects: the power of creating images and the contribution of the senses to the act of perception. In his role as lyric poet, at least, he approached Locke from a subversive perspective, and it is probable that he never regarded the mind as a passive artifact of experience. His inheritance from the empirical tradition was a conception of the mind as both active and passive, a conception that was in turn invested with highly personal moral and religious significance by his own experience. It is not difficult, then, to see why in 1798 he should stress both roles of the mind. Since his Cambridge days he had celebrated the power of natural influence, and now he passionately exhorts a "wise passiveness" that receives "nature's shapes as she has made them." It is equally clear, however, that Wordsworth never minimized the active powers of the mind. Since the first *Salisbury Plain* his dramatic characters exemplify, one after the other, the derangement and introversion of these powers, whether they take the form of the "meddling intellect," the delusive imagination, or the egotism of the will, and in 1798 he seeks to discipline and redeem these powers by placing them in contact with the authentic and complementary powers of the external world. As Wordsworth presents the act of perception at this time, therefore, it is both active and passive. He emphasizes the formative power of natural imagery and traces images as they move into the observing mind. But he is equally insistent, in contradiction of Locke, that the reception of such images is itself an action, an excursive affirmation of the human spirit. A poem like *A Night-piece* makes quite clear that the very passivity with which a sublime revelation is received is intensely active, and that objective and subjective energies reciprocate in the act of perception. He thus insists that the young pedlar had an "active power" to fix images on his mind, and in *Tintern Abbey* echoes Edward Young's salute to senses that "half-create the wondrous world they see." In a fragment of blank verse perhaps composed during the spring he describes the senses as "godlike faculties" that "colour, model, and combine / The things perceived" with an energy that is "absolute" and "essential" (*PW* V, 343). Here, and in other passages, he goes far beyond his models and seeks to define a way of seeing that is itself an act of love and reverence.

Like the immanence of a transcendent God, the activity of a "wise passiveness" is a mystery, which Wordsworth's most successful poetry succeeds in dramatizing. In February or March, for example, he described the young pedlar's perception of the moon:

> there would he stand
> In the still covert of some [?lonesome] rock,
> Or gaze upon the moon until its light
> Fell like a strain of music on his soul
> And seem'd to sink into his very heart.
>
> (*PW* V, 340)

Like *The Ruined Cottage* or the *Lyrical Ballads,* this short paragraph is a presentational structure, which employs imagery, rhythm, sound effects and syntax to govern point of view and to imply feeling. In the first two lines the boy is presented as a passive onlooker, who stands in the shelter of a natural enclosure that is equally passive. But in the third line he appears in a situation of visual exposure, a change signaled by long modulated vowels and a euphonious repetition of [n]—"or gaze upon the moon." Both of these first finite verbs, " [would] stand" and "gaze," emphasize the active powers of the subject. In the subordinate clause that follows, however, the vector of relationship is reversed, and light moves into the mind with a power that is extrinsic. "Fell," in effect, stands in apposition to "gaze"; both verbs describe different modes of the same process. The conjunction "until" suggests not only a lapse of time but causation; the boy's gaze is so intense that the moon responds abundantly and charitably. He asks, and nature gives.

We may note, furthermore, that Wordsworth's diction is strictly disciplined according to the epistemological status of its referent. Nouns that refer to sensible objects are absolutely literal—"rock," "moon," "light"—and those that name the subject are only slightly less so—"soul" and "heart." Rhythm and trope emphasize the verbs that link subject and object. Placed in emphatic positions within the line, these form a sequence that traces a crescendo of subjective excitement—"stand," "gaze"—and a diminuendo of objective response—"fell," "sink." As the only initial trochee in the passage, "fell" receives great rhythmical stress, which emphasizes the mass or substance of light. In the following simile, "like a strain of music," synaethesia disciplines the materialistic implications of "fell" and suggests both the strained intensity of hearing and the sensuous pleasure that is sought. Related back to the boy's mind by the finite verb "seem'd," the infinitive "to sink" extends and completes the motion implied by "fell." Light no longer descends toward the surface of the boy's mind, but penetrates, with rich tactile implications, "into" its substance, and approaches a state of rest in his heart.

Whether our terms are rhetorical or philosophical, such a poetry is extremely difficult to define. Here as in other work of 1798 "one feels," in David Perkins' words, "that the symbolic becomes literal." [8] Our rhetorical tools seem inadequate, as is suggested by the oxymoronic coinages prompted by the attempt to describe this style: "objective metaphor," "reality-metaphor," or "concrete-metaphor." [9] Nor does this passage permit us to describe the poet's conception of the mind as either active or passive, because it is so clearly both. His style seeks, indeed, to preclude such questions, and dramatizes the living vacillations that embody epistemological equilibrium, and, for Wordsworth, human dignity and liberty in the natural world. Although imagery suggests the physical contact of the two substances of Cartesian dualism, it refuses to surrender the distinction between them; as it sinks into the mind, external substance retains a distinct and independent being. Neither mind nor object trespasses on the existence of the other, and yet both enjoy intimate communion. Herbert Lindenberger has described this "rhetoric of interaction" as a "radical attempt to fuse inner and outer," and John Jones has said of Wordsworth that "he never clutches, he shows no eagerness to merge." [10] The process dramatized in this passage falls somewhere between these two extremes, in a realm that preserves the mystery of experience.

It is noteworthy, too, that this passage is rendered unique not by its philosophical assumptions, but by the passionate interpretation imposed on those assumptions. The "fact" assumed here is a commonplace of Lockean psychology, that images are literally sent into the mind by experience, or, as Wordsworth had put it at Hawkshead, that life throws pictures on the "mental tablet" (*Vale of Esthwaite*, l. 566). It is the poet's feelings that transfigure this fact, and the quality of these feelings belongs to Wordsworth and no one else. Behind the trochee that weights "fell," for example, lies the personal gratitude that awoke in 1794 when such gravitational imagery first appeared in his poetry. The tactile implications of "sink into" embody the appeal to touch that rescued the schoolboy from the "abyss of idealism," and, more broadly, a desire to unite image and substance, secondary and primary qualities, and "to combine / In one appearance, all the elements /

And parts of the same object" (*Prelude* II. 247–249). In other metaphorical verbs that appear in 1798, "feed" and "drink," Wordsworth calls not only upon Christian and sacramental associations, but on the imagery of physical and spiritual starvation that had shadowed the Racedown poems. Such verse is "philosophical" in that it dramatizes a scientific fact toward which it directs intense feeling. Its effect may be described in terms Wordsworth applied in later years to the epitaph: "The object being looked at through this medium, parts and proportions are brought into distinct view which before had been only imperfectly or unconsciously seen: it is truth hallowed by love" (*PW* V, 452). In Coleridge's fine metaphor, Wordsworth's poetry is his "Philosophy under the action of the strong winds of Feeling—a sea rolling high" (*STCL* II, 957).

Coleridge himself regularly displays philosophical aspirations in the poetry composed at this time, but such passionate dramatizations of the act of perception are quite foreign to his genius. When he attempted to celebrate the "language of the sense," for example, the result was this:

> With other ministrations thou, O nature!
> Healest thy wandering and distempered child:
> Thou pourest on him thy soft influences,
> Thy sunny hues, fair forms, and breathing sweets,
> Thy melodies of woods, and winds, and waters,
> Till he relent. . . .
>
> (*The Dungeon*, ll. 20–25)

As Lindenberger points out, Coleridge has "merely explained the process of interaction without successfully reenacting it." [11] It is evident from both the form and diction of the passage that he is not moved as Wordsworth is by his subject, the process that links nature and mind. As he surveys a series of nature's gifts, his diction betrays a sense that a philosophical vocabulary is inappropriate to verse and that it must be adorned. He personifies nature far more violently than his friend and draws his language from the conventional poetic vocabulary of natural influence that Wordsworth had employed in 1792, when he had personified a "doubly pitying Nature" that showered its "healing pow'r" on the human heart (*Descriptive Sketches,* ll. 13–14). Such terms shunt feeling away from the object to a conventional human interpretation of that object and suggest what is plain in the letters of the time, that Coleridge did not share a "matter-of-factness" that proceeded from Wordsworth's highly personal feelings for nature.

Like other aspects of his philosophy, then, Wordsworth's epistemology cannot be separated from the poetic and often presentational form in which it appears, a form that tends to render it equivocal when subjected to systematic analysis. In each of the cases we have examined, it is also clear that failure to appreciate the conditions imposed by his poetry encourages interpretations that cast what John Jones has called "a conventional romantic haze" over his art.[12] Overemphasis on the pantheism, mysticism, or animism of the naturalism leads to the charge that Wordsworth's poetry is "primitive" or indeed "infantile" in character.[13] It is worthwhile, therefore, to remind ourselves that the poet was deeply serious in his claim to "truth, general and operative," and that the work of 1798 is the product not only of a private vision of nature but of a concerted attempt to reconcile that vision with the established general truths of human experience. To condescend to Wordsworth on the ground that he was less than intellectually responsible is not only profoundly unjust, but it seriously limits our understanding of his greatest poems.

It is seldom recognized, for example, that the language in which Wordsworth presents his vision of nature is selected with the semantic precision and the etymological sophistication that appears elsewhere in the *Lyrical Ballads.* When the speaker of *The Tables Turned* claims that "there are powers / Which of themselves our minds impress," the term "powers" is not intended to represent the passionate personification of an uncritical animist.[14] Wordsworth uses it as Locke had used it, to denote the forces that act upon consciousness from without, without assuming unjustified knowledge of the intrinsic nature or cause of those forces.[15] The term thus implies a reluctance to personify that is hardly characteristic of an animist. A grander example of Wordsworth's linguistic rigor is offered by the philosophical centerpiece of *Tintern Abbey,* in which he weaves a passionately personal confession of faith out of three distinct vocabularies that reconcile the traditions that had shaped his intellectual and emotional life: Protestantism, humanism, and empirical science.

> And I have felt
> A presence that disturbs me with the joy
> Of elevated thoughts; a sense sublime
> Of something far more deeply interfused,
> Whose dwelling is the light of setting suns,
> And the round ocean, and the living air,
> And the blue sky, and in the mind of man,
> A motion and a spirit, that impels
> All thinking things, all objects of all thought,
> And rolls through all things.
>
> (ll. 93–102)

Wordsworth's first name for the object of his perception is "presence," a word that calls upon memories of the Old and New Testaments and *Paradise Lost,* where it implies man's power to perceive the immanence of God:

> God is as here, and will be found alike
> Present, and of his presence many a sign
> Still following thee . . . .
>
> (*Paradise Lost* XI. 350–352)

Attention then passes, in a characteristic movement, from object to subject; the effect of this "presence" upon the mind is "joy" and "elevated thoughts." In the next sentence this relation is stated in the reverse order: the speaker's "sense" of the object, which he now calls "something." Although this unassuming noun frequently disguises intellectual apathy, it here reflects an attempt to adhere rigorously to the limits of human knowledge. Like "powers," it draws its significance from the empiricist's attempt to discriminate what can be known from what cannot. "It is past controversy," Locke had written, "that we have in ourselves *something* that thinks; our very doubts about what it is, confirm the certainty of its being." [16] In his *Light of Nature Pursued,* Abraham Tucker had employed the word to designate the other substance of Cartesian dualism: "the word Something, if then there be a meaning in the word, you may take . . . for your idea of Substance." [17] As J. W. Beach and B. R. Schneider have pointed out, the participle that qualifies this "something" calls upon the authority of the classical tradition. "Interfused" echoes Anchises' celebrated description of the universal mind, which is to the visible world as the soul is to the body: "totamque infusa per artus / mens agitat molem." [18] This passage was by no means esoteric; it spans the history of eighteenth-century naturalism, from Shaftesbury, who cited it in his *Moralists,* to Erasmus Darwin, who selected it as the epigraph for his *Zoonomia,* a work Wordsworth consulted when composing *Goody Blake and Harry Gill.* Virgil's term is in turn compatible with the Newtonian conception of the created universe as the sensorium of God, as is implied by the rigorously defined and immensely comprehensive categories of Wordsworth's climactic lines. He presents a universe in which physical "motion" is paralleled to theological "spirit," asserts the existence of both motion and spirit in all living consciousnesses, in all "objects" perceived by those consciousnesses, and states, finally, that it is communicated "through" all "things" that possess corporeal substance.[19] In the *Lyrical Ballads* Wordsworth sought to bind poet and audience together in a community of Christian charity. Here he binds classical, Protestant, and empirical ideas into a grand consensus or "commonalty" of truth, which recovers the confident syncretism of his first surviving poem, the "School Exercise." Inspired by a highly personal vision of nature, he nevertheless presents this vision in terms that are not only public but normative and comprehensive. Unlike Blake, who sought to "Create a

System" in the fear of being "enslav'd by another Man's," Wordsworth constructs a language that is Miltonic in historical and philosophical scope, a language that testifies to the urgency with which he sought to locate "truth" beyond the confines of the individual mind.

One may observe, furthermore, that here, as throughout the work of 1798, Wordsworth adopts a rhetorical perspective that is epistemologically critical, in that it continuously distinguishes between object and subject. At the outset of the passage he informs us that what follows is something he has "felt," ascribing it to his own subjective experience. The effect of this admission is not to invalidate what follows, but to establish the speaker as a man who can distinguish between what is in his own mind and what is out of it, a man of reason, truth, and good sense. The uncritical enthusiast, on the other hand, would predicate the truth of his vision flatly, without self-consciousness. He might say, simply, that "there is a presence there," or in the *Lines Written in Early Spring* that "there is pleasure there" in the wind and trees (1. 20). He would not inform his reader that he was struggling against such an impression: "And I must think, do all I can, / That there was pleasure there" (ll. 19–20). Nor in the poem, *To My Sister,* would the enthusiast affirm the existence of a "blessing" that "is" in the air, and then delicately modulate his assertion by noting that it "seems" to yield its joy to visible objects (ll. 5–6). All such terms focus our attention on the mind of the observer, whose perspective on a given object is both defined and dissociated from ours. We are urged, that is, to look into another mind from a point of view that is self-consciously external to that mind, a point of view that is implicitly critical and normative.

John Jones has noted Wordsworth's "instinct to place the thinking subject on his one hand and the object of his thought on the other." [20] If we consider its implications, however, such a perspective would seem to involve more than instinct. Because it comprehends both object and subject in a single field of view, it is epistemologically critical; it offers the hope, that is, of separating object from subject and is the characteristic posture of the philosopher who seeks *a priori* knowledge of the external world (or the possibility of such knowledge), and indeed of any man who suspects the "idols of the mind" and seeks to bind it to nature. When the subject disappears from the field of view, on the other hand, point of view becomes uncritical; as seen from the subject, the object can be either appearance or reality, projection or substance. If this is the characteristic posture of the unselfconscious enthusiast or mystic, it is a rare and temporary extreme in those of Wordsworth's earlier poems that claim philosophic authority. Since 1793 he had dramatized deranged modes of perception from a viewpoint that insisted upon its autonomy from the subject and its own lucid view of the object, and in 1798 the critical perspective provides the prevailing norm. When the moon appears in *A Night-piece,* for example, it is at once set in opposition to the mind of a "musing man." In implicit tribute to the sublimity and power of the skyscape, however, the poet's point of view then joins the "man's" in rapt and comparatively uncritical contemplation. In the concluding lines we see the "mind" settling into calm from a perspective that is once again external and critical. Similar perspectives govern the credal lyrics, the philosophical blank verse of early spring, and many of the great blank verse pictures of the first book of *The Prelude.* In the stolen boat episode, for example, point of view shifts delicately between that of the boy, who suffers delusion, and that of the adult speaker, who perceives this delusion naturalistically, as the effect of an optical illusion brought on by the boy's own activity.

Although Coleridge is seldom accused of primitivism or animism, his perspective is characteristically less critical than Wordsworth's. His poems tend to depart from a philosophical and empirical perspective, on behalf of an idealism that ultimately loses all sense of the equilibrium between mind and object. He begins, that is, by adopting the subject's point of view, and moves toward an apprehension of its object so intense as to annihilate self-consciousness altogether. This happens not only in the supernatural poems, but in the so-called conversation poems, where the "common range of visible things" repeatedly suffers a sea-change toward or into the marvelous. In *The Nightingale,* for example, Coleridge employs a deliberately presentational style, and with Wordsworthian techniques achieves an intensity of effect quite foreign to Wordsworth's genius:

> On moonlight bushes,
> Whose dewy leafits are but half disclos'd,
> You may perchance behold them on the twigs,
> Their bright, bright eyes, their eyes both bright and full,
> Glistening . . . .
>
> (ll. 64–68)

From Wordsworth's point of view, such transfiguration of mundane reality very probably seemed reprehensible on both philosophic and moral grounds. By enhancing nature surreptitiously, Coleridge is not only courting the solipsism that Wordsworth would regard as the characteristic posture of a mind "debarr'd from Nature's living images" (*Prelude* VI. 313), but, in adorning the external thing, is condescending to it and to its creator. Coleridge is not at all concerned to subject the imagination to the discipline of sensible phenomena, and the theoretical differences between the two prophets of nature, if here only incipient, are quite profound. Like Blake, Coleridge's deepest affiliations are to an idealistic tradition that identifies naturalism with materialism, and in the passage above he employs a style that implicitly asserts the hegemony of the mind over its objects. His purpose, he would recall, was to secure a species of belief in the "shadows of the imagination"—a purpose that assents in principle to the gulf between poetry and objective truth that Wordsworth sought to bridge. It is just such a "suspension of disbelief" that Wordsworth's characteristic perspective avoids imposing on the reader; he does not seek to "build that dome in air," but to celebrate what is given, "the bare trees, and mountains bare, / And grass in the green field." In the stolen boat episode of *The Prelude,* for example, he does not seek to impose the boy's vision on the reader—to secure a "belief" that a mountain has become an avenging pursuer —but to secure an appreciation of the role of such visions, considered as subjective facts, in the growth of the mind. It is Wordsworth's distrust of a subjective poetry that in 1800 led him to subtitle *The Ancient Mariner* a "Poet's Reverie"—a dream—and in 1798 inspired him to the virtually impossible task of rewriting Coleridge's ballad within a naturalistic and philosophical perspective in *Peter Bell.* It is frequently assumed that Wordsworth is a consummate impressionist; as Donald Davie has written, "he renders not the natural world but (with masterful fidelity) the effect that world has upon him." [21] This is of course true; if we believe that all viewpoints are equally subjective, it is true of all poetry and indeed all human utterance. Wordsworth, however, does not in 1798 assent to such relativism. He offers us an impression, but he also offers us the opportunity to look at this impression from a normalized and implicitly universal perspective, in which object and subject mutually guarantee one another's authenticity. He would gradually surrender this emphasis, and in 1815 would define the duty of the poet as the presentation of things "not as they *are,* but as they *appear"* (*PW* II, 410; Wordsworth's italics). In 1798, however, he writes in the faith expressed in *Peter Bell,* that "good men" could "feel the soul of nature,/And see things as they are" (ll. 764–765).

As a last reminder that Wordsworth cannot be considered an uncritical enthusiast, we may take the obvious corollary of his philosophical perspective, the fact that in 1798, as throughout the Racedown years, he engages in a deliberate and rigorous disciplining of the fabricative or creative imagination. His emphasis lies in the passionate reception of nature's shapes "as she has made them" (*Prelude,* p. 566), as the biography of the young pedlar makes clear:

> deep feelings had impressed
> Great objects on his mind, with portraiture

And outline [colour] so distinct that on his thought [mind]
They lay like substances . . . .

(PW V, 381, ll. 81–84; DCP)

These images are a "precious gift" (l. 86); preserved unchanged in
the memory they comprise the boy's "ideal stores" (l. 88)—a
store of ideas—and provide a touchstone of value and significance
in later life.[22] Wordsworth in fact names the imagination itself
quite rarely in 1798 and commonly presents the process of perception as a mysterious interaction of feeling and sensation. But
the power he describes is clearly the imagination in its "primary"
aspect, the mediator of intuitive and comprehensive response to
the sensible world. It was probably in the spring of 1798 that he
added to his *Lines* on the yew-tree a reference to the "holy forms
/ Of young imagination" (ll. 48–49), that is, the images given to
the young mind by nature. In the additions to *The Ruined Cottage*
the term describes the power nourished by local "legend," and is
associated with that "apprehensive power / By which [the mind]
is made quick to recognize / The moral properties and scopes of
things" (*PW* V, 383, ll. 169–73). The imagination of the mature
pedlar "condenses" the conclusions of his thought into a "passion" (*PW* V, 403, ll. 108–110), mediating between reason and
the heart, and implicitly fusing both thought and feeling with sensation. Thus Wordsworth does not deny the imagination any more
than Samuel Johnson denied it; without an "atmosphere of sensation in which to move his wings" the poet is helpless, and within
the terms of the vocabulary inherited by Wordsworth his necessary
dependence on sensation and feeling was a dependence on "imagination." But he strictly disciplines the visionary power he had indulged at Hawkshead, the transformational power he would celebrate in 1804 and after, and the "romantic imagination" as it is
loosely conceived by modern readers. His fear of subjective delusion and his reverence for the images given by nature combine to
produce a passionate empiricism. Only rarely, when he is imitating the language of undisciplined minds, such as those of the In-

dian Woman or the speaker of *The Thorn,* does the Wordsworth of 1798 impose the rhetorical effect of an imagination excited to the point of delusion, passionate personification, upon his readers.

Wordsworth's distrust of the fabricative imagination may be inferred from his style, but it is made explicit by one of the few theoretical observations on this subject that survive from these years, a marginal comment on a landscape in *Paradise Lost.* Noting that Milton's work is "inimitably picturesque," he continues:

> It has been said of poets as their highest praise that they exhausted worlds and then imagined new, that existence saw them spurn her bounded reign &c. But how much of the most valuable part of the poet's province [consists in] how much of the real excellence of Imagination consists in the capacity of exploring the world really existing & thence selecting objects beautiful or great as the occasion may require.[23]

Such sentiments are thoroughly classical in spirit, and they in fact echo the critic John Scott, whose epistemological rigor had influenced the style of *An Evening Walk.* In the course of his commentary on *Lycidas,* Scott had cited Milton as evidence of the fact that "imagination, properly directed, will not be employed in producing impossible fictions, but in exploring real existence, and selecting from it circumstances grand or beautiful, as occasion may require." To this observation he appends a note that could be duplicated in the writings of Pope, Addison, or Johnson, and which quite accurately summarizes Wordsworth's attitude toward the imagination in 1798: "without imagination, no man can be a poet at all; without imagination and judgement, no man can be a good poet."[24]

It is noteworthy, moreover, that the enthusiastic encomium of the visionary imagination which Wordsworth cites as a foil to Scott's realism does not derive from a "pre-romantic" source, from the Wartons or the young John Aikin, for example. As Bishop Hunt has pointed out, it is found in Samuel Johnson's *Prologue,* "spoken by Mr. Garrick at the opening of the theatre in Drury Lane, 1747":

Each Change of many-colour'd Life he drew,
Exhausted Worlds, and then imagin'd new;
Existence saw him spurn her bounded Reign,
And panting Time toil'd after him in vain.

(ll. 3–6)

Now, although Wordsworth repeatedly disagreed with Johnson on matters of diction and taste, he was not under the impression that such an "enthusiastic" encomium of Shakespeare was representative of Johnson's criticism. He was not unaware that Johnson agreed with Scott, as the latter frequently acknowledges, or that the author of *The Vanity of Human Wishes, Rasselas,* and the Preface to Shakespeare had devoted his life to the reclamation of the imagination to truth, defined as "things really existing." We must read this comment, that is, in the paradoxical spirit Wordsworth had demonstrated in the *Lyrical Ballads,* or indeed in *An Evening Walk,* where he had directed his reader to Scott in order to emphasize his own superiority to the greatest nature-poet of the century, James Thomson. He deliberately quotes Johnson in an "enthusiastic" moment, in order to place himself to the classical side of the greatest classicist of the century. He turns the tables on Johnson, implying that he has carried his premises to their logical and ultimate conclusions.

That Wordsworth should now cite John Scott does not imply that this particular critic had a dominant influence on his development. It was the poet's own experience that rendered "things really existing" a supremely adequate object for poetry, and Scott's views are by no means unique. But the reference does suggest that in 1798 Wordsworth perceived his poetic development since 1788 as a continuous discipline of art on behalf of truth, and, more specifically, on behalf of the classical, Protestant, and scientific truths he had upheld since his Hawkshead years. He repeatedly attributed his development to his determination to look steadily at the object, and we do not mistake his purposes if we compare them to those of the only philosopher he had mentioned in the "School Exercise" of 1785, and to the comprehensive and

exalted ambitions that inspired the *Great Instauration:* "And all depends," Bacon wrote, "on keeping the eye steadily fixed upon the
facts of nature and so receiving their images simply as they are.
For God forbid that we should give out a dream of our own imagination for a pattern of the world; rather may he graciously grant
to us to write an apocalypse or true vision of the footsteps of the
Creator imprinted on his creatures." [25]

It is this union of religious vision with scientific positivism
which survives in the philosophical poetry of 1798, and which
presents modern criticism with its most formidable task—that of
simultaneously honoring values that have become even more
deeply estranged in our day than in the poet's. An authentic and
living spiritual illumination, Wordsworth's philosophy is private,
idiosyncratic, and enthusiastic. And yet it is also the product of a
mind that, in 1798, was deeply concerned to avoid idiosyncrasy
and relativism, a mind that sought rest in the stability and permanence of truth. If he offers us a lofty and esoteric vision of the
"one life," he nevertheless viewed his art as a "science of feelings"
(*PW* II, 513), presented it as an "experiment" (*PW* II, 383), and
asked that he be understood in no "mystical and idle sense" (*Prelude* II. 235). And some years later, in the course of a prayer not
to nature but to God, he described his highest purpose as that of
parting "inherent things from casual, what is fix'd / From what is
fleeting, " so that his song might live

> and be
> Even as a light hung up in heaven to chear
> The world in times to come.
>
> (*PW* V, 5–6, ll. 88–92 *app. crit.*)

II

The great milestones of Wordsworth's life are his homecomings.
In 1788, 1789, and 1794, returns to the Lakes had issued in work

that not only celebrated his "native regions" but confronted and assessed subjective change. In the spring of 1797 he embarked on a series of imaginary returns to the yew-tree of Esthwaite and the river Derwent, and, a year later, to the sublime landscapes that begin the pedlar's biography. In two ballads of 1798 he returned in thought to a landscape nearer in time and space, the River Wye.

There is thus an element of premeditation in his decision, early in July, to revisit the "green pastoral landscape" that had received him five years earlier, after his lonesome journey across Salisbury Plain. It is as if Wordsworth again sought an authentic occasion for a comprehensive summing-up, an affirmation of recovery from the third and greatest crisis of his life. And the poem came, as Albert Gérard has noted,[26] as if it were something given. Composition began at once, and ended as he and Dorothy walked down the hill into Bristol, where the poem was written down without altering a line and given to Cottle, the publisher of the *Lyrical Ballads* (*PW* II, 517). A month later it appeared as the concluding poem in the volume, under the title of "Lines, written a few miles above Tintern Abbey, on revisiting the banks of the Wye during a tour, July 13, 1798."

It is the element of premeditation that illuminates the many paradoxes of this great poem, which may be approached as a deliberate attempt to reenact the returns of the past. Like *An Evening Walk*, *Tintern Abbey* begins by asserting return to a concrete landscape. Its second movement, which itself has three parts, is shaped by the reverent obedience of the pedlar; the speaker enumerates the gifts he has received from nature, relinquishes his own past in the consciousness that any protest against "ruin and change" constitutes an indictment of natural law, and builds to a triumphant assertion of continued faith and love. Like several of Wordsworth's ballads, the *Lines* on the yew tree, and the conclusion of Coleridge's *Frost at Midnight*, the concluding movement is a benediction which confers these gifts on a human listener, the poet's sister. So described, the poem may be regarded as the imitation of an ideal response to a given object, a response that by 1798 had become a well-defined ritual of gratitude and love. It dramatizes an "enthusiastic admiration of Nature, and a sensibility to her influences" that Wordsworth would in later years oppose to the assumed enthusiasm of such imitators as the author of *Childe Harold* (*LY*, I, 130) and venture to compare in form and intensity to an ode (*PW* II, 517).

What we hear in the poem, however, is not simply this premeditated ritual of gratitude, affirmation, and benediction, but the struggle of the speaker to adhere to it, in the presence of adversaries that render his success a triumph. And this effect is in turn dependent on the form of the poem, a presentational structure of immense complexity and eloquence which for the first time in Wordsworth's career is allowed to imitate the full range of his own consciousness. He now surrenders the two technical devices that in earlier poems had disciplined subjective response, a fictitious persona and an emphatic meter. He relies, as it were, completely on himself, and the form of his blank verse therefore registers a new depth of personal response: fear of psychological disequilibrium, of betrayal by natural law, and, most obviously, of personal decay and loss. The poem is thus autobiographically comprehensive in a dramatic sense: as Wordsworth struggles toward and attains psychological and epistemological equilibrium, trust in nature, and hope, he reenacts not only past returns to a beloved landscape but the great psychological and moral crises of his life.

The opening paragraph is both crucial and controversial, and it is well to quote it in full:

> Five years have passed; five summers, with the length
> Of five long winters! and again I hear
> These waters, rolling from their mountain-springs
> With a sweet inland murmur.—Once again
> Do I behold these steep and lofty cliffs,
> Which on a wild secluded scene impress

Thoughts of more deep seclusion; and connect
The landscape with the quiet of the sky.
The day is come when I again repose
Here, under this dark sycamore, and view
These plots of cottage-ground, these orchard-tufts,
Which, at this season, with their unripe fruits,
Among the woods and copses lose themselves,
Nor, with their green and simple hue, disturb
The wild green landscape. Once again I see
These hedge-rows, hardly hedge-rows, little lines
Of sportive wood run wild; these pastoral farms
Green to the very door; and wreathes of smoke
Sent up, in silence, from among the trees,
With some uncertain notice, as might seem,
Of vagrant dwellers in the houseless woods,
Or of some hermit's cave, where by his fire
The hermit sits alone.
                                        (ll. 1–22 *app. crit.*)

Although Danby finds this landscape "strangely inert" and several details "scarcely in fact relevant," most critics have read it as an enthusiastic affirmation of nature, an overture to the grand confession of faith that follows. "After the 'soft inland murmur,' the 'one green hue,' the 'wreathes of smoke . . . ,'" writes W. K. Wimsatt, "it is an easy leap to the 'still, sad music of humanity,' and

                    a sense sublime
Of something far more deeply interfused,
Whose dwelling is the light of setting suns."

In the speaker's matter-of-factness Hartman finds "an affection to external nature which cannot be more than stated, nor can the objects of it be more than described." Taking issue with both Danby and Hartman, Gérard reads the poem as an organic dialogue between Wordsworth's empirical and prophetic voices, and finds this landscape a quintessential specimen of romantic symbolism, which unites the concrete and the universal, and embodies a "cosmic unity" of man, God, and nature.[27]

If we examine closely the style of the passage from *Tintern Abbey,* however, asking not only what it says but what it does, such readings are difficult to sustain. The form of the paragraph is molded by passionate attention not to natural objects, but to an idea: a distinction between transience and permanence, between what has changed and what remains. The objects of feeling implied by the four massive, rolling cadences are things and actions that have not been altered by time. It is "these" very images that were perceived five years before by a speaker who now repossesses the physical situation of past time, "here, under this dark sycamore," and engages in acts of sensation that precisely reenact the past. Five times he names these actions—he hears, beholds, reposes, views, and sees—and four times he prefaces these powerful verbs with the adverb "again." We are thus invited to appreciate the immense significance of those elements in his present situation that reproduce the past, and, less obviously, to sense the equally immense range of what is not mentioned and what may have suffered change.

In the light of Wordsworth's past, what is not mentioned is as important as what is. Nowhere in the passage, for example, is an "affection to external nature" named or indeed implied. Nowhere does the speaker's language embody a response that transcends sensation. Although he will ascribe "beauty" to these "forms" a few lines later (l. 22), the only hint of sensuous pleasure here is the single adjective "sweet," which modifies an invisible sound, not a visible "form," and remains unconfirmed by what follows. Nor is there any evidence in the motion of the speaker's attention that a single natural object has the power to capture his attention, as did the moon in *A Night-piece.* His eye moves almost at random, horizontally and vertically, without settling on any one image. More remarkable is the total absence of syntax or imagery that suggests natural response to the speaker's presence, or the tactile and kinesthetic meeting of mind and external power.

One cannot say that the landscape is "inert," but verbs of natural motion are tangential in vector ("connect") or openly fugitive ("lose themselves"). We look in vain for active verbs that move toward or into the mind, for

> How sweetly *breathes* the air—it *breathes* most sweet

or

> shall *lull* thy mind
> By one soft impulse saved from vacancy.

Here, on the contrary, repeated participles ("rolling," "run wild," "sent up") present nature as a continuous activity that knows no past or future, and suggest its indifference to the speaker's cyclical returns and his repeated "agains." In February or March the verb "impress" had denoted the charity with which nature stamped images on the responsive mind, but here it is bent back upon itself, as the cliffs "impress" the speaker's thoughts on the landscape, not their own images on his mind. Nothing balances the powerful outward vector of the poet's perceptions. He gives, but the landscape does not respond. Nature is passive, problematic, and, at the conclusion of the passage, openly "uncertain."

Such stylistic changes strongly qualify the views of Hartman and Gérard and suggest that this passage dramatizes a state of psychological and epistemological disequilibrium. Judging from *Salisbury Plain,* it was as a literal (and not a symbolic) witness to the unity of nature, man, and God that Wordsworth saw the Wye Valley in 1793, but here such unity is implicitly questioned. As the echoes of Gilpin's *Tour of the Wye* suggest,[28] the harmonies of this scene are aesthetic and indeed picturesque. Like the cold pastoral of Keats's *Grecian Urn* they are self-enclosed, exclusive of the probing energies of the speaker's mind. The state of mind dramatized here closely resembles that which produced Wordsworth's most picturesque poem, *An Evening Walk,* where exclusive emphasis on sensation accompanied return to a landscape that intimated subjective loss. And this, I would suggest, is the implication of the present landscape, which provides the starting point for a struggle to redeem and recreate an "enthusiastic admiration of Nature" in the face of disappointment and implicit decay.

Like those that follow, the second paragraph of *Tintern Abbey* incorporates a dramatically significant strophe, or "turn," of attention, which introduces new temporal and psychological modalities. As the speaker turns away from the visible landscape, he also turns away from sensation and from present time, in order to list the "gifts" he received from this landscape in the past: "sensations" (l. 27), "feelings" (l. 30) and a sublime vision into "the life of things" (ll. 35–49). Such deliberate accumulation of particulars is at once a litany of blessings received and a statement of evidence, and it forms the structural skeleton of the poem, a kind of meditative ladder which ascends emotionally and intellectually toward the "therefore" of line 102 and the triumphant profession of faith that follows. Its immediate effect, furthermore, is to reconstruct both nature and mind. By enumerating nature's gifts, the speaker attributes charity to the unresponsive landscape just described, a charity embodied by an organic imagery that now traces the sensuous penetration of external influence into the heart and mind:

> Felt in the blood, and felt along the heart,
> And passing even into my purer mind
> With tranquil restoration.
>
> (ll. 28–30)

The order in which these gifts are named in turn brings into our field of view a host of subjective responses that transcend sensation and imply the psychological integrity that had been denied by the style of the previous section.

In two respects, however, this measured ascent toward integrity and relationship is qualified as it proceeds. This paragraph does not demonstrate a broader range of subjective response, but recalls it. Feeling and vision are named, not enacted. As the organic imagery suggests, moreover, the poet succeeds in celebrating nature only by turning away from it, and engaging in his most sustained and deliberate act of introspection since the Hawkshead poems. The incompleteness and vulnerability of this subjectivism are emphasized, furthermore, by recurrent glimpses of the object-world of past time, a world of individual isolation ("lonely rooms"), of social confusion and dislocation ("the din/Of towns and cities") and of a mystery that is cosmic in scope and suffocating in effect; a "burthen" and a "heavy and weary weight/Of all this unintelligible world." For the first time in Wordsworth's poetry, kinesthetic imagery embodies a weight of externality that threatens to crush the growth and indeed the existence of mind. Contrasted to this outer world, which grows in scope and power as he proceeds, the speaker's meditative ascent is ironically qualified as subjective and potentially vulnerable to the intrusion of truth.

Dramatic evidence of uncertainty therefore grows in power throughout the first and second paragraphs. Implied in the former by the speaker's insistent positivism, it here takes the visible form of remembered imagery. At the beginning of the third paragraph, however, it encroaches on the speaker's mind itself, and brings his celebration of nature's gifts to a sudden and unpremeditated halt:

> If this
> Be but a vain belief, yet, oh! how oft,
> In darkness, and amid the many shapes
> Of joyless day-light; when the fretful stir
> Unprofitable, and the fever of the world,
> Have hung upon the beatings of my heart,
> How oft, in spirit, have I turned to thee
> O sylvan Wye! Thou wanderer through the woods,
> How often has my spirit turned to thee!
>
> (ll. 49–57)

Wordsworth described this paragraph as a dramatic action, "ejaculated as it were [fortuit]ously in the musical succession [of precon-

ceiv]ed feeling" (*MY*, II, 385), and it constitutes the first spontaneous response in a poem that has so far followed a measured and
"preconceived" course. In the opening lines

> If this
> Be but a vain belief

the "burden of the mystery" takes possession of his mind and
threatens to end his meditation in despair. His response is immediate and powerful:

> yet oh! how oft
> In darkness . . . .

With an alacrity that bespeaks depths of consciousness hitherto
concealed, he corrects an error of thought by appealing to the empirical evidence of remembered feelings—that is, by repeating the
psychological action of paragraph two. But the form of his appeal
is no longer introspective. In the final lines of the paragraph his
memory of the spiritual apostrophes of past time merges before
our eyes with the rhetorical apostrophe of present time:

> How oft, in spirit, have I turned to thee
> O sylvan Wye!

At "O sylvan Wye" he "turns" outward, to the visible landscape
of the first paragraph, with an intensity of feeling embodied by
repetition and the closest approach to passionate personification in
the poem:

> Thou wanderer through the woods,
> How often has my spirit turned to thee!

Although to Gérard this section "gives a definite sense of
anticlimax," [29] it is rather a first conclusive climax and a first victory, as the speaker not only names but demonstrates his capacity
to fuse thought, feeling, and sensation in a single action, and offers visible evidence of the love for nature he will proclaim in the
following lines.

In the fourth paragraph he resumes the meditative ascent of the second, and confronts the fear that has shadowed the poem: that he may have suffered essential decay. For the first time he looks into the future, and asserts that

> in this moment there is life and food
> For future years.

(ll. 64–65)

But retreat begins at once. He qualifies this hope as something dared (l. 65) and admits what was implied at the outset, that he is "changed" (l. 66). He then assesses this change, in a synoptic autobiography that distinguishes three stages of life: boyhood, youth, and maturity. The first of these he dismisses in a parenthesis as a time of "coarser pleasures" and "glad animal movements," but his treatment of youth, which he identifies with his first visit to the Wye, is extended and equivocal. In a justly celebrated passage he recalls its freedom and vitality, a "passion" and a "love" for nature that was indescribable in intensity. But he also distinguishes less exalted responses: "fear" rather than love; "appetite" rather than feeling; and a devotion to visible imagery that justifies his final epithet of "thoughtless youth." To the third stage, maturity, he then assigns two compensating "gifts": a vision of nature that is chastened by consciousness of human mortality, and the sublime vision into the "motion and the spirit" that climaxes the poem.

Although this retrospect has been read as literal autobiography,[30] it is clearly shaped by the speaker's dramatic situation, that of a man who assesses loss in the consciousness that complaint will indict natural law and that protest is morally unacceptable. Wordsworth therefore rearranges the past in a sequence that in several respects is new to his poetry. Although he had celebrated a vision of the "motion and the spirit" since 1792, and earlier in 1798 had assigned a similar vision to the nine-year-old pedlar, he here reserves it to maturity. On the other hand, he subjects the historical past—the state of mind reflected in the poems of 1793 and 1794—to a moral criticism it by no means deserves. The twenty-three-year-old who came to the Wye then was not a "thoughtless youth," nor was he in any sense deaf to the "still, sad music of humanity." The visual "appetite" that drove the traveler across Salisbury Plain was not, as Wordsworth now implies, a naïvely thoughtless naturalism, but the product of traumatic confrontation with an alien nature and with human suffering, and it sought not the lonely and secluded landscape that opens this poem but a pastoral world that bore the "trace of human hands." A few months after leaving the Wye, we may recall, Wordsworth had protested his sense of "mortal change," looking back on the joys of his youth as he now looks back on 1793. At both times, that is, he construes the past, like his eighteenth-century predecessors, as a thoughtless paradise that has been replaced by a conscious humanism.

The motives for such rearrangement would seem clear. By appropriating both a chastened humanism and a sublime vision of nature to maturity, and by subjecting the naturalism of 1793 to an essentially unjust moral criticism, Wordsworth cuts his losses, losses which if acknowledged openly would render impossible the goal to which he aspires, the restoration of relationship to nature. He thus constructs a past that he can relinquish without protest:

> That time is past,
> And all its aching joys are now no more,
> And all its dizzy raptures.
>
> (ll. 83–85)

By uttering these words, which testify to a fortitude that yields to the passage of time without complaint, Wordsworth earns the right to use the language of reason, and indeed of Euclidean demonstration, to introduce the triumphant assertion that climaxes the poem:

> Therefore am I still
> A lover of the meadows and the woods,
> And mountains; and of all that we behold

From this green earth; of all the mighty world
Of eye and ear, both what they half-create,
And what perceive; well pleased to recognize
In nature and the language of the sense,
The anchor of my purest thoughts, the nurse,
The guide, the guardian of my heart, and soul
Of all my moral being.

(ll. 102–111)

It is the ability to say these words, which in their enthusiasm con-
cede virtually no loss at all, that Wordsworth painfully and at
times perilously reconstructs in the presence of a landscape that
had implied a far more problematical view of nature and the "language of the sense." And to pronounce these words with feeling
and sincerity is to reenact the past. By relinquishing what he has
lost, Wordsworth redeems it.

This great testament stands on the meridian-line of the poem,
and, as Gérard has observed, the following and final movement
modulates at once into a lower key of imaginative and emotional
intensity.[31] Intensified accents of uncertainty reappear immediately:

Nor, perchance,
If I were not thus taught, should I the more
Suffer my genial spirits to decay:
For thou art with me. . . .

(ll. 111–114)

The faith so triumphantly affirmed in the previous paragraph
suddenly takes on the status of a hypothesis, as Wordsworth now
names—for the first time in the poem—the object of his fear,
"decay," and simultaneously transfers his deepest trust from nature
to his sister. This "turn" from nature to humanity alters the tone
of the poem fundamentally. A brooding, solitary reconstruction of
relationship to nature now becomes an act of human love, which in
turn permits a far more candid assessment of a loss incident to all

human beings. For a moment, in words that echo the Twenty-third Psalm, all of Wordsworth's trust is reposed in his love for Dorothy, and then the drama of reconstruction begins again. As Dorothy is placed beside the speaker on the banks of "this fair river" (ll. 114–115), love for humanity is enfolded into love for nature, and we begin a second meditative ascent toward the benediction that lies ahead.

As in the third paragraph, however, this forward movement is at once interrupted by an ambush of the speaker's intentions. His apostrophe to Dorothy has involved a return to sensation. What the senses suddenly reveal to him, however, is his own past:

> in thy voice I catch
> The language of my former heart, and read
> My former pleasures in the shooting lights
> Of thy wild eyes.
>
> (ll. 116–119)

In the preceding paragraph he had with great circumspection reconstructed a picture of his "former heart," compared it to the present, and relinquished it without complaint. Now, however, when the same comparison is forced on him by his own senses, "powers which of themselves our minds impress," he is unable to sustain such discipline. Spontaneously and involuntarily, he seeks to halt the flow of time:

> Oh! yet a little while
> May I behold in thee what I was once,
> My dear, dear Sister!
>
> (ll. 119–121)

Wordsworth reaches out toward a vision of his own past that is also Dorothy's present: both brother and sister are by implication suddenly recognized as vulnerable to a temporal flux that sweeps them on even as he watches. This second "ejaculation" of "fortuitous" passion is a profound concession, which acknowledges far more candidly than in paragraph four the immensity of what has been lost, and briefly surrenders the struggle to relinquish it without protest.

Discipline, however, returns, as the speaker, like the pedlar, recovers natural piety. This "prayer" for exemption from natural process, he protests, is made in the knowledge that process is benign:

> And this prayer I make,
> Knowing that Nature never did betray
> The heart that loved her.
>
> (ll. 121–123)

Although this sentiment has been interpreted as a statement of "absolute conviction," which expresses "complete assurance of the benevolence of nature," [32] it is painfully inconsistent with the fear implied by the preceding line and itself wavers uncertainly in tone. The cognitive force of "knowing" is absolute, but it applies purely to past time: the speaker is unable to use the future tense of hope, and to say "Nature never *will* betray / The heart that loves her." He then traces his sister's progress into the future and for the third time in the poem builds through a litany of gifts to a climactic assertion that again merits the language of logical necessity:

> Therefore let the moon
> Shine on thee in thy solitary walk;
> And let the misty mountain winds be free
> To blow against thee.
>
> (ll. 134–137)

This look into Dorothy's future (and by implication into his own past) briefly evokes an imagery that embodies the joy of sensuous contact between mind and nature.

The concluding cadences of the poem imply further concessions to time. Movement of attention now yields to temporal process, exploring a more distant future in which both lives, Dorothy's and

his own, will suffer decay. If she will be ambushed by the pain he
has survived, he takes joy in the knowledge that her memories of
the present moment will heal this pain (ll. 143–146). As he
briefly contemplates his own future, however, the language of
naked uncertainty reappears for the last time, together with negative formulations that refuse to name his fate, and summarize it
simply as deafness and blindness to the object of his love. Like the
Lucy of "A slumber did my spirit seal," he will neither hear nor
see:

> Nor, perchance,
> If I should be, where I no more can hear
> Thy voice, nor catch from thy wild eyes these gleams
> Of past existence, wilt thou then forget . . . .
>
> (ll. 146–149)

Attention then returns to an object that permits hope—Dorothy's
mind in future time—and to the memories that will preserve the
present moment. As the speaker prescribes these memories, he
restates the significance of the entire poem:

> Nor . . . wilt thou then forget
> That on the banks of this delightful stream
> We stood together; and that I, so long
> A worshipper of Nature, hither came,
> Unwearied in that service: rather say
> With warmer love, oh! with far deeper zeal
> Of holier love.
>
> (ll. 146–155)

Wordsworth would defend these lines against the charge of
pantheism by describing them as a dramatic utterance, a "passionate expression uttered incautiously" (*MY*, II, 188). And although
the lines continue to be cited as evidence of his pantheism, a dramatic reading of the poem suggests that they are indeed "uttered
incautiously." Their enthusiasm issues, that is, from the speaker's
consciousness that he is inscribing what amounts to an epitaph for

the present moment, and that his words will not only preserve but delineate what he was at this place and time, a few miles above Tintern Abbey on July 13, 1798. In later discussions of the decorum of epitaphs, Wordsworth would defend a loving idealization of the past,[33] and here, looking back on the present, he impulsively corrects himself twice, exalting the quality of his love for nature within a context that implies the inevitable transience of that love. The sudden outburst of comparatives—

> rather say
> With warmer love, oh! with far deeper zeal
> Of holier love—

testifies, like Martha Ray's unceasing cry, to the indomitable power of the human heart in the face of loss. But Wordsworth's triumph here is still grander, because he insists upon uttering his love for nature in the consciousness that it will inevitably betray him.

Enthusiasm disappears from the speaker's final sentence, which recovers the plain and literal language proper to truth, and restates the essential facts of the poem in a spirit of final acceptance: "speak of them as they are; nothing extenuate."

> Nor wilt thou then forget,
> That after many wanderings, many years
> Of absence, these steep woods and lofty cliffs,
> And this green pastoral landscape, were to me
> More dear, both for themselves, and for thy sake.
> (ll. 155–159)

We again recapitulate the structure of the poem, on a more empirical level, and end on a line that condenses its significance into a last assertion of love, which builds even as the poem dies ("more dear"), and a binding-together of nature and man in a parity that is delicately offset by the intimacy of the final spondee: "aňd fŏr thy sakè." The last word is given to Dorothy and to man.

It is clearly impossible to comprehend this poem within categories of optimism or pessimism. It is above all a dramatic action in which the balance of positive and negative forces changes from line to line and often from word to word. Read purely at the level of statement, it seems a poem of "steady and shining optimism," crossed only by a few fleeting shadows of doubt.[34] If we respond to its form, however, and acknowledge the cost of this optimism, it becomes the journey through "dark passages" that Keats perceived, a struggle for "particles of light in a great darkness." What is sure in *Tintern Abbey,* as in Shakespeare's sonnets, is the inevitable triumph of devouring time, the greater triumph of human love, and the power of art to immortalize human love. In theme as in form the poem recalls the pastoral psalm it echoes. Here, once again, Wordsworth attempts to affirm the goodness of the created universe and yet to acknowledge that it is a realm of transience, insufficiency, and suffering. The Wye Valley is at once a place of green pastures and a valley of the shadow of death, and his utterance is prepared quite literally in the presence of the enemies that shape its form, enemies he would personify in a few years as "Death the skeleton and Time the shadow." Like the psalmist, he succeeds in confronting these fears without surrendering either the power of affirmation or the power of poetic utterance.

However we approach *Tintern Abbey,* it is also a poem of transition. In form it represents a unique blending of mimetic and expressionistic modes, as Wordsworth in effect imitates the activity of his own mind and moves toward the openly personal voice of the years to come. His art once again dramatizes the struggle toward psychological equilibrium, instead of presuming such equilibrium, as he had in the lyrics of March. The emotional constellations of earlier crises reappear: fear, doubt, and potential despair. If the object-world continues to offer support to the mind, as it had throughout Wordsworth's apprenticeship, it now begins to threaten consciousness of loss and mortality, and at several points in the poem renders the mind a place of refuge. Although Wordsworth celebrates nature passionately, the sense of immediate communion that dominated the work of the early spring has disappeared and only briefly does he employ a style that dramatizes love for the "language of the sense." Reconciliation of nature and man has become extremely difficult, and throughout the poem relationship to nature and terrestrial hope are restored only by looking into the past. Memory, rather than immediate sensation, has become the agency of redemption, and the entire poem constitutes an attempt to imitate and thus redeem the feelings of the past. In each respect *Tintern Abbey* suggests that the consummation of 1797 and 1798 has come to an end and that the poet stands on the verge of yet another crisis of hope, the history of which will be written in the poetry of the great decade.

Epilogue

Looking back on the course of Wordsworth's development from the vantage-point of *Tintern Abbey,* one is struck by the justice of his reply to Anne Taylor three years later. The growth of his mind and art was truly "slow and insensible," a process of organic unfolding that mingles change with continuity and that belies the categories of our analysis. His mature opinions have their roots deep in his past, and yet they undergo continuous transformation before the pressures of his experience. The development of his art reflects both the history of his mind and that of his times, and is oversimplified by an interpretation that relies exclusively on either. The cyclical variation of his style records the continuous struggle of a great mind to know itself and its world, to comprehend and articulate the depths of its own unconscious, and to affirm its integrity in the face of temporal existence. And yet Wordsworth's persevering assault on the literary conventions of his age proceeded on political and social grounds as well; it is no coincidence, for example, that he first broke the couplet in 1793, shortly after England betrayed the cause of France. Above all, his history testifies to the depth and the continuity of his feelings and to the pain with which a man "slow to love and slow to cease loving" reconciled himself to the fact of mutability.

We may observe, too, that the great paradoxes of Wordsworth's mature poetry are products of his development and that their origins are not as baffling as the contradictions they present to practical criticism. The history of Wordsworth's attitude toward the mind, and its transaction with its objects, clearly suggests why he

246

would come to be the exemplar of the "egotistical sublime." He was born into an age in which a poetry of truth necessarily began with the facts of individual consciousness. Morally and temperamentally, as Protestant and poet, he was furthermore deeply concerned with the health of his own mind and soul. But we do him a great injustice if we press the charge of egotism beyond this point, and doubt the authenticity of his concern for man or the immense energies he devoted to the resurrection of a genuine community of man. The poetry of 1797 and 1798 is a passionate attack on pride, a pride that isolates man not only from his fellows but from the objects of his perceptions and from himself. In *The Ruined Cottage* or the *Lyrical Ballads* Wordsworth is the poet of the greatest of the theological virtues, *caritas*.

It is evident, as well, that Wordsworth's attitude toward nature becomes complex early in his career, as literary conventions were transformed by his experience at Cambridge and by the decisive fact of the French Revolution. From 1792 onward, he regards nature as an active and purposive order, which furthers ends that are both human and divine and which transcends the categories of an orthodox dualism. As early as 1788, on the other hand, his style betrays an apprehension of the gulf between the human mind and a nature that offers respite from self-consciousness, and during the war years his optimistic trust in natural law is repeatedly chastened by profound disappointment. However passionately he celebrates its beneficence, the normative nature of 1798 is not a primitivistic paradise but an order that inexorably and at times tragically purges away the accidental and false in its complement, human nature. The essential drama of Wordsworth's naturalism lies in his struggle to affirm this process, and to uphold the possibility of a created world that is a home to man, in the face of a deepening awareness of its cost.

We may observe, finally, that this development resists definition in terms of either of the two broad movements that framed Wordsworth's age, romanticism and neoclassicism. It is of course true that he shared many of the aspirations of the great poets who are commonly grouped with him as romantics, and that he sought with historic effect to undermine several premises of neoclassic art, particularly those advanced on authoritarian or rationalistic grounds. But it is equally true that the poetry of 1798 constitutes a passionate protest against subjectivism, indulgence of the creative or visionary imagination, and a formless and undisciplined emotionalism—all vices of which the romantic poets and Wordsworth in particular have been accused. The fundamental premises that guided his development cut across both romanticism and neoclassicism, and represent a commitment to values that are rooted not only in the Enlightenment but in the Renaissance. If Wordsworth's developed conception of an organic, purposive nature differed radically from that which inspired the neoclassic exhortation to imitate nature, he nevertheless succeeded in enlarging the conception of *mimesis* itself and recovering much of its classical meaning. Although he sought to deny the Baconian conception of art as a pleasing and useful fiction, and to shape an art that like natural philosophy buckled the mind to the nature of things, he proceeded in a Baconian spirit that evinces a profound distrust of subjective aberration and a patient humility before the power, divinity, and potential beneficence of nature. He precisely inverted the Neoplatonic distinction between nature's brazen and the poet's golden world, but he did so on behalf of Sidney's faith in the ethically formative power of art. The principal purpose of the *Lyrical Ballads* is to teach as nature teaches, and thereby to redeem. Few men are as unlike in temperament and taste as Wordsworth and Samuel Johnson, and yet the former's development after 1793 may be described as a concerted attempt to carry Johnson's broad and empirical classicism to a logical conclusion, to "distinguish nature from custom, or that which is established because it is right from that which is right because it is established." Tempered and deepened by suffering, Wordsworth's conception of human nature drew close to that presented in *Paradise Lost* and the New Testament, as he continued to uphold the belief that man's dignity consists in a firm and charitable openness to the truth of temporal experience ordained by his creator. In each respect he disciplined both romantic and neoclassic practice on behalf of a Christian humanism that is rooted in the Renaissance. However we classify him, therefore, it is abundantly clear that he was not an isolated figure in the history of English poetry or thought. Even during the years of spiritual exile, as he pursued his "lone and perilous way" with massive independence, he traveled in the high road of Western humanism, and his greatest accomplishment during the early years was the reconstruction and the restatement of this tradition in a form and language consonant with the straitened realities of a new age.

If we glance ahead from *Tintern Abbey* across the years of the great decade, we see few essential changes in the direction of Wordsworth's development. His work between 1798 and 1804 recapitulates earlier crises of hope, but does so in the orthodox form exemplified by Gray's Eton College ode, that of a recognition of personal mortality. Adumbrated but successfully averted in *Tintern Abbey,* the profound effects of this recognition dominate the work of the fall of 1798 and later years: a suddenly sharpened consciousness of mortality that renders loving relationship to the temporal world a thing of the past and ultimately a subjective vision, presses Wordsworth to emphasize the transcendent rather than the immanent attributes of divinity, and endears the hope offered by "another and a better world." In the work of 1804 and 1805 he briefly recovers the ability to affirm a loving relationship between man and nature, but the balance of this equilibrium is now that of an orthodox dualism, which views nature as a way-station on the journey to a God who is our home. Such a crisis was not unforeseen; as we have observed, Wordsworth assumed it in his schooldays. But the task of surviving and affirming it would appear to have been extremely painful. Time forced him toward the realization that the vision of 1792 was in part subjective and threatened the repetition of the reversals of 1793 and 1795: the repudiation not only of nature, but of what he had been and loved.

The work of the six years after 1798 is therefore characteristically divided, as it was in 1795. Although Wordsworth insists on the continuity of his relationship to nature, and in discursive contexts continues to celebrate its power, the imagery and situations of his poems frequently imply powerful feelings of estrangement and even hostility toward a nature that offers only "the memory of what has been and never more can be." It is not until 1804 that he recovers the power he had demonstrated in *Tintern Abbey,* and in the Immortality Ode and the later *Prelude* he once again affirms the order that had formed and impoverished him.

The gradual emancipation of Wordsworth's deepest feelings from the temporal world has two profound effects on his art, both of which effectively reverse the direction of his earlier development. As he turns for hope from the objective world to the power and the immortal destiny of the mind, like Arnold, Tennyson and Yeats after him, the epistemology implied by his style gradually becomes idealistic. Instead of affirming the equality of objective and subjective powers, he progressively invests greater value in the mind's contribution to perception, and, in the years after 1804, in the creative and autonomous imagination. This aspect of his thought comes full circle in the Immortality Ode, where he finds "joy" and hope in the memory of an "abyss of idealism" that now testifies, in precise antithesis to its significance in his childhood, to the mind's hegemony over the sensible world and thus to its immortality. A corresponding change comes over the decorum that molds his style, which gradually ceases to embody a reverent imitation of "nature's shapes as she has made them," and instead relies upon language and art to dignify, elevate, and spiritualize the external world. In both respects Wordsworth surrenders his earlier protest against the "mighty stream of tendency" that throughout the eighteenth century had transferred the grounds of human hope from the outer to the inner world.

He does so, however, on behalf of the central commitment of his apprenticeship and his life, to man. His poetry remains "a motion of hope," undertaken in the light of truth. In his greatest later poems, the odes of 1804, *The Prelude,* the *Elegaic Stanzas,* and *The White Doe of Rylstone,* he succeeds in mastering the desire to escape an existence that had steadily grown more painful, and continues to devote his art to the task that Johnson regarded as the end of all writing, that of enabling man "better to enjoy life or better to endure it." His considered response in 1806 to the death of his brother a year earlier finds hope and the possibility of poetry in the role of a happy warrior who stands his ground in a darkened world:

> But welcome fortitude, and patient chear,
> And frequent sights of what is to be borne!
> Such sights, or worse, as are before me here.—
> Not without hope we suffer and we mourn.

Wordsworth remains what he was at the age of seventeen, when he bid farewell to Esthwaite, put the "flowery lays" of a pastoral fancy behind him, and for the first of many times dedicated his genius to the task of confronting, surviving, and ennobling the human condition, not as it might be, but as it is.

Notes   Index

Notes

I: HAWKSHEAD: 1785-1787

1. Christopher Wordsworth, *Memoirs of William Wordsworth* (London, 1851), I, 10; II, 304. Henceforth cited as *Memoirs.*
2. *The Early Wordsworthian Milieu,* ed. Z. S. Fink (Oxford: Clarendon Press, 1958), p. 116.
3. John Locke, *Essay Concerning Human Understanding,* bk. IV, ch. xvii, sec. 3. Cited henceforth in the text.
4. Ben Ross Schneider, Jr., *Wordsworth's Cambridge Education* (Cambridge [Eng.] University Press, 1957), pp. 4–6; *Memoirs,* p. 14; *The Works of Francis Bacon,* ed. James Spedding, R. E. Ellis, and D. D. Heath (London, 1857–1874), III, 343–344.
5. Fink, *Early Wordsworthian Milieu,* pp. 97, 144. At the close of *The Vale of Esthwaite* Wordsworth compares death to the gradual decay of motion in a bouncing ball (ll. 522–527) and the mind to a "mental tablet" (l. 566), and endows the Pedlar of *The Ruined Cottage* (1798) with knowledge of geology and optics (*PW* V, 384–85, ll. 212–235).
6. In *The Simple Wordsworth* (London: Routledge & Kegan Paul, 1960), John Danby writes that the "universe of Newton was a complete, settled thing," and describes Wordsworth's poetry as the product of an age of chemistry, of "action and re-action, of formation and transformation" (p. 12). But the universe of the *Optics* is not fixed and dead: "The changing of Bodies into Light, and Light into Bodies, is very conformable to the Course of Nature, which seems delighted with Transmutations" (bk. III. pt. 1, quest. 30). Newton conceived nature as an active system, immediately dependent for its activity on the influx of a beneficent power that continually forestalls stasis and decay. The relation of God to this universe he compared not to a watchmaker and watch, but to a mind and its thoughts. And in a ringing conclusion to the *Optics* he virtually identifies the truth of natural philosophy with that of revelation and condemns a naturalistic

pantheism that identifies God with the sun and moon (bk. III, pt. I, quest. 31). We need not attribute Wordsworth's shock, when his poetry was accused of a similar pantheism, to a late orthodoxy; it is entirely consistent with the view of nature he would have learned at Hawkshead.

7. John Aikin, *Essays on Song-writing: With a Collection of Such English Songs as are Most Eminent for Poetical Merit* (London, n.d.), pp. 20, 29. The first edition is dated "early in 1772" in Lucy Aikin's *Memoir of John Aikin, M.D.* (London, 1823), I, 19.

8. F. W. Bateson, *Wordsworth: A Re-interpretation* (London: Longmans, 1954), pp. 55, 69; Geoffrey Hartman, *Wordsworth's Poetry 1787–1814* (New Haven: Yale University Press, 1964), pp. 76–89, esp. 87; John and Lucy Aikin, *Miscellaneous Pieces in Prose* (London, 1775), p. 126; Helen Maria Williams, *Poems* (London, 1786), II, 30.

9. The "pattern of alternation" noticed by Hartman (*Wordsworth's Poetry,* p. 81) may, for example, be interpreted as a straightforward attempt to imitate the rapid and vehement transitions appropriate to an excited imagination and the more passionate lyric genres. The grisly episode in which "Edmund" blinds his brother (ll. 369–372), which Hartman regards as an initiation ceremony (p. 89), may seem an equally straightforward allusion to the local history of Cumberland, in the manner of Gray's *Bard* or Helen Maria Williams' *Fragment.* Edmund, it may be noted, was the Saxon invader who deposed the last king of Cumberland, Dunmail, an event commemorated not only by Wordsworth but by a cairn along the high road not far from Hawkshead, as was explained in contemporary guidebooks such as Thomas West's *Guide to the Lakes* (3rd. ed. [London, 1784], pp. 81–82).

10. Ernest de Selincourt, *Wordsworthian and Other Studies* (Oxford: Clarendon Press, 1947) p. 15; *The Works of Francis Bacon,* III, 343–344. Schneider has summarized the evidence for Taylor's sentimental tastes (*Wordsworth's Cambridge Education,* pp. 76–78).

11. Hazlitt repeatedly censured Wordsworth's "devouring egotism" on moral and personal as well as critical grounds (*The Works of William Hazlitt,* ed. P. P. Howe [London: Dent, 1930–1934], V, 53; see Herschel Baker's *William Hazlitt* [Cambridge, Mass.: Harvard University Press, 1962], pp. 342–350); and Keats described him as the "egotistical sublime" (*The Letters of John Keats,* ed. Hyder E. Rollins [Cambridge, Mass.: Harvard University Press, 1958], I, 387). In recent years the question has been explored from widely different perspectives. In *The Egotistical Sublime* (London: Chatto & Windus,

1964), John Jones describes solitude as the "theme" of Wordsworth's life (p. 31). Geoffrey Hartman defines the poet's imagination as a "consciousness of self raised to apocalyptic pitch," and in his chronological survey of the career traces Wordsworth's progress toward the "discovery" that the imagination is essentially autonomous from nature (*Wordsworth's Poetry*, pp. 17, 41). In his *Re-interpretation*, on the other hand, F. W. Bateson tends to regard the poet's subjective "voice" as a symptom of neurotic estrangement from a sane and objective Augustan humanism.

12. Josephine Miles, *Wordsworth and the Vocabulary of Emotion* (Berkeley: University of California Press, 1942); Prior, "Alma; Or the Progress of the Mind," 1. 21.

13. Gray, "Ode on the Pleasure arising from Vicissitude," 1. 46. Here and below I cite the text as edited by H. W. Starr and J. R. Hendrikson, *The Complete Poems of Thomas Gray* (Oxford: Clarendon Press, 1966); Langhorne, "Owen of Carron" (1778), 1. 4: "Ye Maidens fair of MARLIVALE,/Why stream your Eyes with Pity's Dew?"

14. Williams, "Edwin and Eltruda, A Legendary Tale," *Poems*, I, 71.

15. Miles, *Vocabulary of Emotion*, p. 93.

16. Throughout the following discussion I am indebted to four studies of the psychological implications of eighteenth-century figures: Bertrand H. Bronson, "Personification Reconsidered," *Journal of English Literary History*, 14 (1947), 163–177; Earl R. Wasserman, "The Inherent Values of Eighteenth-Century Personification," *Publications of the Modern Language Association*, 65 (1950), 435–463; Chester F. Chapin, *Personification in Eighteenth-Century English Poetry* (New York: King's Crown Press, Columbia University, 1955); and Ralph Cohen, *The Art of Discrimination: Thomson's* The Seasons *and the Language of Criticism* (Berkeley: University of California Press, 1964).

17. Molded in part by Locke's distinction between primary and secondary qualities, this conception of the imagination can be found in Thomson's *Seasons*, Akenside's *Pleasures of the Imagination*, Young's *Night Thoughts*, and elsewhere, including a letter written by Dorothy Wordsworth in 1793, where she describes her brother's "pleasures," in Akenside's words, as "chiefly of the imagination" (*EY*, p. 52). See Marjorie Nicholson, *Newton Demands the Muse* (Princeton: Princeton University Press, 1946), pp. 144–164, and Colin C. Clarke, *Romantic Paradox* (New York: Barnes & Noble, 1963), pp. 94–95.

18. Alexander Gerard, *An Essay on Taste* (1759), ed. Walter J. Hipple, Jr. (Gainesville, Fla.: Scholars' Facsimiles & Reprints, 1963), p. 154.

19. *Idler*, No. 44, *Works of Samuel Johnson*, 9 vols. published (New Haven: Yale University Press, 1958–   ), II, 137; Joshua Reynolds, *Discourses on Art* (London: Everyman Library, 1906), p. 31; Akenside, *Pleasures of the Imagination* (1744), I. 329–331; Aikin, *Essays on Song-writing*, pp. 6–7. Akenside's passage was among the selections anthologized by Vicesimus Knox in his *Elegant Extracts of Poetry*, which Christopher Wordsworth used a few years later and which William would call "the poetical library of our schools" (*The Prose Works of William Wordsworth*, ed. A. B. Grosart [London: Macmillan, 1876], II, 64). On Collins' idealism, see A. S. P. Woodhouse, "The Poetry of Collins Reconsidered," in *From Sensibility to Romanticism: Essays Presented to Frederick A. Pottle*, ed. Frederick W. Hilles and Harold Bloom (New York: Oxford University Press, 1965), pp. 93–137, esp. 103–108.

20. Hugh Blair, *Lectures on Rhetoric*, ed. Abraham Mills (Philadelphia, 1833), pp. 176–177; Henry Home, Lord Kames, *Elements of Criticism*, 4th ed. (Edinburgh, 1769), II, 235–236; II, 518. Wordsworth's dependence on his sources is particularly evident in his allegorical tableau of "Murder." From Gray's ode on vicissitude he took a "reverted eye," from Collins' *Ode to Fear* a "haggard eye," and combined them, outdoing both his predecessors: "Ha! that is hell-born Murder nigh/With haggard, half-reverted eye" (*Vale of Esthwaite*, ll. 387–388).

21. Earl R. Wasserman, "Nature Moralized: The Divine Analogy in the Eighteenth Century," *Journal of English Literary History*, 20 (1953), 71.

22. Jones, *Egotistical Sublime*, p. 207.

23. See Bateson, *Re-interpretation*, p. 60, and Moorman, p. 42.

24. Coleridge, *Philosophical Lectures*, ed. Kathleen Coburn (New York: Philosophical Library, 1949), p. 372.

25. *Boswell's Life of Johnson*, ed. G. B. Hill, 2nd ed. rev. (Oxford: Clarendon Press, 1934–1950), I, 471.

26. Fink, *Early Wordsworthian Milieu*, p. 104.

27. Joseph Warton, *An Essay on the Genius and Writings of Pope*, 4th ed. (London, 1782), I, 42; Aikin, *Essay on the Application of Natural History to Poetry* (Warrington, 1777), p. 25; Hugh Blair, *A Critical Dissertation on the Poems of Ossian*, reprinted in *The Poems of Ossian* (New York, 1846), p. 154. That the criterion of "correctness" sharpened during the years of Wordsworth's apprenticeship is

suggested by the fact that in 1805 Richard Payne Knight could argue against the poem's authenticity on precisely the same grounds, pointing out that it lacks the "scrupulously exact" observation that a truly ancient bard would have displayed (*Analytical Enquiry into the Principles of Taste* [London, 1806], pp. 285–286). See Cohen, *The Art of Discrimination*, chap. III, "Things, Images and Imagination: the Reconsideration of Description."

28. William Gilpin, *Observations relative chiefly to Picturesque Beauty, made . . . on . . . the Mountains, and Lakes of Cumberland, and Westmoreland*, 3rd. ed. (London, 1792), p. xxix. In other passages, as well, Wordsworth corrects literary images by looking at the object. In his *Dirge*, for example, he compares the mind of his heroine to the calm surface of a lake, as Helen Maria Williams had done in "An American Tale" (*Poems*, I, 10–11). But Wordsworth refines this by adding a Lake country detail he would note in his *Guide* to the Lakes, many years later: the "dimple" that is made on the lake's surface by the "influx of a rivulet" (*A Guide Through the District of the Lakes* [London: Hart, 1951], p. 69). This "dimple" he compares unconvincingly to the last smile of a dying heroine (*Dirge*, ll. 15–19). His description, in *The Vale of Esthwaite*, of a "summit brown and bare" that is transformed by mists into an "island in the air" (ll. 11–24) extends Beattie's description of an "ocean" of mist in *The Minstrel* (I. 21), and in phrasing and rhyme echoes Dyer's "summit soft and fair" in *Grongar Hill* (l. 123). In each case Wordsworth looks at landscape through categories set by literary precedent.

29. *The Works of Anacreon, translated . . . by Mr. Addison* (London, 1735), Ode XXVIII, ll. 13–14. Wordsworth amplified this simile still further in *Beauty and Moonlight* (ll. 5–14). One may add that Professor Bateson's attempt to identify "Mary of Esthwaite" on the basis of such descriptions again confronts the problem that they were quite conventional. See his *Re-interpretation*, p. 66.

30. Johnson, "Life of Denham," in the *The Lives of the Poets*, ed. Arthur Waugh (Oxford: World's Classics, 1959), I, 58; Langhorne, "Observations on the Odes," *Poetical Works of William Collins*, ed. Alexander Dyce (London, 1827), p. 143; Blair, *Lectures on Rhetoric*, p. 176.

31. Aikin, *Essays on Song-writing*, pp. 4–5; Kames, *Elements of Criticism*, II, 236.

32. Even here, at his most "apocalyptic," Wordsworth is derivative. His whirlwind is modeled on Collins' "Vengeance," in the *Ode to Fear* (ll. 20–21), and his "terrific Sire" on Gray's "Nature," in the ode on vicissitude (l. 19). In both cases Wordsworth exalts their significance.

33. Catullus, III. 1–2: "Lugete, o Veneres . . . et quantumst hominum venustiorum" (Mourn, ye Graces . . . and all you whom the Graces love) [tr. R. W. Cornish]; Horace, *Odes,* III.xiii.13: "Fies nobilium tu quoque" (You, too, shall be numbered among the famous).

34. Jones, *The Egotistical Sublime,* pp. 17–19.

35. Earl R. Wasserman, "The English Romantics: The Grounds of Knowledge," *Studies in Romanticism,* 4 (1964), 18.

36. Compare *Aeneid,* VI. 272, and "Winter," ll. 1685–1693.

37. *Vale of Esthwaite,* ll. 65–68. De Selincourt prints "round" for "roused" in line 67, an error tacitly corrected by Moorman (p. 62). Line 66, however, has no end-stop; Wordsworth deliberately emphasizes the unusual pause after the first foot in line 67, stressing the abrupt emergence from a subjective trance.

38. Hartman, *Wordsworth's Poetry,* p. 79.

39. In *William Wordsworth: His Doctrine and Art in Their Historical Relations,* 2nd ed. (Madison: University of Wisconsin Press, 1927), Arthur Beatty notes that Hartley attributes imagination to youth (pp. 112–113), and argues that Wordsworth follows him, but that in his later years he exalts this conception of imagination far above his "master" (p. 180). Insofar as a perennial distinction between youth and age may be assigned a particular historical form, however, the assumption that "fancy" is dominant in youth was an obvious and widespread inference from Locke's psychology, and it does not itself establish Hartley's primacy as a Wordsworthian source.

40. *The Poetry and Prose of William Blake,* ed. David V. Erdman (New York: Doubleday, 1965), p. 544.

41. Wordsworth quoted Beattie's sage—"Nor less to regulate man's moral frame/Science exerts her all-composing sway" (II. 53)—in describing the power of the Hawkshead curriculum "to regulate the mind's disordered frame" ("School Exercise," l. 79).

42. Dorothy made this comparison in 1793, recalling Wordsworth as he was when she first knew him after leaving Halifax, that is, in the late spring of 1787 (*EY,* pp. 100–101).

43. *Elegaic Stanzas, Suggested by a Picture of Peele Castle,* ll. 16, 36.

II: CAMBRIDGE AND FRANCE: 1787–1792

1. *Eclogue* X, 72–74. In these lines the pastoral poet consecrates his poems to his beloved friend, Gallus, a reference, perhaps, to Wordsworth's Hawkshead classmate, John Fleming.

2. Wordsworth freely expanded Virgil; Eurydice's two-line farewell (*Georgics* IV. 497–498) grows, for example, into six lines (*Orpheus*, ll. 33–38). His guide in doing so was probably Joseph Warton, who had criticized Pope's abbreviated version (in the *Ode on St. Cecelia's Day*) in his *Essay on the Writings and Genius of Pope,* 4th ed. (London, 1782), I, 58–59. He emphasizes all the "striking incidents" Warton had missed in Pope: the "dismal shriek" heard by Eurydice, the "vast darkness" about her, and the "wild, savage," and "dismal" settings of Orpheus' lamentations. Twice he follows Warton's emendations of Pope's diction (of *vocabat* and *miseram, Georgics* IV. 526), and in general stresses what Warton called the "natural and pathetic exclamations" of Eurydice (I, 58). In imitating Virgil, Wordsworth is concerned not only with "classic niceties" (*Prelude* VI. 127) but with the real language of passion.

3. Several versions of this scene appear in use during 1788 and 1789, and it may have been conceived as part of a longer narrative, in which a traveler, possibly the father of this family, approaches a romantic castle, which seemed "like some grim Eagle on a naked rock/ Clapping its wings & wailing to the storm" (DCP). It eventually becomes part of *An Evening Walk,* and may have contributed to the still later tale of the Female Vagrant.

4. DCP; a passage on which Wordsworth lavished much attention. Darwin's description is drawn from fact: the wreck of the Halsewell East-Indiaman, on the 6th of January, 1786, "when Capt. Pierce the commander, with two young ladies, his daughters, and the greatest part of the crew and passengers perished in the sea" (*Botanic Garden,* 4th ed. [London, 1799], I, 202n). Wordsworth was attracted to this passage not only because it exemplifies Darwin's extreme emphasis on the importance of visual imagery to poetry, but because its theme is the heroic strength of familial love:

> With brow upturn'd to Heaven, "WE WILL NOT PART!"
> He cried, and clasp'd them to his aching heart,—
> —Dash'd in dread conflict on the rocky grounds
> Crash the shock'd masts, the staggering wreck rebounds;
> Through gaping seams the rushing deluge swims. . . .
>
> (Pt. I. IV. 233–237)

As Jonathan Wordsworth has pointed out, this passage contributed to *An Evening Walk* (*The Music of Humanity* [London: Nelson, 1969], pp. 50–51), and it may help us to understand Wordsworth's response to the shipwreck of his brother John in 1805.

5. Elsie Smith, *An Estimate of William Wordsworth by His Contemporaries* (Oxford: Blackwell, 1932), pp. 14–15.

6. In MS Vs 4 "accordant" is added to the octosyllabics Wordsworth had written at Hawkshead, before he converted them into pentameter couplets:

(1) Now o'er the ~~saddened~~ [accordant] heart we feel

(2) But o'er th' sooth'd accordant heart we feel

"Sympathetic" appears for the first time in *An Evening Walk,* composed in 1788 and 1789 (1. 382).

7. Samuel Taylor Coleridge, *Poetical Works,* ed. E. H. Coleridge (London: Oxford University Press, 1912), II, 1139.

8. Although this poem was published in 1793, the manuscripts date its composition during Wordsworth's first two college vacations (*PW* I, 318). See Reed, App. V.

9. Robert A. Aubin relates the poem and the tradition in *Topographical Poetry in XVIII-Century England* (New York: Modern Language Association of America, 1936), p. 219. Émile Legouis regarded the selection of the couplet as an aesthetic error (*The Early Life of William Wordsworth,* tr. J. W. Matthew, 2nd ed. rev. [1921; rpt. New York: Russell, 1965], p. 128, and Geoffrey Hartman describes its stylistic effects in his discussion of *Descriptive Sketches* (*Wordsworth's Poetry 1787–1814* [New Haven: Yale University Press, 1964], pp. 110–112). In the course of a sensitive and engaging discussion of the poem, Frederick Pottle notes that the couplet is inappropriate to its subject and attributes Wordsworth's choice of it to the influence of the French alexandrine, which he encountered in his reading of Delille, Rosset, and other pastoral poets, presumably in 1791 and 1792. ("Emergent Idiom," in *The Idiom of Poetry* [Ithaca, N.Y.: Cornell University Press, 1946], pp. 129–130). As the above discussion makes clear, Wordsworth very probably turned to the couplet in 1788, when his models were largely, if not wholly English. We may recall that the couplet was an accepted form for the topographical poem: among the thirty-five "region poems" that Aubin catalogues as having been composed between 1770 and 1790, fourteen are in pentameter couplets. Wordsworth was employing the couplet at the time for his translations of Virgilian landscapes, and he was certainly aware that it had provided a successful medium for another poem of nostalgic return, *The Deserted Village*—which he echoed twice in his own.

10. In his note to the "Lines Written at Shurton Bars," as in the *Biographia Literaria,* Coleridge praised its "novel" imagery (*Poetical Works,* I, 97; *BL,* I, 56). Dorothy praised its use of the "Poet's pencil" (*EY,* p. 89). The *Critical Review* found the imagery "new and pictur-

esque" and *The Gentleman's Magazine* remarked on its "accurate and well-marked description" (Smith, *Estimate,* pp. 7, 15). And Wordsworth himself praised its "new images" in later years (*EY,* p. 327).

11. James Clarke, *A Survey of the Lakes of Cumberland, Westmorland, and Lancashire,* 2nd ed. (London, 1789), p. viii. Clarke is mentioned in Wordsworth's note to l. 187 (1793).

12. All references to the poem in this chapter are to the 1793 edition, designated by de Selincourt as A.

13. The word "blue" appears five times in *An Evening Walk,* four in *The Prelude* of 1850; corresponding figures for "red," three and two, and "purple," four and two. This proportion is forcefully reversed, however, in the case of "green," which appears seven times in the earlier, and twenty-six times in the later poem—an indication of the symbolic importance of this color to the poet of 1798 and after. Such attention to color reflects Wordsworth's adherence to the maxim *ut pictura poesis,* and probably the particular influence of Thompson, who in Jean Hagstrum's words "rendered the *color* of the natural world with greater eloquence and fidelity than any other writer on so large a scale" (*The Sister Arts* [Chicago: University of Chicago Press, 1958], p. 252; Hagstrum's italics).

14. Thomas West, *Guide to the Lakes,* 3rd. ed. (London, 1784), p. 78.

15. A closer attention to detail is evident, too, in Wordsworth's references to places, which had been quite general in 1787, when Grasmere was a "heavenly vale" (*Vale of Esthwaite,* l. 291) and Windermere a "stream" (*Idyllium,* l. 6). In *An Evening Walk,* Windermere takes on distinctive form: "Where, bosom'd deep, the shy Winander peeps/ 'Mid clust'ring isles, and holly sprinkl'd steeps" (ll. 13–14). To further particularize this description, Wordsworth adds a note limiting it to the "middle part" of the lake.

16. Legouis, *Early Life,* pp. 133–147.

17. Many lines simply have too many images in them: "Cross the calm lakes blue shades the cliffs aspire"(l. 158). Wordsworth's reliance on adjectives is suggested by another passage, in which he converted the octosyllabics of 1787 into heroic couplets simply by adding an epithet to each line:

No ~~visions~~ [purple prospects] now the mind employ
Array'd in [golden] evening tints of joy
But o'er the [sooth'd] accordant heart we feel
A tender twilight ~~gently~~ [[unexpected] steal.

(DCP)

It may be noted that this passage bears on the hypothesis, presented by Reed (p. 308), that Wordsworth altered *The Vale of Esthwaite* into blank verse before transforming it into couplets. These lines suggest that on this occasion, at least, the transformation was direct. I have been able to find no occasion on which the octosyllabics of 1787 become blank verse and then couplets; the one passage that does become blank verse is the allegorical procession exemplified by the portrait of "moody madness," which does not appear in *An Evening Walk* and which Wordsworth may have intended for a different poem. The other passages of blank verse that appear in these manuscripts take up subjects that do not appear in the Hawkshead poem. One of these—the description of the benighted mother—is transformed into couplets, as Reed points out, in MS Vs 7.

18. John Scott, *Critical Essays on Some of the Poems of Several English Poets* (London, 1785). Cited henceforth in the text.

19. Of analogy, Wordsworth's favorite figure a year earlier, Scott writes that "parallels between different subjects are seldom natural or just enough to be pleasing; they exist oftener in the fancy of the person comparing, than in any actual resemblance of the things compared" (*Critical Essays,* p. 189). Elsewhere he attacks personification (p. 48), "far fetched and unnatural comparisons" (p. 19), and "that species of nonsense, ludicrously styled Hibernicism" (p. 14).

20. Like several early passages, this first occurs in prose: "Human life is like the [plate?] of a dial, hope brightens the future, reflection the hour that is past—but the present is always marked with a shadow" (DCP). The poet does not stand in an "evening" that threatens the loss of nature, as Geoffrey Hartman suggests, but in a present that threatens the loss of hope (*Wordsworth's Poetry,* p. 90). If the poem begins by stating the loss of hope, it ends by recovering it.

21. In the course of his discussion of *The Seasons,* Samuel Johnson noted that "Thomson's wide expansion of general views, and his enumeration of circumstantial varieties, would have been obstructed and embarrassed by the frequent intersection of the sense, which are the necessary effects of rhyme" (*The Lives of the Poets,* ed. Arthur Waugh [Oxford: World's Classics, 1959], I, 358).

22. I here adopt a position between that of the two critics who have commented most fully on the psychological implications of this poem, Geoffrey Hartman and F. W. Bateson. Although he finely suggests the psychological precariousness of the poem, Hartman emphasizes the doubtful adequacy, to the needs of the poet's apocalyptic imagination, of a darkened nature that threatens to dissolve into fantasy or apocalypse (*Wordsworth's Poetry,* p. 101), and overlooks Wordsworth's

vastly greater sense of the value of the "common range of visible things" in 1788. The closing lines of the poem may seem to threaten apocalypse, but they certainly do so with far less force than the tempest in *The Vale of Esthwaite*. Fear of loss of visible nature is present, as Hartman points out, but it is not perceptibly greater than the similar fears expressed in 1787. The implied fears in this poem are directed not toward nature, and not obviously toward a world of supernatural vision, but toward the self. Bateson, on the other hand, recognizes the comparative objectivity of the poem, but regards it as a symptom of returning psychic health that takes the form of an Augustan humanism (*Wordsworth: A Re-interpretation* [London: Longmans, 1954], pp. 77–81).

23. All references are to the text of 1793, de Selincourt's A.

24. *Lettres de M. William Coxe a M. W. Melmoth, sur l'État politique, civil et naturel de la Suisse; traduites de l'Anglois, et augmentées des Observations faites dans le même Pays, par le Traducteur,* 2 vols. (Paris, 1782), II, 140 (my translation). Cited henceforth in the text. Legouis first pointed out Wordsworth's debt to Ramond (*Early Life,* pp. 113–114, 475–477), which Arthur Beatty documented in detail (*Wordsworth: Representative Poems* [Garden City, New York: Doubleday, 1937], pp. xxxviii–xliii, and in the notes to the poem). This debt, according to Beatty, includes the "ruling ideas and the general ordering of the poem" (p. 34), a view G. W. Meyer has questioned (*Wordsworth's Formative Years* [Ann Arbor: University of Michigan Press, 1943], pp. 78-79). Wordsworth refers to Ramond in 1798 (*EY*, p. 235) and again in 1823 (Note to "Desultory Stanzas," *PW* III, 488). The book was in his library at his death.

25. Other landscapes are peopled by personified abstractions, tutelary spirits, or animated natural objects. The sun not only walks but stands "tiptoe on an Alpine spire" (l. 662). "Desolation" and "Terror" stalk through the gorge of the Reuss (ll. 245, 252). The "irresistible power" and "controuling influence" of Mont Blanc evoke clustered personifications: Ruin, Havoc, and Chaos (ll. 693-695). Again, however, it should be noted that such figures no longer betoken the autonomy of the fabricative imagination, but the response of the imagination to external power.

26. Joseph Warren Beach, *The Concept of Nature in Nineteenth-Century English Poetry* (New York: Macmillan, 1936), pp. 110–208. For a brief summary of possible sources, see pp. 11–13 and 569–577.

27. Although Beatty notes that Ramond wrote with his "eye on the object," and argues that Wordsworth learned from him to "render the object in its essential truth, directly and not by figure or circumlo-

cution or comparison" (p. xlii)—a statement that is not borne out by the style of *Descriptive Sketches*—he does not discuss Ramond's conception of nature itself or the scientific assumptions discussed below.

28. For a brief survey of contemporary scientific views, see John C. Greene, *The Death of Adam* (Ames, Iowa: Iowa State University Press, 1959), pp. 39–87. For a comprehensive history of the literary effect of such theories in the eighteenth century, see Marjorie Nicholson, *Mountain Gloom and Mountain Glory* (Ithaca, N.Y.: Cornell University Press, 1959).

29. See *The Minstrel,* I. 21, and compare the landscape seen from Snowdon, *Prelude* XIII. 40–65. The details Wordsworth adds to Beattie—the "gulf of gloomy blue," the emphasis on silence, and the speaker's solemnity and awe—clearly recur in *The Prelude,* where he describes the sea of mist in language that explicitly recalls both creation and deluge as they had been described by Milton (see *Paradise Lost* VII. 285–287; XI. 826–828, 893–894).

30. By Geoffrey Hartman, who here (as throughout his survey of the development) makes the assumption Wordsworth made in 1804, that nature is inadequate to the imagination. He therefore finds Wordsworth's failure to mention the disappointment on the Simplon a "mystery" (*Wordsworth's Poetry,* pp. 104, 361, n6).

31. That the disappointments of 1790 were experienced at the time in terms of the picturesque is suggested by Wordsworth's letter from the Alps to Dorothy. If he had read Coxe by 1790, as has been suggested by Mary Moorman (p. 128), he would, for example, have come to the falls of Schaffhausen with high expectations. "The magnificence of the whole scenery," wrote Coxe, "far surpassed my most sanguine expectations, and exceeds all description" (*Sketches of the Natural, Civil, and Political State of Swisserland* [Dublin, 1779], p. 14). "Magnificent as this fall certainly is," Wordsworth wrote Dorothy, "I must confess I was disappointed in it. I had raised my ideas too high" (*EY,* p. 35). Such a disappointment, which proceeded from the "love/Of sitting thus in judgment" (*Prelude* XI. 164–165) that was implicit in the search for picturesque beauty, would have been transformed by the vision of 1792, which infused all nature with sublimity.

32. See M. H. Abrams, "English Romanticism: The Spirit of the Age," in *Romanticism Reconsidered,* ed. Northrup Frye (New York: Columbia University Press, 1963), pp. 30–37. Geoffrey Hartman has in particular presented Wordsworth's career as a struggle, under "the joint imperative of English Protestantism and the Enlighten-

ment," to "humanize . . . his imagination, and so to abandon the older mythical and cosmological imaginings" (*Wordsworth's Poetry*, p. 75). "There are many," Hartman writes, "who feel that Wordsworth could have been as great a poet as Milton but for this return to nature, this shrinking from visionary subjects" (p. 39).

33. Nearly all commentators on *Descriptive Sketches* have taken its several professions of melancholy seriously, thereby discounting the implications of Wordsworth's enthusiasm for the Revolution. Émile Legouis, for example, regarded much of the melancholy as conventional, but partly reversed himself on the appearance of Annette Vallon (*Early Life*, pp. 157–160, 480). H. W. Garrod attributed this melancholy to the "shock" of the Revolution mingled with emotions stirred by Annette (*Wordsworth: Lectures and Essays*, 2nd. ed. [Oxford: Clarendon Press, 1927], p. 48). Geoffrey Hartman and Mary Moorman agree on the sadness of the poem (*Wordsworth's Poetry*, p. 361, n6; Moorman, p. 198). Several relevant passages, it may be noted, lend themselves to misinterpretation. When Wordsworth offers as his motive for the tour a "heart, that could not much itself approve" (1. 46) he is describing emotions not of 1792 but of 1790: the disappointment that he encountered at Cambridge, and the psychological context of *An Evening Walk*. When he speculates that as a traveler he may seem afflicted by some "stroke of crazing Care," he contrasts the inward joy of the pedestrian traveler with his outward appearance to an uninitiated observer, a village maiden (ll. 42–44). Other expressions of melancholy, such as his statement of sympathy for the Grison Gypsy (ll. 192ff) or the pilgrims at Einseidlen (ll. 676–679), fall under the heading of pathos; they do not imply that Wordsworth was himself saddened, but that he "can afford to suffer with those he sees suffer," as he described the Wanderer of *The Excursion*. It is his refusal to express feeling that in *An Evening Walk* and later poems is the most striking symptom of psychic disturbance, not his cultivation of pathos. One may add, finally, that Meyer is certainly correct in writing that Wordsworth's reference to the superstitious delusions of the Catholic pilgrims at Einseidlen by no means implies his atheism (*Wordsworth's Formative Years*, p. 76), as has been suggested by Garrod (*Wordsworth*, p. 50) and G. M. Harper (*William Wordsworth: His Life, Works, and Influence*, 3rd ed. [1929; rpt. New York: Russell, 1960], I, 138). He is at once echoing the staunch Protestantism of Coxe and tempering it with the humanitarian sympathy of Ramond, who pointed out Coxe's anti-Catholicism, asked "tolerance" for him, and directed an enlightened sympathy toward religious delusions: "Let us pity the

frailties of humanity, and respect the least of its hopes" ("Plaignons les foiblesses de l'humanité & respectons les moindres de ses espérances" [*Lettres*, I, 100, 108–109]).

III: SALISBURY PLAIN AND WINDY BROW: 1793–1794

1. To ask, with Herbert Read, "Why did he desert her as soon as the child was born?" (*Wordsworth*, 2nd ed. [London: Faber, 1949], p. 72), or to imagine, with F. W. Bateson, Annette's "reproachful eyes" following Wordsworth across Salisbury Plain in the summer of 1793 (*Wordsworth: A Re-interpretation* [London: Longmans, 1954], p. 113). is to indict Wordsworth on the basis of conjecture.

2. *Wordsworth: Poetry and Prose*, ed. W. M. Merchant (Cambridge, Mass.: Harvard University Press, 1955), p. 86. Henceforth cited in the text.

3. Edmund Burke, *Reflections on the French Revolution and Other Essays* (London: Dent, 1910), p. 73.

4. Quoted in Émile Legouis, *William Wordsworth and Annette Vallon* (London: Dent, 1922), p. 126. Translation by Moorman (p. 180).

5. All citations of the poem in this chapter refer to de Selincourt's MS 1. For a continuous text of this version, see Stephen Gill, "The Original *Salisbury Plain:* Introduction and Text," in *Bicentenary Wordsworth Studies In Memory of John Alban Finch,* ed. Jonathan Wordsworth (Ithaca: Cornell University Press, 1970), pp. 142–179.

6. Wordsworth dates the vagrant's story "at least two years" earlier (*PW* I, 330). See Reed, App. XII.

7. *Memoirs,* I, 117.

8. Since de Selincourt first noted the existence of these fragments, they have been cited primarily as evidence of Wordsworth's early philosophy of nature. See his *Wordsworthian and Other Studies* (Oxford: Clarendon Press, 1947), p. 27; G. W. Meyer, *Wordsworth's Formative Years* (Ann Arbor: University of Michigan Press, 1943), pp. 167–170; Herbert W. Piper, *The Active Universe* (London: Athelone Press, 1962), pp. 72–74; John Jones, *The Egotistical Sublime* (London: Chatto & Windus, 1964), pp. 75–76; and Jonathan Wordsworth, *The Music of Humanity* (London: Nelson, 1969), pp. 184–188. Despite Frederick Pottle's observation that these revisions make "an absorbing study" (*The Idiom of Poetry* [Ithaca, N.Y.: Cornell University Press, 1946], p. 132), virtually no attention has been given to their style and theme.

9. Throughout this section I indicate whether the cited passages,

which often appear in the *apparatus criticus,* are to be found in the 1793 (A) or the 1849 (B) version of the poem.

10. "There is a little unpretending rill," l. 12 (*PW* III, 4). See Moorman, p. 244. This memory scarcely points to a lack of religious belief, as Piper, for example, suggests (*Active Universe,* p. 72).

11. Several drafts of this passage occur in MS Verse 11. De Selincourt's transcription mistakes "hurry" for "horror," and his placement of it suggests that it forms the concluding lines of the description of the vagrant.

12. De Selincourt detected a "germ" of the mature naturalism in these fragments, but G. W. Meyer finds the poet of 1794 in "full possession and control of the ideas which are basic to *Lyrical Ballads"* (*Formative Years,* p. 168). Piper identifies these ideas with the materialistic pantheism that in his view Wordsworth absorbed from his radical connections in France (*Active Universe,* pp. 73–74). Jonathan Wordsworth agrees, but stresses the later contributions of Coleridge to the poet's vision of the "one life" (*Music of Humanity,* p. 188ff). It may be added that although Piper illuminates the milieu of radical scientific ideas that impinged upon Wordsworth in 1792, he overlooks the many points of contact between these ideas and the Protestant, scientific, and empirical tradition in which the poet had been brought up, and that the lines he cites as evidence that Wordsworth had "absorbed" a "new philosophy" in 1794 are few and problematical. The resemblances between the conception of nature assumed in *Descriptive Sketches,* which Piper dismisses as a "simple Rousseauism" (p. 62), and that of 1794 are far more striking than the differences. In both poems nature is an instrument of the millennium—an order active, purposive, progressive, and psychologically formative. Alterations in the significance of this order between 1792 and 1794 would appear to be far less dependent upon philosophical doctrine than on the passionate alliance between the poet and the landscape that had been forged by the English declaration of war and the wanderings of 1793.

13. As Meyer suggests (p. 167, n17), this and other occurrences of the verb "vibrate" may reflect not only the metaphor of a musical harmony between mind and nature, but Hartley's theory of vibrations, which the poet had very probably encountered in Godwin's *Political Justice.*

14. This is one of two passages cited by Piper as evidence of Wordsworth's materialistic pantheism, which he finds implied by the use of the word "form." As used here, he argues, it diverges from the language of English associationism and seems to mean "an organized natural body" with "life and sensibility" (*Active Universe,* p. 74). It

therefore reflects, he continues, the particular influence of such French pantheists as Diderot and Robinet. One difficulty with this argument is that "form" by no means possessed such a limited meaning; it could describe natural bodies without implying pantheism, as witnessed by Ramond's appeal in 1782 to the inexhaustible variety of natural forms, or Wordsworth's use of virtually the same language in 1790 (see n15, below). The point of the passage, furthermore, is not a proclamation of pantheism but a celebration of capacious sensibility to natural influence, a theme Wordsworth had first used at Hawkshead. The passage may therefore be understood in quite another sense: the common range of visible things ("common forms") moves the "favoured" mind, prolonging the "chain" of feeling that links all things.

One may add that the second passage cited by Piper (B ll 72–85 *app. crit.; Active Universe,* p. 73) also celebrates a comprehensive sympathy for natural objects, and that its language is equally ambiguous. The point to be made is not that Wordsworth was not exposed to the ideas Piper usefully elucidates, but that such ideas mingled with others inherited from earlier years, and that all were transformed by personal experience and feeling. This vision of nature depends above all on the catalyzing fact of the Revolution. If, with Piper, we attribute the changes that appear in 1794 to a "new philosophy of nature" which Wordsworth passively "absorbed" (p. 74), we lose sight of the originality and cost of this vision.

15. Of these terms, only "form" and "object" appear in the first version of *An Evening Walk*—neither in a philosophic sense. Among those we find in the letter of 1790 are: "sublime and beautiful *objects*" (*EY,* p. 32); "Nature in all her various *forms*" (p. 35); and his belief that he will derive happiness from remembered *"images"* (p. 36; all italics mine). One may note, further, that Wordsworth had the language of this letter fixed in his memory, both in 1793, when he revised the poem for publication, and in 1794. In it he ascribed his disappointment with the lower part of Lac Leman to the "weather, which was one of those hot glaring days in which all distant objects are veiled in a species of bright obscurity" (*EY,* p. 33). Higher up the lake, he wrote, this "pale steam" vanished (*EY,* p. 33). In the poem of 1793 a "wan noon . . . Breath'd a pale steam around the glaring hill" (ll. 53–54), and in the additions of 1794 a landscape vanishes before "a flood / Of bright obscurity" (B ll. 100–101).

IV: RACEDOWN: 1795–1796

1. R. D. Havens first pointed to the insufficiency of the evidence for or against Godwin (*The Mind of a Poet* [Baltimore: Johns Hop-

kins Press, 1941], pp. 543–544), an opinion confirmed by Godwin's editor, F. E. L. Priestly (*Enquiry Concerning Political Justice* [Toronto: University of Toronto Press, 1946], II, 102–103). Alan Grob has subjected the question to sensible review ("Wordsworth and Godwin: A Reassessment," *Studies in Romanticism*, 6 [1966], 98–119). Of those who blame Godwin for Wordsworth's crisis the most extreme is perhaps H. W. Garrod, who says of Godwin what Nietzsche said of Wagner, that he was "not a man but a disease" (*Wordsworth: Lectures and Essays*, 2nd ed. [Oxford: Clarendon Press, 1927], p. 67). The principal defenders of Godwin, G. M. Harper and G. W. Meyer, deny the existence of a moral crisis itself (*William Wordsworth: His Life, Works, and Influence*, 3rd ed. [1929; rpt. New York: Russell, 1960], I, 215–216; *Wordsworth's Formative Years* [Ann Arbor: University of Michigan Press, 1943], pp. 154–170).

2. Alexander Grosart, *The Prose Works of William Wordsworth* (London, 1876), I, 116; *Excursion* IX. 23.

3. The style of the passage (*Prelude* I. 1–54) is quite incompatible with this date, although memories of the retirement to Racedown may have contributed to it. John Finch argues convincingly for a date of 1799 ("Wordsworth's Two-Handed Engine," in *Bicentenary Wordsworth Studies In Memory of John Alban Finch*, ed. Jonathan Wordsworth [Ithaca, New York: Cornell University Press, 1970], pp. 1–13).

4. Study of this version is complicated by the fact that the earliest manuscript of the poem (de Selincourt's MS 2) dates from the spring of 1799 at the earliest, and perhaps as late as 1800 (Reed, pp. 335–336). There is, however, evidence that this manuscript incorporates few substantial changes. A prose sketch of the revised plot which occurs early in the notebook Wordsworth used at Racedown (MS Vs 12) and very probably dates from 1795, in no way departs from MS 2. Several revised or added stanzas in the notebook that contains the version of 1793–94 (MS Vs 11) are also very probably work of 1795. These establish the character of the sailor as he appears in MS 2, and the few differences between this intermediate version and MS 2 suggest that the latter mitigated the pessimism of 1795 in some degree, and that we are not mistaken in ascribing such pessimism to 1795. The earliest version of the Vagrant's tale, on the other hand, was published in the *Lyrical Ballads* of 1798. As Wordsworth stated that this was written "several years" before the other poems in that volume (*EY*, p. 328), it would appear to offer our best hope of determining the actual language Wordsworth employed in 1795. I have therefore limited my stylistic observations to this tale. Matters of plot, tone, and character are, I believe, safely inferred from MS 2.

5. In 1793, for example, the vagrant's nostalgic memories of her courtship had impelled personification: "The birds prolonged with joy their choicest lays." In 1795 these feelings no longer confuse themselves with the external world: "We two had sung, like little birds in May" (1. 247 *app. crit.*). Then she had described economic depression as the absence of "Labour's thoughtless hum"; now she speaks idiomatically and to the point: " 'Twas a hard change: an evil time had come" (ll. 271–272). Passionate personification survives only when it is dramatically appropriate: "Murder" and "Rape" continue to seize their "joint prey" at the height of the American war (ll. 351–352 *app. crit.*).

6. *EY,* p. 159. See the conclusion of the first version, where Wordsworth criticizes both war and the penal law (*PW* I, 340, Stanzas 57, 58), and the letter to the Bishop of Llandaff (ed. Merchant, pp. 89–90). As Garrod first pointed out, the poem owes a clear debt to Godwin's *Caleb Williams* (*Wordsworth,* p. 83), and its indignation is no doubt informed by the attack on the penal system in Book VII of *Political Justice.*

7. One may point out that the sailor's victim is not his own son, as Meyer inferred from l. 599 of the 1842 version (*Formative Years,* p. 126). Cf. MS 2: "a man," and l. 70, a "traveller."

8. He simply removed the ironic aside, and let the encomium of the social order stand:

> Of social Order's care for wretchedness,
> Of Time's sure help to calm and reconcile,
> . . . .
> 'Twas not for *him* to speak . . . .
>
> (ll. 453–456)

9. O. J. Campbell and Paul Mueschke interpreted this stanza as a sudden outburst of repressed remorse for having deserted Annette (" 'Guilt and Sorrow': A Study in the Genesis of Wordsworth's Aesthetics," *Modern Philology,* 23 [1926], 303–305. G. W. Meyer explained it as the effect of prostitution (*Formative Years,* p. 132).

10. Since G. M. Harper revealed Annette's existence (1916) and Émile Legouis documented it (1922; *William Wordsworth and Annette Vallon,* 2nd ed. rev. [New York: Archon, 1967], her influence has been employed repeatedly to "rescue the poet from the philosophers," as O. J. Campbell and Paul Mueschke described their purpose in 1926 (" 'Guilt and Sorrow,' " p. 293). The great and sometimes uncritical stress laid on her influence, and on Wordsworth's remorse, by

Herbert Read and others, may be regarded as a partial cause of the vigorous opposition of such critics as Willard Sperry (*Wordsworth's Anticlimax* [Cambridge, Mass.: Harvard University Press, 1935], pp. 79–99) and R. D. Havens (*Mind of a Poet*, pp. 508–513). Recent students of Wordsworth's development have largely ignored Annette (see, for example, Geoffrey Hartman's *Wordsworth's Poetry* 1787–1814 [New Haven: Yale University Press, 1964], p. 370, n37, and Carl Woodring's *Wordsworth* [Cambridge, Mass.:· Harvard University Press, 1968], pp. 7–8). As Pierre Legouis has pointed out, only Mrs. Moorman, among recent English critics, has viewed Annette with some "equipoise" (*William Wordsworth and Annette Vallon*, pp. 175–176). The point I seek to make is not, of course, that Annette's influence is in any sense a sufficient cause of the poetry, but that it must be recognized as a contributory cause of the psychological crisis that did shape the poetry of 1797 and 1798, and a way of understanding the significance of certain symbolic actions and images.

11. The only textual evidence that has been cited to show that his passion for Annette had "cooled" by 1794 (*PW* I, 371) is the lyric *Septimi Gades* (*PW* I, 296–298), in which Wordsworth invites "Mary" to share his rural retreat at Grasmere. Both the style and the sentiments in this poem seem to me to corroborate Reed's argument that it, together with several other poems copied in the Windy Brow notebook (MS Vs 11), dates from the later Cambridge years (pp. 302–303). Like the "Ode to Apollo," which occurs in a Cambridge notebook (MS Vs 7), it translates Horace; it mingles images and diction, furthermore, that recall the Hawkshead poems (ll. 49–51) as well as the walking tour of 1790 (ll. 13–18).

12. "Nothing in his writings suggests that among the troubles of his conscience, in the period following his return to England, moral concern . . . was predominant . . . . I am inclined to suppose that, to Wordsworth, reviewing the history of his spiritual development [in *The Prelude*], the Annette episode did not present itself as a part of his life in which his passions and his feelings had been seriously engaged" (Garrod, *Wordsworth*, p. 72).

13. On the dates of these fragments (*PW* I, 292–295) and the "Gothic Tale" see Reed, pp. 344–345, and Carol Landon, "Wordsworth's Racedown Period: Some Uncertainties Resolved," *Bulletin of the New York Public Library*, 68 (1964), 100–109. In the blank verse fragment he strictly avoids the syntactical "distortion" that Samuel Johnson regarded as the great danger of blank verse, and shows no sensitivity at all to the charge that his poetry may be prosaic. See the passage quoted in *Prelude*, p. xlii, n2.

14. This event is mentioned in an early draft of *The Borderers* (*PW* I, 351).

15. The earliest complete manuscript of *The Borderers*, like that of *Salisbury Plain*, dates from 1799 or 1800, and may represent the "curtailed" version of the play Wordsworth had sent off to Covent Garden by November 20, 1797 (*PW* I, 343; *EY*, p. 194; see Reed's comprehensive summary in Appendix X). What fragments survive of the first draft that was nearly finished in February 1797 (*EY*, p. 177) suggest that this curtailment involved changes of plot and form, but that the central action—the subversion of Mortimer by Rivers—and those elements in the play that develop the "Gothic Tale," including the role of the external universe, were present in Wordsworth's first conception, that of late 1796 and early 1797. Unless otherwise noted, all references below are to the manuscript of 1799, de Selincourt's MS B. Names of the central characters are taken from this version: Mortimer, Rivers, and Matilda. In the final version of the play (and in numerous works of criticism) these characters are named, respectively, Marmaduke, Oswald, and Idonea.

16. Roger Sharrock locates the play's origins in the Revolution, regards it as a critical dramatization of anarchic psychology, and suggests that Mortimer's final withdrawal constitutes the passage of a crucial and irreversible moral frontier (*"The Borderers:* Wordsworth on the Moral Frontier," *Durham University Journal*, n.s. 25 [1964], 170–183). Peter L. Thorslev, Jr. compares Rivers to the conventional Gothic villain of the time and finds him a prophetic type of modern individualism and existential estrangement from nature ("Wordsworth's *Borderers* and the Romantic Villain-Hero," *Studies in Romanticism*, 5 [1965–66], 84–103). Geoffrey Hartman takes a similar view on psychological grounds; Rivers, he suggests, is a type of the modern intellect in its necessary growth beyond nature, and the play a myth of the birth of this intellect (*Wordsworth's Poetry*, pp. 125–135). To these should be added Robert Osborn's recent study of Rivers' character in relation to the themes and sources of the developing play, "Meaningful Obscurity: The Antecedents and Character of Rivers," in *Bicentenary Wordsworth Studies*, pp. 393–424.

17. Emphasis on the modernity of Rivers' skepticism may obscure the fact that he is enslaved. Although Geoffrey Hartman acknowledges that Rivers is compelled by the past, and that "the independent intellect, as [Rivers] conceives it, is an illusion" (*Wordsworth's Poetry*, p. 130), he nevertheless holds him up as a type of necessary psychological individuation and intellectual emancipation from nature, a "natural man who has to be alienated from nature in order to know

himself" (p. 131). In the play, however, Rivers knows neither himself nor anything beyond himself; he is quite blind to the true significance of what he does and what he says. This is not to say that he does not incorporate powers and aspirations that Wordsworth (and Godwin) admired, but that he perverts these to justify a "great crime."

18. DCP (transcribed by Thomas J. Rountree, in *The Mighty Sum of Things* [University, Alabama: 1965], p. 124).

19. Geoffrey Hartman takes Rivers' attack on remorse at face value, and therefore seriously underestimates, I believe, the significance of humility in the play: "But once [Mortimer] has reached self-consciousness, he is offered only impossible options. These are remorse, an essentially Christian solution which Coleridge was exploring at about the same time . . . complicity [with Rivers] . . . and a radical, self-decreed exile from the common life of humanity" (*Wordsworth's Poetry*, p. 129). One may note that these three solutions are in fact two (the third, penance, follows from the first, contrition), and that neither is "impossible" to a man suffering from guilt. Although it is not dramatically convincing, Mortimer's self-exile is no more a "stalemate" (p. 130) than the chastened exile of Adam and Eve or the penance undertaken by the Red Crosse Knight. He is not so much a generic type of "consciousness of self" (p. 126), that is, as of consciousness of sin, and separation from grace.

20. I wish to thank Mr. Robert Osborn for pointing out this debt.

21. The pessimistic implications of nature in this play have been noted by Thorslev ("Wordsworth's Borderers," p. 101) and the optimistic implications by Meyer (*Formative Years*, p. 209), Mrs. Moorman (p. 306), and John Jones, who observes the importance of the star that recalls Mortimer to himself, suggests the struggle between nature and Rivers' "abstract creed," but finds that this hint goes unsupported in the play (*The Egotistical Sublime* [London: Chatto & Windus, 1964], pp. 76–78). Enid Welsford acknowledges both views, and concludes, correctly, that Wordsworth's attitude toward nature, God or Fate was equivocal (*Salisbury Plain: A Study in the Development of Wordsworth's Mind and Art* [Oxford: Blackwell, 1966], pp. 55–64). Here, as elsewhere, Geoffrey Hartman regards nature as little more than a foil for the mind: "What is great and strong in [Rivers] is certainly related to his hatred of nature, of natural law and natural piety" (*Wordsworth's Poetry*, p. 128).

22. See Aldous Huxley, "Wordsworth in the Tropics," in *Holy Face and Other Essays* (London: Fleuron, 1929).

23. Roger Sharrock observes that the border of the title "represents

the ambiguous, borderline character of [Mortimer's] effort to harmonize knowledge and right action" ("Moral Frontier," p. 178), but its theological, epistemological, and psychological significance has not to my knowledge been discussed.

24. William Blake, "A Little Boy Lost," ll. 3—4.

V: RACEDOWN: 1797

1. Quoted from Thomas Poole's account of the story by William Luke Nichols, who also recalls Wordsworth's poem, in *The Quantocks and Their Associations* (London, 1891), p. 47. See Jonathan Wordsworth's "A Wordsworth Tragedy," *Times Literary Supplement,* 21 July 1966, p. 642.

2. I follow the authoritative chronology reconstructed by John A. Finch (" 'The Ruined Cottage' Restored: Three Stages of Composition, 1795—1798," *Journal of English and Germanic Philology, 66* [1967], 179—199). Finch shows that the version of the poem completed by June 1797 was 174 lines long. Of these, all but about 25 lines survive in MS (a short introduction, and two transitional passages amounting to perhaps fifteen lines). Although Jonathan Wordsworth arrives at a figure of from 370 to 400 lines, the evidence on which he bases this correction of Finch is not clear (*The Music of Humanity* [London: Nelson, 1969], p. 16).

3. Émile Legouis, *The Early Life of William Wordsworth,* tr. J. W. Matthews, 2nd ed. rev. (1921; rpt. New York: Russell, 1965), pp. 343—344. F. R. Leavis finds it Wordsworth's finest poem (*Revaluation: Tradition & Development in English Poetry* [London: Chatto & Windus, 1936], p. 179), and F. W. Bateson calls it "poetry of the very highest quality" (*Wordsworth: A Re-interpretation* [London: Longmans, 1954], p. 123). The most ambitious study of the sources of the poem, its manuscript history, and its themes is Jonathan Wordsworth's *The Music of Humanity.* Virtually no attention, however, has been paid to the version of 1797.

4. G. W. Meyer noted Wordsworth's attempt to "cushion" the reader against pain (*Wordsworth's Formative Years* [Ann Arbor: University of Michigan Press, 1943], p. 225), and Herbert Lindenberger describes the pedlar as a human "filter" (*On Wordsworth's Prelude* [Princeton: Princeton University Press, 1963], p. 228), a term Geoffrey Hartman applies to the devices that "intervene between the strange imagination and its strange object" (*Wordsworth's Poetry 1787—1814* [New Haven: Yale University Press, 1964], p. 140).

5. Here and below I refer to lines that remain unchanged in the

published version of the manuscript of 1798 (de Selincourt's MS. B, *PW*, V, 379–404).

6. The order in which these fragments were composed has been disputed. John Finch argues that they constitute a first stage of *The Ruined Cottage* (" 'Ruined Cottage' Restored," pp. 182–183), as Geoffrey Hartman, too, appears to assume (*Wordsworth's Poetry*, pp. 135–137). But as Thomas M. Raysor first pointed out, both passages clearly developed out of the pedlar's tale in manuscript and were then transferred to the fragment de Selincourt entitled "Incipient Madness" ("Wordsworth's Early Drafts of *The Ruined Cottage* in 1797–98," *Journal of English and Germanic Philology*, 55 [1956], 4; see Jonathan Wordsworth, *Music of Humanity*, pp. 7–8). No explanation of this sequence has yet been offered.

7. *EY*, p. 684. Although this letter was dictated by Coleridge, it expressed what he called "our notions" and was signed by Wordsworth (*STCL*, II, 665).

8. Jonathan Wordsworth cites the passage as a possible source (*Music of Humanity*, pp. 61–62), and Robert Mayo compares Kate to the heroines of several Lyrical Ballads ("The Contemporaneity of the Lyrical Ballads", *Publications of the Modern Language Association*, 69 [1954], 498n).

9. Jonathan Wordsworth, *Music of Humanity*, pp. 62–65. *Hannah* was compared to the tale of Ellen in *The Excursion* by Judson Lyon (*The Excursion: A Study* [New Haven: Yale University Press, 1950], p. 39), and to *The Thorn* by Robert Mayo ("Contemporaneity", pp. 496–497).

10. T. E. Hulme, *Speculations*, 2nd ed. (London: Routledge, 1936), p. 134.

11. *Old Cumberland Beggar*, ll. 44–51 *app. crit.* On the manuscript history of the poem, see Reed, pp. 342–43.

12. DCP, fragmentary essay on the sublime. I am indebted to Mrs. Maureen Andrews for permitting me to consult her transcription of this essay.

13. Wordsworth did not go north in 1797, and this return to the Derwent was very probably imagined. It may represent a stylistic overhaul of an unpublished sonnet he had composed at Windy Brow, or before, "Derwent again I hear thy evening call."

14. This last line recalls an inverted negative in *An Evening Walk* —"They not the trip of harmless milkmaid feel" (A l. 226).

15. De Selincourt writes, for example, that "the poem as a whole represents his revulsion from the intellectual arrogance and self-sufficiency of Godwinism" (*PW* I, 329).

VI: ALFOXDEN: 1798

1. "We pass there," wrote H. W. Garrod, "suddenly and surprisedly, into the sunshine . . . Indeed, it is notable that all Wordsworth's crises fall unawares. Like the visitation of angels and demons, they happen without the just accumulation of their antecedents" (*Wordsworth; Lectures and Essays,* 2nd ed. [Oxford: Clarendon Press, 1927], p. 74). F. W. Bateson finds the work of 1798 a mixture of realistic humanitarianism and social propaganda, exemplified by *Goody Blake and Harry Gill,* and the "nature-mysticism" of the naturalistic poems (*Wordsworth: A Re-interpretation* [London: Longmans, 1954], p. 140). The latter he elsewhere describes as an "instinctive regression to childhood" (p. 183). Hartley has been cited as the dominant influence on this period by Herbert Read (*Wordsworth,* 2nd ed. [London: Faber, 1949], p. 107) and G. W. Meyer (*Wordsworth's Formative Years* [Ann Arbor: University of Michigan Press, 1943], pp. 237–239), as well as by Arthur Beatty. Coleridge's philosophical influence has been emphasized by many critics, since Émile Legouis argued that Coleridge "provided, or rather assisted [Wordsworth] to find, the only thing still needful to make him the poet he finally became, namely, a philosophy" (*The Early Life of William Wordsworth,* tr. J. W. Matthews, 2nd ed. rev. [1921; rpt. New York: Russell, 1965], p. 319). Numerous critics have agreed, including Garrod (*Wordsworth,* p. 104), B. R. Schneider, Jr. (*Wordsworth's Cambridge Education* [Cambridge: Cambridge University Press, 1957], pp. 230ff), and Jonathan Wordsworth (*The Music of Humanity* [London: Nelson, 1969], pp. 184–201).

2. Wordsworth recalled that he composed the poem "extempore," walking along the highroad from Coleridge's cottage to Alfoxden (*PW* II, 503), but he may have written it shortly thereafter, following the description in Dorothy's journal (*DWJ* I, 4). For the early versions of this poem and the episode of the discharged soldier, see Beth Darlington's "Two Early Texts: *A Night-Piece* and *The Discharged Soldier,*" in *Bicentenary Wordsworth Studies in Memory of John Alban Finch,* ed. Jonathan Wordsworth (Ithaca, N.Y.: Cornell University Press, 1970) pp. 425–448.

3. W. J. Bate, *Criticism: The Major Texts* (New York: Harcourt, Brace, 1952), p. 5.

4. This unpublished passage occurs in de Selincourt's MS A of *The Borderers* (DCP MS Vs 14), and was replaced in MS B by ll. 1985 ff.

MARGARET: You said a sudden turning of the road
             Down in the neighbouring dingle to your eye
             Did first present him
PEASANT: And at such short distance
             That I could mark him well, myself unseen.
             He leaned upon the bridge that spans the glen . . . .

Although Edward Bostetter views the first part of this episode as an anesthetizing prelude to the painful meeting with the soldier (*The Romantic Ventriloquists* [Seattle: University of Washington Press, 1963], p. 59), it is more accurately described as a deliberate contrast to what follows, as David Perkins points out (*The Quest for Permanence* [Cambridge, Mass.: Harvard University Press, 1959], p. 19). One may add that the first part (IV. 363–399) was composed in 1798, and that it therefore does not represent a rationalization of 1804, as Bostetter suggests. See Reed, pp. 63–64.

5. Here and below I refer to MS B of the poem as cited at *PW* V, 379–404.

6. See Colin Clarke's discussion of the psychological diction in the passage (*Romantic Paradox* [New York: Barnes & Noble, 1963], pp. 35–36).

7. This passage has been cited by a number of critics as evidence of Wordsworth's complacent optimism, or of the ambiguity of his moral vision, but all deal with it in its final position, at the end of the poem. Its original significance, as an immediate natural response to the pedlar's grief, has not been discussed. See n8, below.

8. Herbert Lindenberger cites this poem as an example of the way in which Wordsworth "came to skirt the tragic consequences of his material" (*On Wordsworth's Prelude* [Princeton: Princeton University Press, 1963], p. 227). Cleanth Brooks has asked, more specifically, how Wordsworth could reconcile the optimistic naturalism of the poem with Margaret's suffering ("Wordsworth and Human Suffering," in *From Sensibility to Romanticism: Essays presented to Frederick A. Pottle,* ed. Frederick W. Hilles and Harold Bloom [New York: Oxford University Press, 1965], pp. 385–386). In answer to Brooks, Jonathan Wordsworth argues that "in death [Margaret] becomes, or can be seen as being, part of a total pattern; but her suffering is not retrospectively explained or condoned" (*Music of Humanity,* p. 148). The manuscript history of the poem would suggest, I believe, that Wordsworth himself was not at all certain of the answer to the prob-

lem of evil: it is part of the "burden of the mystery." But it is clear that he was no easier than his critics with the optimism of the pedlar.

9. Elsie Smith, *An Estimate of William Wordsworth by His Contemporaries* (Oxford: Blackwell, 1932), p. 51n. Although this point is made by Stephen Parrish ("Dramatic Technique in the 'Lyrical Ballads,'" *Publications of the Modern Language Association,* 74 [1959], 87), it has so frequently been overlooked that it bears repeating. See, for example, F. W. Bateson (*Re-interpretation,* p. 137) and Robert Langbaum (*The Poetry of Experience: The Dramatic Monologue in Modern Literary Tradition* [New York: Random House, 1957], p. 56), who regard the Ballads as deliberate and innovative attempts to render a narrative form lyrical. But the ballad was classified as a song in the anthology Wordsworth used at Hawkshead, Knox's *Elegant Extracts;* by John Aikin, in his *Essay on Song-writing* (1772); and, as Parrish notes, by Wordsworth himself in the *Preface* of 1815 (PW II, 433). The point to be emphasized is that the ballad was a form that was both lyrical and objective, and that Wordsworth's indisputable attempt to intensify the emotional dimensions of the form by no means implies an indulgence of romantic subjectivism. Campbell and Mueschke observed, for example, that the title reflects an intention to employ the ballad "not so much for purposes of pure narration as for the vehicle of personal emotion" ("Wordsworth's Aesthetic Development, 1795–1802," University of Michigan Publications, Language and Literature, 10 [1933], 22). Albert Gérard cites Eliot's theory of the "objective correlative," and confirms that their subject matter is "not there for its own sake but for the sake of the emotion it produced" (*English Romantic Poetry* [Berkeley: University of California Press, 1968], p. 65). This emphasis is correct, but it diverts attention from the fact that the emotion developed in the ballads is not "personal," and that they are not expressionistic but pragmatic in mode, presentations of pre-selected artistic forms to an audience for the sake of highly complex and premeditated effects.

10. *PW* II, 435; *Complete Works of William Hazlitt,* ed. P. P. Howe (London: Dent, 1930–1934) XVII, 118–119.

11. Robert Mayo, "The Contemporaneity of the Lyrical Ballads," *PMLA,* 69 (1954), 486–522.

12. John Danby, *The Simple Wordsworth,* (London: Routledge & Kegan Paul, 1960), pp. 38–47.

13. The poem appears in Knox's *Elegant Extracts,* and Wordsworth echoed it in the first version of *Salisbury Plain.*

14. Danby notes the play on "gentle," but he does not stress the

ironies involved, or their function in the transformation of the speaker (*Simple Wordsworth*, pp. 44–45).

15. See Wordsworth's letter to Wilson (*EY*, pp. 357–358), and *BL* II, 35.

16. Francis Jeffrey, "Thalaba the Destroyer" (rev.), *Edinburgh Review*, 1 (October 1802), 66.

17. Ramond praises the kindness shown by the Valaisiennes toward the idiot, and notes man's universal respect for those innocent of the crimes of the earth (*Lettres de M. William Coxe a M. W. Melmoth, sur l'État politique, civil et naturel de la Suisse* . . . [Paris, 1782], II, 65–66).

18. To this powerful nexus of private symbols one may add the heroine's name, Martha Ray. Her namesake, Basil Montague's mother, was, like the heroines of the Racedown poems, the victim of a crime of passion, and her grandson, little Basil Montague, was in Wordsworth's charge throughout the Racedown years. Although the poet's use of Martha's name has been regarded as "completely inexplicable" (R. L. Brett and A. R. Jones, eds., *Lyrical Ballads* [New York: Barnes & Noble, 1963], p. 285), it clearly falls into the symbolic pattern that dominates *Salisbury Plain* and its successors.

19. Wordsworth insisted on the autonomy of the "loquacious narrator" both in 1798 and in 1800 (*PW* II, 384, 512–13), and a major focus of criticism since has been the analysis of his role in the poem. To S. M. Parrish (" 'The Thorn': Wordsworth's Dramatic Monologue," *Journal of English Literary History*, 24 [1957], 153–163), the primary function of the poem is the dramatic presentation of the psychology of superstition, as Wordsworth suggested (*PW* II, 512). In his brief comment, Geoffrey Hartman recognizes the narrator's ambivalence ("a mind shying from, yet drawn to, a compulsive center of interest"), but interprets him as a "caricature of Wordsworth's own imagination-in-process" (*Wordsworth's Poetry* [New Haven: Yale University Press, 1964], pp. 147, 148). Both John Danby (*Simple Wordsworth*, p. 58) and Albert Gérard stress his role in guiding and organizing response to the imagery and the plot of the poem (*English Romantic Poetry*, pp. 64–88). That his primary function is to exalt response to Martha Ray, however, has not been considered.

20. *BL* II, 36; Smith, *Estimate*, p. 31. Recalling Crabb Robinson, who, after "gently alluding" to the lines, confessed to Wordsworth that he could not "read them out in company" (*Henry Crabb Robinson on Books and Their Writers*, ed. Edith J. Morley [London: Dent, 1938], I, 166), James A. W. Heffernan cites their "unendurable banality"

(Wordsworth's Theory of Poetry: The Transforming Imagination [Ithaca: Cornell University Press, 1969], p. 6).

21. See ll. 89–90, 105, 114, 155–156, and 247.

22. Geoffrey Hartman refers the telescope not to the narrator but to Wordsworth: "The captain is the ocular man in Wordsworth, searching for a sacred or secret spot, spying on nature (his telescope is a big eye)" (*Wordsworth's Poetry,* p. 148).

23. Several critics have emphasized the horror of the poem. Johnathan Wordsworth, for example, calls it a "horror story" (*Music of Humanity,* p. 76), and John Danby argues that Swinburne was "right to record 'the dreadfulness of a shocking reality' in his response to the poem, 'an effect of unmodified and haunting horror' " (*Simple Wordsworth,* p. 70). Albert Gérard, on the other hand, regards the poem as an attempt to construct an "attitude of pity and sympathy, focussed on the woman's misery . . . because what matters is not guilt and punishment but sorrow and compassion" (*English Romantic Poetry,* p. 81). Neither interpretation accounts for the heroic element in the poem, which carries Martha Ray, like Simon Lee and the Idiot Boy, far above pity or lurid horror.

24. Smith, *Estimate,* p. 36.

25. Ibid., p. 31.

26. Francis Jeffrey, "Thalaba," pp. 66–67.

VII: RETURN TO THE WYE: 1798

1. G. M. Harper, *William Wordsworth: His Life, Works, and Influence,* 3rd. ed. (1929; rpt. New York: Russell, 1960), II, 467. With Harper we may group Arthur Beatty and G. W. Meyer. Geoffrey Hartman makes a similar assumption, that "Wordsworth came under the joint imperative of English Protestantism and the Enlightenment" (*Wordsworth's Poetry, 1787–1814* [New Haven: Yale University Press, 1964], pp. 74–75), but traces their effects on the poet's imagination from a perspective unsympathetic to the Enlightenment.

2. Here again we find a single assumption being viewed in two ways. A host of critics have sympathetically described Wordsworth's naturalism as "pantheism" or "mysticism," among them Legouis, Garrod, Stallknecht, E. D. Hirsch, Jr., and Jonathan Wordsworth. F. W. Bateson, however, uses the term in a pejorative sense; for him Wordsworth's naturalism is the product of a regression into romantic subjectivism.

3. The most useful of these are J. W. Beach's *The Concept of Na-*

ture in Nineteenth-Century English Poetry (New York: Macmillan, 1936); and Melvin Rader's *Wordsworth: A Philosophical Approach* (Oxford: Clarendon Press, 1967).

4. John Jones, *The Egotistical Sublime* (London: Chatto & Windus, 1954), p. 92.

5. Alfred North Whitehead, *Science and the Modern World* (New York: Macmillan, 1925), p. 122.

6. R. L. Brett and A. R. Jones, eds., "Introduction," *Lyrical Ballads* (New York: Barnes & Noble, 1963), p. 1 (L).

7. Arthur Beatty, *Wordsworth: His Doctrine and Art in Their Historical Relations,* 2nd ed. (Madison: University of Wisconsin Press, 1927), p. 108; René Wellek, *A History of Modern Criticism: 1750–1950* (New Haven: Yale University Press, 1955–65), II, 145; Rader, *Wordsworth,* p. 149.

8. David Perkins, *Wordsworth and the Poetry of Sincerity* (Cambridge, Mass.: Harvard University Press, 1964), p. 195.

9. N. P. Stallknecht, *Strange Seas of Thought* (Durham: Duke University Press, 1945), p. 86; Jones, *Egotistical Sublime,* p. 85; Roger N. Murray, *Wordsworth's Style: Figures and Themes in the "Lyrical Ballads" of 1800* (Lincoln: University of Nebraska Press, 1967), pp. 105–106.

10. Herbert Lindenberger, *On Wordsworth's Prelude* (Princeton: Princeton University Press, 1963), p. 90; Jones *Egotistical Sublime,* p. 33.

11. Lindenberger, *On Wordsworth's Prelude,* p. 48.

12. Jones, *Egotistical Sublime,* p. 33.

13. Bateson writes that "the Wordsworthian religion of nature seems to be implicit in these recurrent metaphors. Their primitive, infantile character, for one thing, shows how personal and subjective it was" (*Wordsworth: A Re-interpretation* [London: Longmans, 1954], p. 183).

14. As Bateson suggests (*Re-interpretation,* p. 183).

15. See Locke's *Essay,* bk. II, ch. xxi, sec. 1–3. He defines a sensible "quality" as "the *power* to produce any idea in our mind" (II, viii, 8; my italics). Secondary qualities, furthermore, are "nothing . . . but powers" (II, viii, 10).

16. *Essay,* IV, iii, 6; Locke's italics. The word takes on great importance in his demonstration of the existence of God, as well. See IV, x, 2, 8.

17. Abraham Tucker, *The Light of Nature Pursued* (London, 1836), I, 278.

18. J. W. Beach, *Concept of Nature,* p. 576; B. R. Schneider, Jr., *Wordsworth's Cambridge Education* (Cambridge: Cambridge University Press, 1957), p. 261; *Aeneid* VI. 726–727.

19. Following Newton, Locke had defined "body" or material substance in terms of its power to communicate motion by impulse (II, xxiii, 17).

20. Jones, *Egotistical Sublime,* p. 47.

21. Donald Davie, *Articulate Energy: An Inquiry into the Syntax of English Poetry* (London: Routledge & Kegan Paul, 1955), p. 107.

22. Here again Wordsworth takes a commonplace of the empirical philosophy with passionate literalness. The conception of the mind as a storehouse or receptacle of images was of course implied by Locke's "cabinet." It appears, for example, in Burke's discussion of how to enlarge our "stock" of images (*A Philosophical Enquiry into the Origin of Our Ideas of the Sublime and Beautiful,* ed. J. T. Boulton [London: Routledge & Kegan Paul, 1958], p. 18). Tucker describes the imagination as a "receptacle of images" (*Light of Nature Pursued,* I, 16); and Johnson's Imlac recalls his youthful attempt to "store his mind with inexhaustible variety," that is, with ideas.

23. Bishop C. Hunt, Jr., "Wordsworth's Marginalia on *Paradise Lost,*" *Bulletin of the New York Public Library,* 73 (1969), 170. On the basis of handwriting, Hunt assigns this comment to the years 1798–1800 (p. 168).

24. John Scott, *Critical Essays on Some of the Poems of Several English Poets* (London, 1785), p. 59.

25. *The Works of Francis Bacon,* ed. James Spedding, R. E. Ellis, and D. D. Heath (London, 1857–1874), IV, 32–33 (tr. James Spedding).

26. Gérard, *English Poetry,* p. 100.

27. John F. Danby, *The Simple Wordsworth* (London: Routledge & Kegan Paul, 1960), p. 97; W. K. Wimsatt, *The Verbal Icon* (Lexington: University of Kentucky Press, 1954), p. 111; Geoffrey Hartman, *The Unmediated Vision* (New Haven: Yale University Press, 1954), p. 4; Gérard, *English Romantic Poetry,* pp. 95–101.

28. Allusions to Gilpin are cited by Brett and Jones (*Lyrical Ballads,* p. 291) and Carl Woodring (*Wordsworth* [Cambridge, Mass.: Harvard University Press, 1968], p. 63).

29. Gérard, *English Romantic Poetry,* p. 107.

30. See, for example, Arthur Beatty, who derives his theory of the "three ages of man" from this passage (*Doctrine and Art,* pp. 71–73).

31. Gérard, *English Romantic Poetry,* p. 113.

32. Ibid., p. 117.

33. "The character of a deceased friend or beloved kinsman is not seen, no—nor ought to be seen, otherwise than as a tree through a tender haze or a luminous mist, that spiritualises and beautifies it; that takes away, indeed, but only to the end that the parts which are not abstracted may appear more dignified and lovely; may impress and affect the more" (*PW* V, 452).

34. Jones, *Egotistical Sublime,* p. 94.

Index

Abrams, M. H., xvi n, 71
Abstractions, 126, 208; in Cowper's
  Task, 143-144; redeemed by poetic
  form, 158-160
Action, disappears from W's style,
  56; as sign of feeling, 142-143
Addison, Joseph, 24, 226
Aikin, John, 5, 14, 22, 23, 61, 226,
  280 n9
Aikin, Lucy, 256 n7, 8
Akenside, Mark, 14, 101, 207,
  257 n17
Allegory: allegorical imagery, 14; at
  Cambridge, 45
Alliteration: in *The Ruined Cottage,*
  146-147; in yew-tree *Lines,* 155;
  and Southey's *Inscription,* 156; in
  Lyrical Ballads, 186, 194
Ambush: as conventional metaphor
  for maturation, 34; in W's poetry,
  39, 40; of war, 75; in syntax, 144-
  145; as function of poem, 157; by
  nature, 166; literal, 170-171; in
  Lyrical Ballads, 185, 199; by sensation, 240
Anacreon, 5
Analogy: in Hawkshead poems, 14,
  15, 24-25, 29; in *An Evening
  Walk,* 55; in *Salisbury Plain,* 1793,
  86, 87, 91, 94; John Scott on,
  264 n19; divine analogy, as solution to problem of maturation, 35;
  divine analogy in Hawkshead

poems, 39, 40; divine analogy, ab-
  sent from *Descriptive Sketches,* 70
Animism: as effect of form, 209-
  210; as effect of diction, 218
Apocalyptic imagery, 27; in Hawks-
  head poems, 259 n32; in *An Eve-
  ning Walk,* 264-265 n22; in Cole-
  ridge's *Religious Musings,* 119
Apostrophe, 103; in *Tintern Abbey,*
  234, 236
Aristotle, 206
Arnold, Matthew, xi, xii, 205, 250
Association of ideas: in Hawkshead
  poems, 12-13; in *An Evening
  Walk,* 1794, 269-270 n14
Aubin, R. A., 262 n9
Austen, Jane, 203; *Emma,* 196

Bacon, Francis, 3, 4, 63; *The Great
  Instauration,* 228; and epistemology of art, 9, 37, 93; and W's development, 227-228, 248
Baker, Herschel, 256 n11
Ballad, 5; as lyric, 184-185; and W's
  radicalism, 181
Banality, in *Lyrical Ballads,* 185,
  189, 198-199, 281 n20
Bate, W. J., 168
Bateson, F. W., xiv n, 258 n23,
  259 n29; on W's neurosis, 256 n8,
  257 n11; on *An Evening Walk,*
  264-265 n22; on Annette Vallon,
  261 n1; on *The Ruined Cottage,*

Bateson, F. W. (*continued*)
276 n3; on *Lyrical Ballads,* 278
n1, 280 n9; and W's naturalism,
282 n2, 283 n13, 14
Baudelaire, Charles, 204
Beach, J. W., 62, 220, 282-283 n3
Beattie, James, 1, 5, 14, 29, 33, 44,
62; lack of fortitude, 36-37.
WORKS: *The Minstrel,* 12, 29, 66,
259 n28, 260 n41; theme of maturation in, 33; rational hope in, 34-
35, 36-37; cited by W, 38, 39;
Ode to Hope, 39; *Retirement,* 31
Beatty, Arthur, 213, 260 n39,
265 n24, 27, 278 n1, 282 n1, 284
n30
Beaumont, Lady, 166
Beaupuy, Michael, 63, 69, 85, 106
Beerbohm, Max, 196
Beggar's Petition, The, 189-190
Berkeley, George, 18, 36, 178
Blair, Hugh, 13, 22, 25
Blake, William, 17, 27, 40, 110, 220-
221, 223; view of W duplicated in
recent criticism, xiv and n, 266-
267 n32; idealism of, 36, 38, 71,
134-135; on W's impiety, 212-213.
WORKS: *America,* 71; *Holy Thurs-
day,* 109; *A Little Boy Lost,* 134;
*The Marriage of Heaven and
Hell,* 77
Blank verse, 119; and lyrics, 180-
181; in poetry after 1798, 187;
and syntactical distortion, 273 n13
Boehme, Jacob, 205
Bostetter, Edward, 278-279 n4
Bowles, William, 48, 56, 62, 80
Boyle, Robert, 18
Bradley, A. C., xi and n
Brett, R. L., 281 n18, 283 n6,
284 n28
Bronson, Bertrand, 256 n16
Brooks, Cleanth, 279 n8
Browne, Moses, 54, 61
Bürger, Gottfried A., 184

Burke, Edmund, 78, 284 n22
Burney, Charles, 202
Burns, Robert, 32
Byron, George Gordon, Lord:
Childe Harold's Pilgrimage, 230

Calvert, William, 79, 83
Cambridge, University of: links to
Hawkshead, 4; W attends, 43-44;
W's disappointments at, 43-44, 46,
49
Campbell, O. J., 272 n9, 10, 280 n9
Carbonnières, Ramond de, 61, 73;
and *Descriptive Sketches,* 63-65,
68, 265 n24; and *Prelude* VI. 571,
64; and *The Idiot Boy,* 195,
281 n17; on Coxe's intolerance,
267-268 n33
Cartesian dualism. *See* Dualism
Catullus, xv, 5, 27, 39
Chain, image of, 111, 115, 140, 152
Chapin, Chester, 257 n16
Charity of W's art, 204, 247
Chatterton, Thomas, 6, 24
"Children of the Wood, The," 35
Cicero, 3
Clarke, Colin, 257 n17, 279 n6
Clarke, James, 263 n11
Classicism, W's, 226-227, 248. *See
also* Mimetic theory, Neoclassical
tradition
Classics, W's early imitation of,
261 n2. *See also* Virgil
Cohen, Ralph, 257 n16
Coleridge, Samuel Taylor, 74, 94,
104, 110, 119, 160, 162, 176, 183,
210, 217, 277 n7; on reason, 3;
on Berkeley, 18; on Bowles, 48;
on Godwin, 107; on guilt, 110;
W's independence of, 120, 163,
175; idealism of, 134, 222-223;
generosity of, 163; on nature, 166,
168; on novelty, 207; praises *An
Evening Walk,* 262 n; on *Descriptive Sketches,* 52, 59; on *The Idiot*

Boy, 194; on *Lyrical Ballads,* 199, 202; praises W, 93, 108, 137, 205; influence in 1798, 162-163, 174-175, 278 n1; style of, 217-218, 222-223. WORKS: *The Ancient Mariner,* 116, 179, 224; *The Dungeon,* 217; *The Nightingale,* 223; *Religious Musings,* 118, 178; *Frost At Midnight,* 229

Collins, William, 5, 13, 21, 25, 46, 72, 258 n19, 20, 259 n32; idealism of, 13-14, 38

Cooper, Anthony Ashley, Earl of Shaftesbury, 220

Cottage, image of, 91, 94, 116, 117, 138, 153

Cottle, Joseph, 229

Covenant, biblical: confirmed by Alpine landscape, 66, 68; breach of, by man, 81; embodied in external nature, 166

Cowley, Abraham, 24

Cowper, William, 32; poetic diction of, 87; style of *The Task,* 143-145

Coxe, William, 61, 266 n31, 267 n33

Crabbe, George, 32

Critical Review, The, 262-263 n10

Cumberland, Richard, 21

Danby, John, xiii, 189, 231, 255 n6, 280-281 n14, 282 n23

Dante, 183

Darlington, Beth, 278 n2

Darwin, Charles, xi, 129

Darwin, Erasmus, 45, 220

Davie, Donald, 224

Deluge: biblical and geological, effect on Alpine landscape, 64, 66; reenacted in *Descriptive Sketches,* 66; W's understanding of, 65; as metaphor for freedom, 68-69; as hallucination, 111; as metaphor for feeling, 194; and the Snowdon ascent, 266 n29

Deserted woman (or wife), figure of, 112-114, 116, 137, 140, 197

Diction, W's: vices of, 52; incremental, 60, 70, 243; "poetic," 87; colloquial, 100, 119, 121, 272 n5, 273 n13; Latinate, 155; psychological, 169, 279 n6; stock, in *Lyrical Ballads,* 191-192; in descriptions of perception, 215; and philosophy, 217-218, 270 n15; precision and scope of, 203-204, 218-221; Newtonian, 219-220

Displacement, psychological, in Racedown poems, 114

Dualism: as conventional end-point of maturation, 33; and Revolution, 70-71, 247. Cartesian: 220; instability of, 18; and Protestant conscience, 133; respected by W, 216

Dyer, John, 259 n28

"Egotistical sublime," 12, 247, 256 n11. See also Subjectivism, Idealism

Eliot, T. S., 204

Ellipsis, 87

Emotion, W disciplines and purifies, 77, 128, 139-141, 185, 187, 189, 248; W's distrust of, 134-135

Empiricism, 3, 4; and poetry of sensibility, 10; and the "abyss of idealism," 17-18; and W's epistemology, 213-214; language of, 219-220; W's 225

Enlightenment, the, 3, 9, 248, 282 n1

Epistemology, W's, 275-276 n23; and isolation, 117; of crime, 120; and hope, 129-130, 133; mystery of, 216; and presentational style, 213-217; compared to Coleridge, 217-218, 221-222; after 1798, 250. See also Idealism, Realism, Subject-object relation

Euclid, 4, 238

Exposure: to landscape, moral significance of, 89, 94, 131, 139; as an end of W's art, 157, 161

Expressionistic theory: in poetry of sensibility, 16; in early poems, anachronism of, xiv-xvi; in 1798 and after, 175, 182-183; in *Tintern Abbey*, 244

Fancy: and imagination, in early poems, 12; and primary qualities, 18; in human maturation, 33-37; W indulges, 6, 37-38; and rejects, 38-40, 55, 62, 72, 251

Figures: in early description, 25-27; in mature descriptions of perception, 215. *See also* Alliteration, Analogy, Apostrophe, Ellipsis, Hyperbole, Irony, Metaphor, Personification, Repetition, Synaesthesia, Understatement

Finch, John, 271 n3, 276 n2, 277 n6

Fink, Z. S., 255 n2, 5, 258 n26

Fixation, psychological, 142, 149-150, 157; and meter, 186

Fleming, John, 163, 182, 260 n1

French Revolution, xv, 65, 76, 85, 89, 94; and nature, 47, 62-63, 96, 104; impact on W's style, 59-61, 72-74, 247; W's millennial interpretation of, 68-69, 71-72; and Annette Vallon, 76, 115; failure of, 105-106, 139, 150; perpetuated in W's art, 161, 195, 203

Freud, Sigmund, 19

Galileo, 18

Garrod, H. W., xii, 282 n2; on *Descriptive Sketches*, 267 n33; on Godwin, 271 n1, 272 n6; on W's relation to Annette Vallon, 273 n12; on *Lyrical Ballads*, 278 n1

Gentleman's Magazine, The, 23, 263 n10

Gérard, Albert, 280 n9; on *The Thorn*, 281 n19, 282 n23; on *Tintern Abbey*, 229, 231, 236, 239, 284 n32

Gerard, Alexander, 258 n18

Gibbet, image of, 111, 197

Gill, Stephen, 268 n5

Gilpin, William, 24, 233

Godwin, William, 96, 160, 210, 269 n13, 277 n15; influence on W, 106-107; critical views of, 270-271 n1; and *The Borderers*, 121, 125-126, 275 n17; *Caleb Williams*, 109, 272 n6

Goldsmith, Oliver, 184; *The Deserted Village*, 262 n9

Gothicism: W indulges, 6-8, 26; and disciplines, 38, 55, 72; transcends Gothic sensation, 120; draws upon Gothic fiction, 124

Gratitude, decorum of: in *The Ruined Cottage*, 1798 version, 173, 177; in *Tintern Abbey*, 229-230, 237-238

Grave, image of, 111, 115, 196, 198

Gray, Thomas, 5, 9, 10, 14, 33, 40, 45, 62, 101. WORKS: *The Bard*, 11, 256 n9; *Elegy*, 26; *Ode on a Distant Prospect of Eton College*, ambush of hope in, 34, 86, 95, 160, 249; *Ode on the Pleasure Arising from Vicissitude*, 9, 54, 258 n20, 259 n32; *Ode on the Spring*, 23; *Progress of Poesy*, 31

Greene, J. C., 266 n28

Grob, Alan, 271 n1

Hagstrum, Jean, 263 n13

Harper, G. M., 205, 267 n33, 271 n1, 272 n10

Hartley, David, 161, 206, 260 n39, 269 n13, 278 n1

Hartman, Geoffrey, 262 n9; premises of, xiv n, 266-267 n30, 32, 282 n1; on Hawkshead poems, 256 n8, 9,

260 n38; on imagination, 257 n11; on *An Evening Walk,* 264 n20, 22; on *Descriptive Sketches,* 267 n33; on Annette Vallon, 273 n10; on Racedown poems, 274 n16, 17, 275 n19, 21, 276 n4, 277 n6; on *The Thorn,* 281 n19, 282 n22; on *Tintern Abbey,* 231, 233

Havens, R. D., x, 270-271 n1, 273 n10

Hawkshead Grammar School, 1-2; curriculum of, 3-5

Hazlitt, William, 185, 256 n11

Hefferman, J. A. W., 281-282 n20

Hirsch, E. D., Jr., 282 n2

Holbach, Baron d', 63

Hope: odyssey of, in human life cycle, xvi, 33, 40-41; objects of, quest for in eighteenth-century poetry, 35-37, and in W's poetry, 91, 94; as end of poetry, 107, 250; cottage as symbol for, 138-139; task of renouncing, 127, 149, 150; psychopathology of, 149

Horace, xvi, 27, 28, 203, 273 n11

Hulme, T. E., 148

Humanism: classical, 2, 219-220, 249; and W's naturalism, 96, 116-117, 179, 245, 265 n22

Hume, David, 36

Hunt, Bishop C., Jr., 226, 284 n23

Huxley, Aldous, 129

Huxley, Thomas Henry, 129

Hyperbole, 61; as effect of loving retrospection, 243

Idealism, philosophic: as possible anachronism in study of early poems, xiii-xiv, 266-267 n32; W's instinctive fear of, 17-18; transcendental, Coleridge's, 94; Blake's, 134; "abyss of," 16-20, 29, 30, 40, 132, 250

Identity: stylistic parameters of, 56-58; W's recovery of, in 1794, 104;

in 1798, 163, 182-183; in *Tintern Abbey,* 230

Imagery: and imagination, 16; accuracy and detail of, 22-23, 50-51, 258-259 n27, 259 n28, 263 n15; of sensuous deprivation, 29; and external substance, 31, 216-217; gravitational, 99, 216; of starvation, 112, 131-132, 217; as "language" of feeling, 142-143; and of nature, 162; literal, 212-213; novel, 262-263 n10. *See also* Apocalyptic imagery, Sensation

Images, significant and symbolic. *See* Chain, Cottage, Deserted Woman, Gibbet, Grave, Light, Storm, Sunset, Wanderer

Imagination: in 1804 and after, xiii-xiv; autonomy of, xiv n, 13-14, 41; primary, 12, 154, 225, 257 n17; and fancy, 12; creative and visionary, 13-14, 135, 149, 248; W's discipline of, 224-228; apocalyptic, 257 n11; and Hartley, 260 n39

"Intentional fallacy," xiii

Inversion, syntactical, 277 n14

Irony, 46, 82, 92, 125, 129; in *Lyrical Ballads,* 184-185, 190-191, 196, 203

Irrationalism: cultivated by W, 6-9; disciplined, 46

James, Henry, *The Turn of the Screw,* 196

Jeffrey, Francis, 195, 202-203

Johnson, Samuel, xvi, 13, 25, 57, 284 n22; realism of, 18, 19; fortitude of, 36, 37, 40, 106, 134; and W, 134, 227, 248; on imagination, 225; on blank verse, 273 n13; *Preface to Shakespeare,* 227; *Prologue,* quoted by W, 226-227; *Rasselas,* 37, 227; *The Vanity of Human Wishes,* realism and forti-

Johnson, Samuel (*continued*)
    tude of, 36, 151, 227, echoed by
    W, 96
Jones, A. R., 281 n18, 283 n6
    284 n28
Jones, David, 59, 83
Jones, John, 216, 218, 221, 256-
    257 n11, 258 n22, 283 n4, 9; on
    Hawkshead poems, 28; on Windy
    Brow fragments, 268 n8; on *The
    Borderers*, 275 n21; on *Tintern
    Abbey*, 285 n34
Jonson, Ben, 203
Joyce, James, 204
Juvenal, 36

Kames, Henry Home, Lord, 14, 15,
    26
Kant, Immanuel, 3
Keats, John, xi, 16, 244, 256 n11;
    Hyperion, 81; *Ode on a Grecian
    Urn*, 233
Knight, Richard Payne, 259-260 n27
Knox, Vicesimus, 258 n19, 280 n9,
    13

Landon, Carol, 273 n13
Landscape: in Hawkshead poems,
    21-27; mythological, 27-29; and
    Georgics, 46; picturesque, 50; rev-
    olutionary, 60-62; symbolic, 81-
    82, 88-89, 90-91, 130-131; emble-
    matic, 157; in *Tintern Abbey*, 230-
    234
Langbaum, Robert, 280 n9
Langhorne, John, 11, 25, 33
Leavis, F. R., 276 n3
Legouis, Émile, 268 n4, 278 n1; on
    stylistic vices of *An Evening
    Walk*, 52; on *Descriptive Sketches*,
    265 n24, 267 n33; on *The Bor-
    derers*, 121, 125; on *The Ruined
    Cottage*, 137; on Annette Vallon,
    272 n10
Legouis, Pierre, 273 n10

Light and dark, imagery of, 29, 50,
    98-99, 141, 153. *See also* Sunset
Lindenberger, Herbert, 216, 217,
    276 n4, 279 n8
Locke, John, 4, 10, 13, 35, 61, 214;
    and "demonstrative" reason, 3, 4,
    34, 94; primary and secondary
    qualities, 18-19, 257 n17; sensa-
    tionalism of assumed by W, 160,
    207, 213, 216; language of, 218,
    220; W's knowledge of, 255 n5;
    and Hartley, 260 n39
Lonsdale, Lord, 184
Lorrain, Claude, 57, 61
Louis XVI, 78
Lyric form: W's early devotion to,
    5; in later poetry, 104, 187

Macpherson, James: *Fingal*, 24; *Os-
    sian*, 22, 26, 32
Malthus, Thomas, 129
"Mary of Esthwaite," 259 n29
Mason, William, 51
Materialism: monistic, 18; in W's
    revolutionary naturalism, 71; in
    Windy Brow fragments, 269 n12,
    269-270 n14; reductive, 133; dis-
    trusted by Blake and Coleridge,
    xiv n, 134, 223
Maturation: humanistic paradigm
    of, 33; as viewed by poets of sensi-
    bility, 33; crisis of, idealistic solu-
    tion, 35-36, realistic solution, 36-
    37; in *Salisbury Plain*, 86; fixation
    of, 126-127, 149-150; in *Tintern
    Abbey*, 237-238. *See also* Am-
    bush, Analogy, Dualism, Fancy,
    Hope, Imagination, Pastoral, Ra-
    tionalism, Sensibility, Virgil
Mayo, Robert, 188, 277 n8, 9,
    280 n11
Mediation: by landscape, 97, 138;
    by style, 98; by narrator, 139-141;
    by time and memory, 138
Melancholy, 5-6, 72, 267-268 n33

Memory: as type of reflection, 56, 160; imagery generated by, 87; a mode of mediation, 138; assumes greater importance, 228-229; in *Tintern Abbey*, 234, 245
Meredith, George, 81
Metaphor, 14, 145, 192
Meter: octosyllabics, 5, 44, 184; pentameter line, 44; pentameter couplet, 5, 44, in *An Evening Walk*, 50, in topographical poetry, 262 n9; couplet broken, 83, 103, 246; line-ending, 156; rhyme in topographical poetry, 264 n1; in *The Ruined Cottage*, 145-148; disciplinary function in *Lyrical Ballads*, 185; in *Tintern Abbey*, 230. *See also* Blank verse
Meyer, G. W., 282 n1; on *Descriptive Sketches*, 265 n24, 267 n33; on Windy Brow fragments, 268 n8, 269 n12, 13; on Godwin, 270-271 n1; on Racedown poems, 272 n6, 9, 275 n21, 276 n4; on poems of 1798, 278 n1
Miles, Josephine, 10, 11
Milton, John, 63, 183, 203, 221; imitated by W, 5, 44, 45, 71, 148; view of poetry, 37, 148; Protestantism of, 63; fortitude of, celebrated by W, 95-96, 106, 134. WORKS: *Il Penseroso*, 5, 21, 188; *L'Allegro*, 5, 14, 21, 90, 188; *Lycidas*, 27, 226; *Ode on the Morning of Christ's Nativity*, 28; *Paradise Lost*, 90, 99, 219; hope, and immanence of God in, 35, 211; deluge in, 65, 66, 82, 266 n29; and covenant, 66, 68; humanism of, 67, 248; and French Revolution, 72; Satan, alluded to by W, 102; ethics of, 112; reason in, 160; cited by W, 166; W's marginalia, 226
Mimetic theory: 248; in early po-

ems, xv-xvi; implied by landscapes of 1798, 167-168; exemplified by the pedlar of 1798, 175; in *The Idiot Boy*, 203
Mont Blanc, 67-68, 69, 265 n25
Moor, Karl, 123
Moorman, Mary, 258 n23, 260 n37, 266 n31, 268 n4; on *Descriptive Sketches*, 267 n33; on Annette Vallon, 273 n10; on *The Borderers*, 275 n21
Mueschke, Paul, 272 n9, 10, 280 n9
Murray, R. N., 283 n9
Mysticism, 205, 218, 228
Myth: and landscape, 27-29; and French Revolution, 71

Narrative poems, psychological function of, 85
Narrator, function of in *Lyrical Ballads*, 188-202
Natural law: assimilated to Revolution, 62-63; enigma of, 81; as alternative to political revolution, 96; treachery of, 128-129; in *Lyrical Ballads*, 187, 192. *See also* Naturalism
Natural sympathy: a conventional motif, 47, 48; and William Bowles, 48; and Revolution, 69; and W's personal experience, 133; as instrument of redemption, 174, 207; W opposes to humanism, 80, 176-179; W disciplines and reenacts in *Tintern Abbey*, 229. *See also* Gratitude, Naturalism
Naturalism: as temporary stage in human life cycle, 34-35; continuity of in W's development, 206; complexity of, 247; centrality of W's struggle to affirm nature, 247; at Hawkshead, 21-32, 40-41; at Cambridge, 46-48, 62; effect of Revolution on, 62-63, 69, 70, 73; at Windy Brow, 101-102, 269 n12;

Naturalism (*continued*)
in 1798, 32, 175; W's struggle to
humanize in 1798, 179-180, 187,
209; in early *Prelude,* 20; and
Ramond, 63-64. *See also* Natural
law, Natural sympathy, Nature
Nature: as respite from self-consciousness, 57, 247; embodies biblical covenant, 96; impotence of,
117-118; formative power of, 154,
173-174; as art of God, 166; as
language of God, 212-213. *See
also* Naturalism, Natural law,
Natural sympathy
Necessitarianism, 109-110, 112, 172,
175, 176, 179
Negation, 91-92, 155, 169, 187
Neoclassical tradition: W's relation
to, 203, 247-249
Newton, Isaac, xi, 35, 62, 63; and
W's schooling, 4-5; cosmology of,
5, 220, 255-256 n6
Nicholson, Marjorie, 257 n17,
266 n28

Optimism, 279-280 n8; W's suspicion of, 40
Osborn, Robert, 274 n16, 275 n20

Paley, William, 210
Pantheism: scanty evidence for in
W, 211-213; and Newton, 256 n6;
materialistic, in 1794, 269 n12, 14
Parrish, S. M., 280 n9, 281 n19
Pastoral: as conventional metaphor
for youth, 33; and Revolution, 70;
invaded by evil, 118; elegy, 151,
180; French, 262 n9
"Pathetic fallacy," 26
Pathos: as premeditated effect, xvi;
W indulges at Hawkshead, 39; at
Cambridge, 44-45, 261 n2; of
revolution, 72; in *Descriptive
Sketches,* 267 n33; in *The Thorn,*
282 n23
Percy, Thomas, 184

Perkins, David: on W's symbolism,
216; on "discharged soldier," 278-
279 n4
Personification: "decorative," defined, 14; "passionate," defined, 26; W's use of, at Hawkshead, 14-15, 26-27; in *An Evening
Walk,* 54-55; in *Descriptive
Sketches,* 60-61, 265 n25; in 1793,
82, 84, 86, 87, 91, 92, 94, 141-
142; at Racedown, 272 n5; in
1798, 165, 198, 225-226; and W's
philosophy, 212-213, 217; as parody, 155; John Scott on, 264 n19
Philosophy of W, 62, 101-102, 205-
228; continuity of, 206; and feeling, 207-208, 216-217; influence
of poetic form and decorum on,
208-210, 218. *See also* Dualism,
Empiricism, Epistemology, Materialism, Naturalism, Necessitarianism, Pantheism, Rationalism, Sensation, Substance
Picturesque: canons of, in *An Evening Walk,* 50, 57, 263 n13,
266 n13; rejected by W, 61-62;
in *Tintern Abbey,* 233
Piper, Herbert, 268 n8, 269 n10, n12,
n14
Pitt, William, the younger, 184
Plato, 3, 206
Poet, W's conception of: as exemplary, 150, 174, 175-176, 183;
power and authority of, 167, 191;
alters in 1798, 179-180
Poetry, W's conception of: reliance
on nature, 143; as completion of
nature, 168; as a "motion of
hope," 107, 250-251
Point of view: in presentational
style, 91, 92-93; epistemologically
critical, 221-224
Poole, Thomas, 276 n1
Pope, Alexander, 27, 33, 35, 61,
226, 261 n2; *Essay on Man,* 35
Pottle, Frederick, 262 n9, 268 n8

Pragmatic poetic theory, in early poems, xv-xvi
Price, Bonamy, 17
Pride: embodied by style, 53, 155; humbled by nature, 89, 157; W's attack on, 154, 247; of a solitary naturalism, 179, 206-207, 209
Priestley, F. E. L., 271 n1
Primitivism, W's: and Rousseau, 67; and Milton, 67; in *Lyrical Ballads,* 203, 247
Prior, Matthew, 10
Protestantism, W's, 3, 5, 133; and the French Revolution, 71-72; and diction of *Tintern Abbey,* 219. *See also* Covenant, Deluge, Scriptures

Rader, Melvin, 213
Rationalization: W engages in, 112, 123, 279 n4; W attacks, 125, 127
Rationalism: and dilemma of modern poet, xi; an ambiguous term, 2-3; and human maturation, 33-37; French war fortifies, 77-79, 107; Godwinian, 106-107, 160; in W's mature poems, 160, 196-197, 210. *See also* Locke, Reason
Ray, John, 65
Raysor, T. M., 277 n6
Read, Herbert, xiv-xv, 268 n1, 272-273 n10, 278 n1
Realism: social, 85-109; epistemological, 18-19, 36, 37-40, 71, 150-151, 251
Reason: in "School Exercise," 3; ethical and intuitive, 3, 160; demonstrative, 3, 34, 94, 127, 196-197; as agent of painful maturity, 34; dignity of, 36; reconstructed in W's poetry, 160, 209-210. *See also* Rationalism
Reed, Mark, xii, 264 n17, 273 n11, and passim
Reflection: language of, 160; as meliorator of obsessive imagery,

172; as component of psychological recovery, 72, 206
Relativism, moral: as effect of war and guilt, 77-78, 107, 133; W opposes, 183, 224
Renaissance, W's debt to, 5, 9, 248-249
Repetition: and feeling, 57; in *The Ruined Cottage,* 146-148; in the *Lyrical Ballads,* 194, 198, 200-201; in *Tintern Abbey,* 232, 236, 239, 241, 242
Reynolds, Joshua, 13, 24
Robespierre, 106, 121
Robinson, Crabb, 281 n20
Romanticism, xiv, 134-135, 182-183, 247-249
Rountree, T. J., 275 n18
Rousseau, Jean-Jacques, 63, 64, 66, 77-78, 269 n12
Ruskin, John, 26

Saussure, Horace Benedict de, 64
Schneider, B. R., Jr., 4, 220, 256 n10, 278 n1
Science, natural, xi; in W's schooling, 1, 3, 225 n5; language of in *Tintern Abbey,* 219; and art, 248. *See also* Bacon, Newton
Scott, John: influence on *An Evening Walk,* 53-55; epistemological rigor of, 54; precepts rejected by W in 1792, 60-61; W quotes c. 1798, 58, 226-227
Scriptures, the, 171, 203, 219, 248; Ecclesiastes, 138; Psalms, 240, 244; Romans, 212
Selincourt, Ernest de: on W's Gothicism, 8; on the manuscripts, 23, 106, 120, 152, 260 n37, 263 n12, 269 n11, 271 n4, 274 n15, 276-277 n5; on naturalism of 1794, 268 n8, 269 n12; on W's anti-Godwinism, 277 n15
Sensation: as alternative to self-consciousness, 58, 79; imagery of,

Sensation (*continued*)
160, 178, 207; in W's renderings, 213-218; in Coleridge's poetry, 217-218; function of after 1798, 240, 244-245

Sensibility, poetry of: 7; subjectivism of, 10-12; W's imitation of, 10-12; conceptions of maturation in, 33, 37; W disciplines, 56-58, 77-78; introversion of corrected by W, 128, 148-149; and reception of the *Lyrical Ballads,* 202. *See also* Emotion, Melancholy, Pathos

Shakespeare, William, xi, 121, 227, 244. WORKS: *Hamlet,* 120; *King Lear,* 121, 124; *Macbeth,* 121; *Othello,* 120, 121, 123, 124

Sharrock, Roger, 274 n16, 275-276 n23

Sidney, Sir Philip, 248

Smith, Charlotte, 5, 27, 33

Smith, Elsie, 262 n5, 280 n9, 281 n20

Southey, Robert, 199, 202; style compared to W's, 145-148, 149, 156-157

Spenser, Edmund, 112

Sperry, Willard, 273 n10

"Spy Nozy," 184

Stallknecht, N. P., 282 n2, 283 n9

Storm: as analogy for poet, 167

Style, W's: W's view of, x; vices of, 49, 262 n17; and self-consciousness, 56; epistemological and psychological implications of, 58; and the French Revolution, 59-62; and the French war, 80-83; moral force of, 139, 141-149; achievement of, 148-149; and naturalism, 156-157; disciplines subjectivism, 156; and philosophy, 207-210; and politics, 246; after 1798, 250. Presentational style: defined, 87-88; W experiments with, 91-92, 98; in

Racedown poems, 108-109, 141, 143, 154, 158; in Alfoxden poems, 163, 164-167, 175-176, 178, 180; in *Lyrical Ballads,* 185, 187, 204, 280 n9; and W's philosophy, 206, 207-208, 214-215, 218; in *Tintern Abbey,* 230. *See also* Abstractions, Action, Allegory, Diction, Figures, Imagery, Meter, Negation, Reflection, Symbol, Syntax

Subject-object relation: importance of object in eighteenth-century cosmology, 34-36; importance in W's psychology, 19-20; confused in early poems, 29; clarified by W, 48, 53-55; disequilibrium of, 10, 19-20, 57-58, 233, 235; dynamic equilibrium of, 19-20, 93, 165, 178, 216, 221-222; moral importance of object in W's poetry, 128, 129-135; in Coleridge's poetry, 222-223. *See also* Epistemology

Subjectivism: in poetry of sensiblity, 9-12; in W's art, 9-10, 246-247; W indulges, 10-16; W disciplines, 17-19, 56-58, 130-131, 141, 144-149, 183, 248, 280 n9; as effect of psychological trauma, 124-125, 149-150; dramatized in *Tintern Abbey,* 235; in poetry after 1798, 250. *See also* Epistemology

Sublime, the: and French Revolution, 70; W's instinctive attraction to, 73; of duration, 152

Substance: material, in Locke, 18; and solidity, 18; in W's mature work, 19; and image, 31, 216-217; assumes explicit moral force, 132-133, 139, 149; of Cartesian dualism, 216; and language of *Tintern Abbey,* 220

Sunset, W's renderings of: 29-30, 46, 53-54, 59-61, 67-68, 70, 72-82, 96-97, 102-103

Swinburne, Algernon Charles: 282 n23

Symbolism: in W's poetry, 81, 88; constellation of in Racedown poems, 114-116; disciplined and rationalized by W, 139-140, 171-172; character of, in W's art, 143, 216; and Annette Vallon, 272-273 n10

Symbols, particular: *see* Images, significant and symbolic

Synaesthesia: in W's mature studies of perception, 215; of image and substance, 31, 216-217

Syntax: W distorts, 52; simplifies, 82-83, 100; in lyric forms, 180; in *Lyrical Ballads*, 186, 194; in blank verse, 273 n13. *See also* Inversion, Verbs

Taylor, Anne, ix, x, xiii, 246

Taylor, William, 1, 2, 9, 44, 163; tastes of, 256 n10

Tennyson, Alfred, Lord, 250

Theocritus, 6, 27, 47

Thomson, James, 60, 62, 82, 227, 257 n17; and Hawkshead poems, 21, 22, 29, 32; and Cambridge poems, 44, 51, 53, 54; corrected by W, 56

Thorslev, Peter L., Jr., 274 n16, 275 n21

Truth: as object of art, 6, 207; W rejects, as lyrical poet, 6, 8-9; W's dedication to, 213, 227-228, 248; and subjectivism, 247

Tucker, Abraham, 220, 284 n22

Turner, William, 61

Understatement, 139, 187

Vallon, Annette: W's supposed desertion of, xv, 115, 268 n1; W's separation from, 75-76, 78-79; W's feelings toward, 79, 114-115,

273 n11, 12; and the French Revolution, 75-76, 106, 115; and Godwin, 107; influence on Racedown poems, 114-115, 139, 150, 273 n10; W pays tribute to, 150; influence on W criticism, 205, 267 n33, 272-273 n10

Verbs: of motion, 165, 233, 234; significance in W's studies of perception, 215

Virgil: translated by W, xiv, xv, 44-45, 46-47, 261 n2; cited by W, 6, 150; and W's naturalism, 29, 46-47, 155, 220; and paradigms of maturation, 33; objective vision of, 44, 53; and French Revolution, 73; and pastoral elegy, 151; *Eclogues,* cited by W, 44; *Georgics,* xv, 44, 46-4⁻; *Aeneid,* 220, 260 n36

Wanderer, figure of: in W's poetry, 116; as exiled violator of domestic bonds and affections, 116-117; fixation of by guilt and abstraction, 126-127; fixation of by hope and imagination, 149; reconciled to man, 127-128; in *Somersetshire Tragedy,* 136; despair and remorse as *rite de passage* for, 149, 275 n19; as survivor of trauma, 151-153; crime exorcised, 171, 175

Warton, Joseph, 22, 23, 27, 56, 61, 226, 261 n2

Wasserman, Earl R., 15, 29, 257 n16

Wellek, René, 213

Welsford, Enid, 275 n21

West, Thomas, 51, 256 n9

Whitehead, Alfred North, 208

Williams, Helen Maria, 5, 8, 11, 33, 256 n9, 259 n28

Wilson, John, 195

Wimsatt, W. K., 231

Winchelsea, Lady, 168

Woodhouse, A. S. P., 258 n19

Woodring, Carl, 273 n10, 284 n28
Woodward, John, 65
Wordsworth, Caroline, 78
Wordsworth, Christopher, 2, 21
Wordsworth, Dorothy, 37, 79, 89, 173, 229; reunited with W, 95, 105, 108; W's love for, 104, 182, 183, 243; her role at Racedown, 127; in *Tintern Abbey*, 239-243; praises *An Evening Walk*, 262 n10
Wordsworth, John, 40, 251, 261 n4
Wordsworth, Jonathan: on *An Evening Walk*, 261 n4; on the Windy Brow fragments, 268 n8, 269 n12; on the Racedown poems, 145, 276 n1, 2, 3, 277 n6, 8; on the Alfoxden poems, 278 n1, 279 n8, 282 n23, 2
Wordsworth, William: phases of development, xvi, 246; composes first poems, 1; neurosis in early poems, 7-8; passionate nature, 8, 246; ambition, 8, 16, 56; pride, 8, 16; egotism, 9, 183, 204, 246; 256 n11; father's death, 39-40; at Cambridge, 43-44, 46-48; summer vacation, 49; effects of English declaration of war, 75; journey of summer 1793, 83; lyricism of 1794, 102-104, 105; retires to Racedown, 105, 108; loss of hope, 107; guilt, 110, 123; political views, 161, 191, 246, 272 n6; religion, 166, 195, 211-212, 267-268 n33, 269 n10; and isolation from nature, 168; recovery of 1797, 136-138, 153; moves to Alfoxden, 162; fruition of 1798, 162-163, 181-183; returns to Wye, 1798, 229; crisis of great decade, 244-245, 249-250; familial love, 261 n4
WORDSWORTH, WRITINGS OF: *

Anacreon (GCL 11), 24-25
Anecdote for Fathers, 196
Ballad, A (GCL 18), 6
Beauty and Moonlight, An Ode (GCL 10), 13, 259 n29
Borderers, The, 120-135, 139, 151, 154, 157, 162, 171, 175, 180, 190, 196; setting of, 121; as a test of nature, 121-122, 127-129, 180, 187; title of, 133-134; and *The Ruined Cottage*, 141, 143, 149; and "discharged soldier," 170; Prefatory Essay, 124, 125, quoted, 128
Complaint of a Forsaken Indian Woman, 186-187, 188, 225-226
Death of a Starling, The (GCL 10), 6
Description of a Beggar (GCL 53), 151-152, 172
Descriptive Sketches, 59-74, 76, 81, 85, 92, 100, 138, 195, 211, 218; composed, 59; Christian eschatology of, 65, 166; and *Paradise Lost*, 65, 71; naturalism of, 62-63, 101-102, 153; landscape in, 59-63, 164; disappointment in, 266 n31; melancholy in, 267 n33
Desultory Stanzas, 265 n24
Dirge, Sung by a Minstrel (GCL 21), 6, 259 n28
Elegiac Stanzas Suggested by a Picture of Peele Castle, 40; quoted, 251
Essay, Supplementary to the Preface (1815), quoted, 224
Evening Walk, An: Version of 1788-93, 49-52, 62, 70, 72, 95, 138, 227, 229; composed, 49-50; landscape in, 61, 81, 90, 96, 104; naturalism of, 80, 179; objectivism of, 89, 226, 233-234;

* Lesser known works are identified by their number in Reed's General Chronological List (GCL).

point of view in, 93; W's note to, 23; conjectural blank verse version of, 264 n17. Version of 1794, 95-104, 108, 153, 164; composed, 95; fortitude of, 95; naturalism of, 96-102; lyricism of, 102-104, 105, 162; quietism in, 106; promise of, fulfilled, 163

Excursion, The, 28, 71, 72, 137, 179, 184

Expostulation and Reply, 188, 208; quoted, 240

Extract from the Conclusion of a Poem, Composed in Anticipation of Leaving School, 30

FRAGMENTS: "Derwent Again I Hear Thy Evening Call" (GCL 8a), 277 n13; Description of a freezing mother (GCL 28b), 45; Essay on the sublime, 277 n12; Farewell to Helvellyn (prose fragment, GCL 19), 20, 26; Fragment of an Ode to Winter (GCL 14), 21; Gothic Tale (GCL 49), 119-120, 130, 274 n15; Heroic narrative (GCL 2), 5, 24; "How Sweet to Walk along the Woody Steep" (GCL 43), 79-83; "Human Life Is Like the Plate of a Dial" (prose fragment), 264 n20; Incipient Madness (GCL 58), 152-153; composition of, 277 n6; Moral Essay, fragment of a (GCL 77), 126; "Some Men There Are" (PW V, 413; Prelude, p. 566), 178, 224; Storm scene (GCL 22a), 261 n3; Tale, A (GCL 15), 86, 127; "There Are Times When the Heart" (prose fragment), 10-11; "There Is Creation in the Eye" (PW V, 343), 210, 214; "There Would He Stand" (PW V, 343), 214-217; "Trans-

figured by His Feeling" (PW V, 413), 174; XVI a, b (PW I, 292-295; GCL 49), 119; "Yet Once Again Do I Behold the Forms" (GCL 54), 153-154

Goody Blake and Harry Gill, 184, 188, 220

Guide through the District of the Lakes, A, 259 n28

Guilt and Sorrow. See Salisbury Plain

Idiot Boy, The, 193-195, 202, 203

Idyllium, An (GCL 12), 13-14, 25, 27-28, 30, 52, 92; original title of, 6

"In Vain Did Time and Nature Toil to Throw" (GCL 44), 84

Juvenal (GCL 47), 109

Letter to the Bishop of Llandaff, 77-78, 86, 272 n6

Lines Left upon a Seat in a Yew-Tree, 154-161, 166, 176, 185, 188, 208, 210, 225, 229

Lines Written in Early Spring, 187, 221

Lyrical Ballads, ix, 47, 153, 172, 173, 183-204, 205, 208, 214, 218, 220, 227, 229; benign ambush in, 185; purposes of, 22, 185, 187, 248; meter in, 185-187; banality of, 185, 189, 198-199, 281 n20; critical response to, 202-203; art of, 203-204; charity of, 204, 220, 247. Preface to LB of 1798: quoted, xiii, 161, 187, 202; Preface to LB of 1800, ix, 6, 142-143, 156, 175, 176, 183, 184, 185, 202; quoted, 209-210; Preface to LB of 1802, 150; quoted, 8

Mad Mother, The, 187

Night-piece, A, 164-172, 184, 232; and Idiot Boy, 195; perception in, 214; critical perspective in, 222

Nutting, 171; quoted, 19

WORDSWORTH, WRITINGS OF (*cont.*)
Ode to Apollo (GCL 31), 273 n11
Ode. Intimations of Immortality
and Gray, 9, 95; W's note on,
16-17; sunset in, 30; idealism in,
250
Old Cumberland Beggar, The, 172
Old Man Travelling, 151-152, 172
Orpheus (GCL 24), 44
Peter Bell, 120, 202, 224
Prelude, The *, xi, 105, 121, 171,
251; biographical application of,
xiii-xiv; naturalism in, 22, 126,
250; Wordsworth's moral crisis
in, 121, 122; 1850 version, 50
EPISODES CITED: stolen boat
(I.372-427), 222, 223; discharged soldier (IV.363-504),
168-172, 278-279 n4; tour of
Alps (VI.332-657), 69; crossing
of Simplon Pass (VI.488-572),
xiii, xiv n, 69, 74; Vaudracour
and Julia (IX.555-934), 75-76,
114, 116, 123; wait for horses,
and father's death (XI.345-
389), 39; Snowdon ascent
(XIII.10-65), 266 n29
PARTICULAR REFERENCES (line
numbers are italicized): I: 26,
87, 175, 222; *1-54* ("preamble"), 108, 271 n3; *271*, 68;
II: 26, 175; *182-183, 206-207,*
20; *235,* 228; *247-249,* 217;
301-320, 376, 20; *403-405,* 25;
405-430, 20; III: *169-195,* 43;
437, 46; *574-580,* 47; *590-591,*
607-608, 653, 43; IV: *104-105,*
13; *226-227,* 56; *272-273, 292-*
294, 304-305, 49; V: *104,* 4;
599-601, 26; VI: *72-73,* 56;
179-180, 116; *313,* 223; *453,*
69; *486,* 6; *549, 629-657,* 69;
VIII: *454* [1850], 30; *518,* 32;

528-529, 27; *604-605,* 31; *609,*
39; IX: *202,* 63; *252,* 74; *276-*
279, 76; *411-413, 511-519,* 69;
X: *234-235, 238,* 75; *259,* 89;
264-275, 77; *291-307,* 79; *297,*
81; *377-381,* 110; *540-557,* 106;
695-700, 76; *726-728,* 71; *750-*
752, 94; *753-755,* 73; *761-769,*
107; *807-809,* 79; *872,* 114; *873,*
885-889, 901, 107; XI: *6-7,* 107;
55, 119; *97-98,* 130; *172, 195,*
58; XII: *312,* 143, 167; *320,* 85;
359, 84; *371-373,* 93; XIII: *439-*
441, 176; MS JJ: quoted, 212
Poet's Epitaph, A, 202; quoted,
199
Recluse, The, 55, 104, 174, 204;
quoted, 212, 228
Remembrance of Collins (GCL
33), 46
Ruined Cottage, The: Version of
1797: 137-151, 153, 154, 171,
180, 201; composed, 137; fixation in, 142, 149-150; style of,
141-149, 165, 166, 208, 214,
229; humanism of, 139, 150,
179, 247; length, 276 n2. Version of 1798: 172-181, 229;
meter, 185-187; naturalism, 178,
205, 207, 209; theism, 212; and
imagination, 224-225; quoted,
65, 126, 209
Salisbury Plain: Version of 1793-
1794: 84-94, 100, 102, 108,
109, 116, 117, 118, 139, 141-
142, 157, 213, 233, 261 n3;
realism of, 85; three styles of,
85-93, 160; autobiography in,
86; point of view in, 85, 89, 93;
quoted, xiv. Version of 1795:
108-118, 136, 140, 171, 199,
238; composed, 108; pessimism
of, 108-109; naturalism in, 117-

* Unless otherwise noted, all references are to the version of 1805.

118, 120; guilt in, 110, 130, 131; rationalism and rationalization in, 109-114, 127; and *Borderers*, 121, 122, 123; and version of 1793-1794, 108, 109, 116, 117, 118. Version of 1842 (*Guilt and Sorrow*), 110, 272 n8

School Exercise at Hawskhead, Lines Written as a (GCL 5), 1, 2-5, 6, 14, 78, 98, 220, 227

Septimi Gades (GCL 38), 273 n11

Simon Lee, 188, 189-193, 195, 202, 207

Slumber Did My Spirit Steal, A, 242

Somersetshire Tragedy, The, 136-137

"Sweet was the Walk along the Narrow Lane" (GCL 37), 48

Tables Turned, The, 188, 208-209, 210, 218

"There Is a Little Unpretending Rill," 269 n10

Thorn, The, 167, 184, 188, 197-202, 226, 243, 281 n18; horror and pathos in, 283 n23

Tintern Abbey, Lines Composed a Few Miles Above, xvi, 6, 21, 55, 89-90, 96, 154, 163, 205, 214, 229-245, 249, 250; diction of, 219-221; as dramatic autobiography, 229-230; rearrangement of past in, 237-239

To My Sister, 181-183, 187, 221

Vale of Esthwaite, The, 5, 15, 29, 30, 31, 32, 45, 49, 52, 54, 55, 70, 72, 151, 182, 216, 256 n9; Gothicism of, 6-7; fancy in, 12, 38, 39; naturalism of, 20-21; landscape in, 23, 25-27, 50; maturation in, 37-41

We Are Seven, 83, 196, 197

"Western Clouds a Deepening Gloom Display, The" (GCL 44), 84

"When Slow from Pensive Twilight's Latest Gleams" (GCL 35), 48

Whirlblast from behind the Hill, A, 184

White Doe of Rylstone, The, 251

Written in Very Early Youth, 48

Wrangham, Francis, 184

Yeats, William Butler, 204, 250

Young, Edward, 34, 154, 214, 257 n17